MAKING
ART

and

MAKING
A LIVING

MAKING
ART
and
MAKING
A LIVING

*Adventures in Funding
a Creative Life*

MASON CURREY

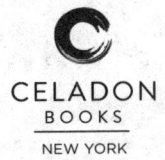

CELADON
BOOKS

NEW YORK

MAKING ART AND MAKING A LIVING. Copyright © 2026 by Mason Currey. All rights reserved. Printed in the United States of America. For information, address Celadon Books, a division of Macmillan Publishers, 120 Broadway, New York, NY 10271. EU Representative: Macmillan Publishers Ireland Ltd., 1st Floor, The Liffey Trust Centre, 117–126 Sheriff Street Upper, Dublin 1, D01 YC43.

www.celadonbooks.com

Designed by Michelle McMillian

The Library of Congress Cataloging-in-Publication Data is available upon request.

ISBN 978-1-250-82452-3 (hardcover)
ISBN 978-1-250-42207-1 (ebook)

Our books may be purchased in bulk for specialty retail/wholesale, literacy, corporate/premium, educational, and subscription box use. Please contact MacmillanSpecialMarkets@macmillan.com.

First Edition: 2026

10   9   8   7   6   5   4   3   2   1

FOR REBECCA

CONTENTS

SCHEMES

MAKING
ART
and
MAKING
A LIVING

INTRODUCTION

Arthur Schopenhauer was in his early teens when he decided that he wanted to pursue a literary career. For his father, Heinrich Floris Schopenhauer, a successful Hamburg merchant, this was bad news; he expected Arthur to take over the family business in due course. So, in 1803, when Arthur was fifteen, Heinrich Floris gave him a choice: Stay in Hamburg and begin regular studies of literature, Latin, and other subjects necessary to a man of letters, or agree to a mercantile career and leave immediately on a long tour of Europe, to see something of the world before settling down to business.

Arthur chose the latter option, as his father suspected he would; even for a bookish teenager, the opportunity to travel was too great to resist. Arthur's European tour lasted two years; when he returned home, his father apprenticed him as a clerk in the office of a local merchant. There, Arthur quickly realized his blunder: The daily work of a merchant, indeed the entire world of trade and finance, held no interest for him whatsoever, and he was plunged into despair as he contemplated the life he had so regrettably chosen.

By all rights, this would be the end of the story, and the world would never have known of Arthur Schopenhauer the philosopher, whose brilliant and deeply pessimistic writings have arrested the attention of readers for more than two hundred years. But four months after Arthur began his clerkship, his father died (of suspected suicide); in the aftermath, the family business was sold and Arthur's mother and sister relocated to Weimar. Arthur was left in Hamburg, in the merchant's office, feeling duty bound to fulfill his promise to his father. For two long years, he kept that promise, all the while loathing the mercantile profession and his place in it. Finally, his mother—who, in Weimar, had started a literary salon frequented by Goethe and would herself become a successful author—intervened, writing to tell Arthur that, if he liked, he could consider his promise to his father fulfilled and pursue a more congenial career.

On receiving this letter, Arthur burst into "tears of joy" and left the merchant's office at once. He resumed the secondary-school education that had been cut short by his apprenticeship and subsequently enrolled at the University of Göttingen, where he discovered his calling as a philosopher. But he did not forget his two-plus years working in an office; to the contrary, the sense of futility and cosmic indifference that he experienced there became the kernel of all his future work. As the scholar R. J. Hollingdale—whose introduction to Schopenhauer's *Essays and Aphorisms* I drew upon in writing the preceding sketch—has argued, "the attitude towards life produced by these two years and more of office misery became, as did everything he felt, a permanent and irremovable part of his make-up: became, in fact, his permanent attitude towards life." In that taste of the ordinary workaday world, Germany's future "philosopher of pessimism" was born.

+ + +

How you feel about Schopenhauer's story probably depends on how you feel about your own lot in life. On the one hand, how delightful that this budding genius escaped a lifetime of uninspired drudgery and that his brief experience of office life inspired an entire philosophy! On the other hand, *how fucking depressing*, because think of the many potential Schopenhauers who are never rescued from their day jobs, who spend their lives feeling in their bones that they're destined for something greater but lack the time and resources to figure out what that might be.

Plus, there is a crucial detail that I neglected to mention in the above summary. At twenty-one, Arthur inherited his portion of his late father's estate, and it was that infusion of capital that enabled his lifelong philosophical investigations. (He worked as a university lecturer for only a brief part of his career.) Indeed, if his mother hadn't released him from the merchant's office at nineteen, it seems likely that Schopenhauer would have made the break himself upon receiving this money at twenty-one. The inheritance was not enormous; Schopenhauer was never a wealthy man. But neither was he in real danger of spending his life at a job he loathed.*

Which leads me to a question I find myself asking with some regularity these days: Did all the celebrated "great minds" throughout history—all the brilliant, groundbreaking writers and artists and intellectuals whose biographies seem so inspiring from afar—enjoy a covert (or overt) source of wealth that they tapped into to realize their creative endeavors? Is the history of art and ideas a history of rich kids?

The answer, of course, is no. Everyone knows the stories: Chekhov was a country doctor, T. S. Eliot worked in a bank, Van Gogh was constantly borrowing money from his younger brother. Speaking of Van Gogh: Weren't a lot of famous writers and artists and musicians, like, really poor? Didn't Mozart die penniless, his body dumped in a pauper's grave? Wasn't Picasso's Paris studio a glorified squat in the Bateau-Lavoir, a dingy, unheated former piano factory?

Actually, contrary to popular lore, Mozart was at the time of his death a celebrated composer with significant earning power, and he was given a perfectly normal burial. As for Picasso: Not long into the Bateau-Lavoir era, the artist was financially secure and would be for the rest of his life. (Picasso liked to live "like a pauper," he said, "but with lots of money.") Inaccuracies aside, the familiar tales of artists' saintly poverty—or writers' respectable parallel careers—are of little use to my target reader for the following pages. This reader is someone powerfully drawn to a life in the arts and at the same time powerfully stumped by the difficulty of

---

* This inherited income allowed the adult Schopenhauer to follow the same routine every day for more than twenty-five years: up at 7:00 AM, a bath, coffee, and writing until noon, then a half hour of flute practice, lunch at a tavern, reading until 4:00 PM, a two-hour walk, more reading, attendance at an evening theater or concert performance, dinner at a hotel or restaurant, and home to bed.

balancing those ambitions with the very real need to pay rent and put food in the fridge. Sure, there are some well-worn paths forward: Get a day job and do your creative work in your spare time. Go to graduate school and try to find a foothold in academia that encourages or at least tolerates your art-making practice. Pursue a sort-of-related career—journalism for writers, say, or graphic design for visual artists—and hope to channel your artistic impulses into this more financially secure profession. Find somewhere extremely affordable to live and get by on as little income as possible. Become a genius at applying for—and winning—grants, fellowships, residencies, retreats, contests, and other funding opportunities. Coax money out of your parents, acquire a patron (how exactly does one do that?), or attract a life partner who's willing to subsidize your art. Or—most elusive of all—*make* your art pay, by tailoring it to the marketplace or somehow forcing the culture to come to you.

None of these paths are straightforward, and none of them are exclusive, either; most unwealthy artists will assemble various combinations of strategies throughout their careers. And what would be valuable to anyone embarking on this journey, I think, is a careful look at how these strategies and others like them have played out for artists over time. Everyone has to figure out their own unique path forward, but it can be tremendously useful—and comforting—to learn how your predecessors have done it.

Hence this book: a quasi-history of making art and making a living—of patrons, day jobs, side hustles, strategic marriages, petty theft, palace intrigue, and other adventures in funding a creative life, featuring a variety of brilliant minds spanning the Renaissance to the present day. Originally, I envisioned it as a proper history, with a straightforward chronological march from fifteenth-century Florence to now. But after much flailing around and more than a few thoughts of abandoning the whole thing, I decided to scrap the chronology and make it more of a romp through art and literary history, landing on figures and moments that illuminate various facets of this eternal dilemma.

A skeptic might say that this approach focuses on precisely the least important aspect of art history. Isn't art supposed to transcend material concerns? Perhaps. But to ignore money is to neglect a huge piece of the context of the art's making, and understanding that context can only serve to enrich our appreciation of the work. Besides, I can't be the only one who feels alternately baffled and enraged by the economics of art-making. The dumb truth is that there is no cultural production without financial support. It is simply not possible to become an accomplished painter or musician or novelist or poet without spending a lot of time experimenting, making false starts, starting over, starting over *again*, absorbing criticism, thinking, reading, talking, and mooning about the house aimlessly. All this time has to be purchased, one way or another. So, yes, money is just one piece of the artist's life, but it's a piece that gets skipped over with annoying frequency; too often, it's a big gaping hole in our knowledge of a career. Too often, looking at an artist's work, I feel like we say: *Here's this beautiful, amazing thing, and, well, somebody must have given the artist some money at some point, who knows?* (I want to know!) Or else we glorify the artist's poverty, or we just straight up lie to people: *Do what you love and the money will follow.* What if you love composing sonnets, making experimental music, or, god forbid, feeling your way toward a new art form that hasn't existed before? The money may follow eventually, or it may not, and it's the artist's job to keep going regardless.

+ + +

Before we begin, a few clarifications: For simplicity's sake, I use the word *artist* throughout these pages to refer to all manner of creative artists: writers, visual artists like painters and sculptors, filmmakers, musicians and composers, and so on. Also, I want to be clear that this is not a book about the dire situation for arts funding at this moment, though certainly that situation informed its writing. (An excellent, if depressing, book on that subject is William Deresiewicz's *The Death of the Artist*, published in 2020, which persuasively makes the case that the twenty-first-century economy has hurt artists as much or more than any other type of worker.) Rather, this book assumes that you, the reader, are living in circumstances unfriendly to the funding of art—because that has nearly always been the case. There have been moments that were friendlier, overall, to artists' incomes, it's true—and we will visit some of them in these pages—but plenty of individual artists struggled mightily even in economies that offered a lower cost of living or more opportunities for profit. As the author and publisher Anne Trubek wrote recently about writers, in a formula that really applies to all artists, "financial stress is the rule, not the exception."

In addition, I want to be clear that this is not a book of advice, because, well, what one-size-fits-all advice could there be? For me, when it comes to the really big dilemmas, I don't want advice, no matter how well-meaning; I want examples of *how to be*. I want to see what attitudes people copped, what their instincts were and whether they listened to them, how they worked with and pushed back against their temperaments, how much latitude they gave themselves versus how strict they were with themselves, how seriously they took their own ambitions, how heavily or lightly they wore their various burdens, how much fun they had, how much energy, how much trust in things working out, how much bitterness or resentment, how much iron willpower versus gentle striving, how much hesitation, how much second-guessing, and, of course, the focus of this book, how all of it was funded, *really* how, and how the funding influenced the making of the work and was in many cases inseparable from it.

In part 1, "Family Money," I look at the best possible strategy for funding a life as an artist: to have inherited wealth, a parental allowance, or a family member or two from whom you can extract the necessary funds—though even these most ideal situations are not without their complications and pitfalls.

And if family money is nonexistent or impenetrable? In part 2, "Jobs," I examine three ways to approach the dreaded day job: working a series of relatively undemanding (but equally unrewarding) odd jobs; pursuing a long-running parallel career in a well-paying profession like medicine, law, or insurance; or trying to unite one's creative interests and money-earning needs by serving a cultural institution like a museum or a university (or a university library). Throughout, I tried to pay special attention to how artist employees found the time and energy to make their own work and how their choice of job influenced the work they made.

In part 3, "Patrons," I turn my attention to several varieties of patronage: from an Italian cardinal, a pair of Hungarian princes, a shipping-industry tycoon, a visionary American president, an impulsive heiress, and the public itself, via one very successful (and a few not-so-successful) audience subscription plans. As with family money, patronage has enabled a great deal of brilliant art that wouldn't have existed otherwise—but it has also, at times, brought out the worst in both patron and artist.

Finally, in part 4, "Schemes," I survey some *other* means of funding the art life: by stealing, by gambling, by going on television game shows, by patenting a profitable invention, by setting out to a write a hit song, and via perhaps the most timeless scheme of all: by absolutely refusing to be pragmatic or to compromise in any direction, and insisting on making a living *from* one's art, regardless of the consequences, and still somehow making it work, perhaps.

+ + +

I started off with Arthur Schopenhauer's near miss on a life of the mind because, looking at the lives of artists, I'm frequently struck by how some of the great works of human thought and ingenuity very nearly did not happen, could have so easily been derailed. Often it is just one person or one event that keeps the artist on the track to completing something of lasting value. And so often the element that proves decisive in whether a work is completed or not is money—stupid money! At any given time, there is so much of it in the world, flowing through hidden channels or stored tight in private vaults, or else being spent openly for all to see, and yet how should one person gain access to it? I know, I know—get a job, start a savings account. "The world doesn't owe you a living." Every time I hear that supposed truism, I find myself thinking, pointlessly: *Oh yeah?*

This book is about individuals who felt at some level that they owed the fruits of their labor to the world. They weren't necessarily selfless or generous in their personal lives—in some cases, far from it—and with a few exceptions they weren't insensitive to material comforts. But their work came first, because they thought it had a greater value, and because when they put the work second, as they sometimes inevitably had to do, their souls suffered. I hope that these stories help readers see some new paths forward for themselves, or at least see their own dilemmas reflected back at them, and draw strength from reading about how those who came before them kept up the effort and came through.

FAMILY MONEY

INHERITANCE

I n 1907, a nineteen-year-old Portuguese aspiring writer named Fernando Pessoa found himself in a position that most artists can only dream of. Following the death of his Grandma Dionísia, in September, Pessoa faced the prospect of receiving a monthly payment, indefinitely, that would cover his basic living expenses and allow him to devote virtually all his time to literature, which he had already determined was his life's purpose. All he had to do was show some financial restraint.

The details were easy to grasp: Upon his grandmother's death, Pessoa stood to inherit an estate worth five million reis, or approximately $140,000 at today's values. Most of the estate was invested in shares in the Bank of Portugal, and the interest on these shares would be just about enough to cover Pessoa's room and board and incidental expenses in Lisbon, where he was born and would spend all his adult life. As he would never marry or have children, Pessoa could have lived off this inheritance for his entire adulthood, supplementing the interest payments with income from occasional freelance writing and translation work. (Pessoa was fluent in English and French as well as his native Portuguese.)

The opportunity to avoid a normal job, forever, would have come as a relief to anyone, but perhaps especially to Pessoa. A few months earlier, he had dropped out of school after two years of rather desultory studies; under pressure from his parents and extended family, Pessoa had next taken an internship at R. G. Dun & Company, which gathered and sold information on businesses around the world. In the firm's Lisbon office, Pessoa's job was to prevail upon local businessmen to accurately fill out a one-page questionnaire, a job that he found stultifying in the extreme. When news of his grandmother's passing arrived, he quit almost immediately—submitting, the biographer Richard Zenith writes, "a huffy, slightly insulting letter of resignation to the agency's director, complaining about the meager pay."

But Pessoa was confident that he could do more with his inheritance than live, rather humbly, on the monthly interest payments. The principal was what interested him—the full five million reis. Think of what a young man of intelligence and ambition could do with it! Under the terms of the estate, Pessoa would not have access to the bank shares until he turned twenty-one. So he bided his time, drawing up a list of inventions that he could realize once the funds were at his disposal. These included his own system of shorthand; something called a "typewriter shifter," the details of which are unrecorded; and a "commercial code" for, Zenith writes, "condensing messages and saving on telegraph costs."

By the time he turned twenty-one, however, Pessoa had decided that his best course of action was to launch his own publishing enterprise. The fateful birthday occurred on June 13, 1909. On August 5, while Pessoa was in a barbershop getting a shave and a trim, he saw a newspaper ad for a used printing press and, Zenith writes, "with his face still partly covered with lather, he jumped out of the chair and, brandishing the paper, ran out of the shop in a mad rush to contact the seller before anyone else did." The seller was in Portalegre, near the Spanish border, one hundred miles east of Lisbon; Pessoa traveled there by train. The press would cost him around one million reis—one-fifth of his inheritance—plus the cost of having it dismantled, shipped, and reassembled in Lisbon. Zenith writes:

> In September, at the latest, he sold his stock in the Bank of Portugal without telling anyone except, in all likelihood, his cousin Mário, swearing him to secrecy. At least half the money went to pay for the used press, additional equipment, and set-up costs, and

the rest would be needed for operating and living expenses until the business began turning a profit. In a small notebook, Pessoa jotted down figures and reckoned these expenses would amount to around two hundred thousand reis per month. It was a disastrously conservative estimate.

Pessoa's printing and publishing operation—which he named Ibis, after the ancient Egyptian symbol for the divine art of writing—opened in November 1909 and almost immediately ran into financial trouble. Pessoa had dramatically underestimated the competitiveness of the printing market in Lisbon, and he showed little interest in trying to secure the commercial clients whose business-related jobs (letterhead stationery, calling cards, flyers, brochures, and the like) would keep the press solvent. Instead, he invented an ambitious scheme of literary publishing, encompassing the plays of Aeschylus and Shakespeare, novels by Robert Louis Stevenson and the Brazilian author Joaquim Maria Machado de Assis, and his own fiction and verse, as well as collections of scientific, historical, political, and philosophical works. His scheme would have required the involvement of a whole team of writers, editors, and translators—it was certainly more than a twenty-one-year-old university dropout could handle alone—but Pessoa had a solution for that, sort of. At this age, he had already begun to invent what he called *heteronyms*: literary alter egos, each with their own fully fleshed-out biographies, points of view, and writing voices. (He preferred the term *heteronym* to *pseudonym*, because a pseudonym was just a different name—Pessoa was writing under entirely distinct personalities.) These heteronyms would prove an inexhaustible source of literary invention for Pessoa, but of course they could not actually permit him to perform the work of multiple employees, and they made no difference in the viability of Ibis.

In the end, Ibis didn't even last six months. In April or May 1910, Pessoa was forced to put his beloved printing press up for sale, securing a buyer for it in June. But the cash from the sale had to go straight to paying the many creditors he had relied upon for operating expenses during the preceding months. Those expenses had been far higher than he had reckoned; when the dust cleared, Pessoa was forced, finally, to face reality. Zenith writes, "In less than a year's time he had spent his entire inheritance of five million reis—and then some. On top of various amounts owed to family members, friends, and several investors, Pessoa had taken out a bank loan that he would be paying off for the next four years."

To get a sense of Pessoa's reaction toward this stark new reality—a lifetime monthly stipend squandered in just six months, with nothing to show for it except an army of creditors breathing down his neck—one needs only read the poem that Pessoa composed on November 17, 1911, a year and a half after the collapse of Ibis, while he was stringing along his creditors and feeling the full weight of his situation. On this day, according to Richard Zenith, Pessoa saw a newspaper wanted ad for a translator and began drafting a letter of application. But, Zenith writes, "some part of him rebelled," and instead of finishing the letter he composed a Shakespearean sonnet, which begins:

> How can I think, or edge my thoughts to action,
> When the miserly press of each day's need
> Aches to a narrowness of spilled distraction
> My soul appalled at the world's work's time-greed?

How indeed? Pessoa goes on to lament that he can't even pause his thoughts upon the task "my soul was born to think that it must do." As a result, he feels "beggared of infinity"—a memorable description of this all-too-common, all-too-depressing collision of glorious possibility and grim necessity.

+ + +

Surely not all artists are so irresponsible with their inherited income, should they be lucky enough to have such a thing—right?

Virginia Woolf is a good example of someone who inherited a situation like Pessoa's and did not blow it to smithereens, despite also falling in love with the idea of running her own publishing enterprise. Woolf was born six years before Pessoa, in 1882, into an upper-middle-class Victorian household—"born not of rich parents, but of well-to-do parents, born into a very communicative, literate, letter writing, visiting, articulate, late nineteenth century world," as she put it in an autobiographical essay. Woolf's father, Leslie Stephen, provided a formidable model of the writer's life and also of the writer's relationship to money: He was a figure of tremendous devotion and tenacity, continually hunched over his literary projects (especially after he assumed the editorship of the *Dictionary of National Biography*, a monumental undertaking that he shouldered for six years before exhaustion finally forced him to hand it off to a successor), and he was continually worried about the family finances. After Woolf's mother died in 1895—Woolf was thirteen—he became a brooding, self-pitying, histrionic presence in the family's London townhome, prone to outbursts of rage, particularly when it came to reviewing the weekly household expenses. As the youngest daughter, Woolf was spared from presenting the "weekly books" to him; after her mother's death, that duty fell first to Woolf's half sister, Stella, and then, after Stella's sudden death, to Woolf's older sister, Vanessa—though the trauma of the experience reverberated throughout the household. In her autobiographical essay, Woolf recalled the awful weekly ritual:

> Over the whole week brooded the horror, the recurring terror of Wednesday. On that day the weekly books were given him. Early that morning we knew whether they were under or over the danger mark—eleven pounds if I remember right. On a bad Wednesday we ate our lunch in the anticipation of torture. The books were presented directly after lunch. He put on his glasses. Then he read the figures. Then down came his fist on the account book. His veins filled; his face flushed. Then there was an inarticulate roar. Then he shouted . . . "I am ruined." Then he beat his breast. Then he went through an extraordinary dramatisation of self pity, horror, anger. Vanessa stood by his side silent. He belaboured her with reproaches, abuses. "Have you no pity for me? There you stand like a block of stone . . ." and so on. She stood absolutely silent. He flung at her all the phrases . . . about his misery, her extravagance,

that came handy. She still remained static. Then another attitude was adopted. With a deep groan he picked up his pen and with ostentatiously trembling hands he wrote out the cheque. Slowly with many groans the pen and the account book were put away. Then he sank into his chair; and sat spectacularly with his head on his breast. . . . I was speechless. Never have I felt such rage and such frustration.

So Woolf grew up seeing writing as a duty and a calling and also something that would keep you on the precipice of ruin, financially and emotionally. ("Like my father, I can always conjure up bankruptcy," she wrote in a 1941 letter.) It was no small thing, then, that she managed, gradually and with great effort and dedication, to make herself into a profitable author, indeed into a virtual one-woman publishing enterprise—this at a time when such a feat was still extremely rare for a woman, as she well knew—and also to co-run an actual publishing enterprise in the Hogarth Press, which began as a hobby in 1917 and became, almost accidentally, a viable and increasingly profitable business.

Of course Woolf benefited from inherited wealth: By the time she was married, in August 1912 (her father had died eight years earlier), she possessed a total inheritance of a little more than £9,000. This was invested in stocks and shares, providing her and her new husband, Leonard Woolf, with an interest income of around £400 a year. This was roughly equivalent to an average middle-class salary today—in the ballpark of $50,000 at present-day values—and just about enough to cover their living expenses in the first year of marriage. But those expenses dramatically increased when Virginia suffered a prolonged breakdown shortly after their marriage and required extensive medical supervision. Thereafter, the Woolfs' expenses hovered at around £700–£800 per year, meaning Virginia's investments would cover only about half of what they needed to live. (Leonard, whom Woolf described to her friends as "a penniless Jew," had about £500 saved when they married.) Unlike Pessoa, the Woolfs would not dream of touching their principal; instead, they set to work making up the annual shortfall through journalism and books. The biographer Hermione Lee writes:

> Both would work extremely hard to make up the four or five hundred pounds' income they needed. . . . Between 1916 and 1929 Virginia Woolf wrote as many as forty-seven articles a year, and hardly ever fewer than ten. For a few months in 1914 she kept a housekeeping book; then Leonard took it over, and for the rest of his life kept scrupulous annual accounts, balancing their actual against their estimated expenditure at the end of every year.

In Leonard, Virginia found an ideal comanager of their household finances: a supremely well-organized bookkeeper—after university, he had been a colonial administrator in the Ceylon Civil Service for four years before returning to England—who did not share her father's over-the-top anxiety about money, even though the Woolfs' finances were considerably more tenuous than the Stephens' had ever been. In his autobiography, Leonard tallied the earnings for all of Virginia's (and his own) writing over the course of their lives together, and they are a fascinating record of just how long it took her to become a profitable author—and just how impossible it would have been for her to have the career she had without that £400 a year. Leonard writes: "Virginia was 40 years old before she earned a living wage by writing; if she had had to earn her living during those years, it is highly improbable that she would ever have written a novel."

Woolf began writing her first novel, *The Voyage Out*, in 1909, when she was twenty-seven, and completed it, after four years and at least ten drafts, in early 1913. (It was published in 1915.) It was barely profitable; according to Leonard, the book took fifteen years to sell two thousand copies, and in all that time her earnings came out to less than £120. Her next novel, *Night and Day*, was published in 1919 and earned only slightly more: £146 over ten years. And this income was not evenly distributed: In 1919, Virginia received no money at all from her books; the following year, she received £106—but the year after that, only £10.

Her earnings from journalism during this time were somewhat better; between 1919 and 1924, she earned a total of about £780. (These earnings were also unevenly distributed: In 1920, for example, she earned £234 from journalism but only £47 the next year.) Leonard's earnings during this time were more robust: After his own attempts at writing novels—he published two, in 1913 and 1914, but they earned even less than Virginia's—he became editor of the *International Review* with an annual salary of £250, and he did a good deal of freelance journalism on top of that. In 1919, for instance, he earned £250 from his editorship, £262 in freelance journalism, and £66 from his books, easily making up the £400- or £500-pound shortfall.

This all began to shift in the 1920s, with the publication of *Mrs. Dalloway* in 1925, *To the Lighthouse* in 1927, *Orlando* in 1928, and *A Room of One's Own* in 1929. Starting in 1926, Virginia's annual earnings from her books rose rapidly: They were £356 in 1926, £545 the next year, £1,434 the year after that, and £2,396 in 1929. *Orlando* in particular sold well; where *The Voyage Out* took fifteen years to sell two thousand copies, *Orlando* sold in six months more than eight thousand copies in the UK and thirteen thousand copies in the United States. Her income from her books was £1,294 in 1930, £1,266 in 1931, £1,795 in 1932, and £2,446 in 1933. These were not extravagant sums; the historian Alison Light points out that at this time a barrister might have made at least £10,000 a year. But during all this time the Woolfs' living expenses stayed largely the same; as a result, the couple never really had to worry about money again. Leonard writes:

After 1928 we were always very well off. In the next ten years our income was anything from twice to six times what it had been in 1924. Neither of us was extravagant or had any desire for conspicuous extravagance; we did not alter fundamentally our way of life, because on £1,000 a year we already lived the kind of life we wished to live, and we were not going to alter the chosen pattern of our life because we made £6,000 in the year instead of £1,000. But life is easier on £3,000 a year than it is on £1,000. Within the material framework which we had chosen for our existence we got more of the things which we liked to possess—books, pictures, a garden, a car—and we did more of the things we wanted to do, for instance travel, and less in the occupations which we did not want to do, for instance journalism.*

As for publishing—this was a labor of love that the Woolfs embarked on in 1917, when they impulse purchased a small handpress, an instruction booklet, and some type and began teaching themselves the rudiments. Almost immediately, they fell in love with the fiddly, laborious process of setting, inking, printing, and binding. Their plan was to produce small editions of their own work and the work of their friends and contemporaries. "But, rather quickly," Hermione Lee writes, "the amateurs began to transform themselves into professionals." For the first several years of its operation, the Hogarth Press was very modestly profitable—but it never lost money, and by the end of the 1920s it began to be quite profitable, contributing on average another £1,000 a year to the Woolfs' bottom line.

Leonard says that 1928 was the year they began to be truly well off; is it any coincidence that it was in that year, in October, that Virginia delivered her two lectures at women's colleges that became the extended essay *A Room of One's Own,* with its famous declaration that "a woman must have money and a room of her own if she is to write fiction"? In fact, it was at this very moment that Virginia was literally adding rooms to Monk's House, the Woolfs' cottage in Rodmell, which, when they bought it for £700 in 1919, had a damp kitchen, no hot water, and no indoor toilet. "I'm out to make £300 this summer by writing, & build a bath & hot water range at Rodmell," Virginia wrote in her diary in April 1925. She did it—and later, after *Orlando,* her book sales enabled her to add a major new extension to Monk's House, with an L-shaped attic study for Leonard

---

* It is worth emphasizing how much Virginia did not want to do journalism. Though she used her reviews and critical essays to work out her own ideas about literature, and though journalism was a valuable training ground for her as a young writer, she came to deeply resent the time it took away from her real writing: "Always to be doing work that one did not wish to do . . . and then the thought of that one gift which it was death to hide—a small one but dear to the possessor—perishing and with it my self, my soul,—all this became like a rust eating away the bloom of the spring, destroying the tree at its heart."

and a two-room brick outbuilding for herself, where she slept and where she wrote in the winter. (In warm weather, she wrote in a small lodge in the garden.)

In *A Room of One's Own*, Woolf identifies £500 a year as the amount a woman ought to have in order to write, just slightly more than what she had from her inheritance; she was keenly aware of how few women could enjoy that amount and just how impossible her own career would have been without it, to what a great extent "intellectual freedom depends upon material things," as she wrote. Still, it took amazing industry for her to convert her fixed income into art and, eventually, profit—and this is the thing that sticks with me, how terrifically hard she worked over all those years. Leonard writes:

> Neither of us ever took a day's holiday unless we were too ill to work or unless we went away on a regular and, as it were, authorized holiday. We should have felt it was not merely wrong but unpleasant not to work every morning for seven days a week and for about eleven months a year. Every morning, therefore, at about 9.30 after breakfast each of us, as if moved by a law of unquestioned nature, went off and "worked" until lunch at 1. It is surprising how much one can produce in a year, whether of buns or books or pots or pictures, if one works hard and professionally for three and a half hours every day for 330 days.

This is what money gave Virginia—the opportunity to arrange her life in service to writing; and when she wasn't literally at her desk writing, she was thinking about writing while taking her long afternoon walks or while engaged in the pleasantly laborious process of setting type in the basement workroom of the Hogarth Press. Her death, by suicide, shortly after her fifty-ninth birthday, should not overshadow the many years of unflagging literary enterprise, of bold experimentation and simultaneous growing prosperity, and her delight in having really done what she set out to do. Despite her breakdowns and her so-called madness, few artists have managed such sustained periods of absolute lucidity, control, and freedom—freedom to write as she wished, and publish what she wrote herself, and gradually continue adding rooms to her cottage.

+ + +

Woolf achieved freedom—both economic and imaginative—through lifelong discipline and hard work. Her near opposite in this regard was Charles Baudelaire, the great nineteenth-century French poet, critic, and translator, who also sought freedom above all else but who viewed self-discipline with a mix of defiance and bewildered yearning. He often wished to achieve steady, reliable work habits, but over and over he found himself simply incapable of doing so.

Like Fernando Pessoa, Baudelaire received his inheritance at age twenty-one; unlike Pessoa, he did not have any entrepreneurial schemes waiting to be funded, unless you count his lifestyle as a young Latin Quarter dandy as an entrepreneurial scheme, which it kind of was: Before he was even publishing his work, Baudelaire was building notoriety as a poetic figure, a dashing young writer of promise not yet fulfilled.

Baudelaire turned twenty-one on April 9, 1842. He had only recently returned to Paris from what was supposed to be a long sea voyage to India, a journey pushed on him by his mother and stepfather, who sought to separate Baudelaire from the life of bohemian excess he had been leading over the previous few years since passing his baccalaureate exam—the equivalent of a high school degree—in 1839. (Baudelaire had been expelled from school several months earlier, after refusing to hand over a note passed to him by a fellow student, defiantly swallowing it instead.) The voyage was supposed to last a year, but after three months Baudelaire jumped ship in Mauritius and refused to travel any farther, making his way back to Paris in time to assume control of his inheritance.

The money was from Baudelaire's father, who had passed away when Charles was six years old. Two years later, Baudelaire's mother remarried, to an ambitious military officer named Jacques Aupick. Before this remarriage, Baudelaire and his mother had been incredibly close. Aupick's arrival—and the decision to send sensitive young Charles away to boarding school—set up an irresolvable tension that would play out for the rest of Baudelaire's life. He was desperate to recapture his mother's full affection, to impress her with his brilliance and renown, but at the same time he needed to utterly reject his stepfather's disciplined, rational worldview.

Baudelaire's inheritance was substantial: a mix of cash and investments, plus four pieces of land at Neuilly-sur-Seine, on the western edge of Paris, worth approximately one hundred thousand francs in total (in the ballpark of a half million dollars at present-day values). From the investments, Baudelaire could have drawn an annual interest payment that would have permitted a comfortable though not lavish lifestyle. Unfortunately, lavish was exactly what Baudelaire liked, and between his love of spending (especially on clothes and paintings) and the repayment of the considerable debts he had already accumulated, he began to blow through his inheritance at an alarming rate. Before long, he was forced to sell the land at Neuilly to cover his expenses; within eighteen months of receiving the inheritance, he had spent more than half of the total.

At this point, Baudelaire's mother and stepfather decided to intervene, using a previously established family trust to place Baudelaire on a strict allowance. If he wanted any funds beyond the allowance, Baudelaire would have to apply to the *conseil de famille*, a middle-aged lawyer named Narcisse Ancelle, who would have sole authority to veto or approve his requests. Baudelaire was devastated, furious, disbelieving. They couldn't do this—could they? It was *his* money, so surely he could spend it as he saw fit. If that meant that the entire inheritance was gone within a few years, so be it—that was his choice, not theirs. Writing to his mother in the summer of 1844, as the lawyer Ancelle was taking control of his fortune, Baudelaire fumed at this turn of events:

> You've told me you see my anger and grief as passing moods; you're assuming that you're just giving me a little pain as one might hurt a child for its own good. But for heaven's sake convince yourself of this one truth, that is, in very truth and to my own sorrow, I'm not like other men.—What you consider a necessary and fleeting pain, I cannot, I really cannot bear. . . . When we're alone you can treat

me as you like—but I furiously reject anything that encroaches on
my freedom.

It goes on from there—indeed, it never really stops. For the rest of
Baudelaire's life (a tragically short one; he died at forty-six after years of hard
living and increasingly dire side effects from the syphilis he contracted
around age eighteen), the poet would continue to implore his mother to
understand his position, to understand how unjust it was to place his inheritance under the control of a mere administrator. Worse than the lack
of familial understanding was the public humiliation he felt. Baudelaire
still had plentiful creditors, and now when they demanded repayment he
had no choice but to dodge them, to move from lodging to lodging in
a never-ending game of hide-and-seek. He was no longer a respectable
member of society but a perpetual outcast, forever fleeing his obligations
but unable—he thought—to choose any other path. As he insisted to
his mother, he was not like other men; to treat him as such was a gross
disservice.

"I'm writing to you as my last two logs burn, and my fingers are fro-
zen," Baudelaire informed his mother by post on March 26, 1853. It was
a familiar refrain. In Baudelaire's copious letters to his mother, the usual
pattern is: inquiries after her health and happiness, statements of his love
and admiration for her, and then a lengthy series of laments, about his
own poor health, his lack of productivity, and of course his lack of money,
always, and the grim conditions under which he must live—"the horrible
life I lead, which leaves me so little time for work"—and the unfairness of
the *conseil* arrangement, "that shocking error that ruined my life, withered
all my days, and gave all my thoughts the colors of hatred and despair,"
often followed by vows to do better and unrealistic-sounding plans for
how his financial situation will soon right itself, provided that the letter
yield an immediate loan, which will be the key to unlocking a new world
of possibility. "I need to be saved, and you alone can save me," Baudelaire
wrote to her on May 6, 1861. (These entreaties were often successful:
Baudelaire's mother is estimated to have forked over more than twenty

thousand francs over the course of the poet's adulthood, around $100,000 in today's currency.) Mixed into this, at times, were thoughts of ending his own life, sometimes outright threats that this would be his only option if things did not improve—and indeed he did attempt suicide once, at age twenty-four, by stabbing himself in the chest, though he recovered quickly and no one seemed to take his subsequent threats very seriously.

Baudelaire was clearly suffering—but did a part of him enjoy writing these letters? They are bravura performances of a kind: beseeching, self-rationalizing, darkly humorous, and occasionally quite insightful, at least when it came to his own torpor. He is a great observer of procrastination, of the special flavor of that self-defeating habit, how it is at once a torment and a kind of friend.

> When I'm unfortunate enough to neglect a duty, the following day it's even harder to perform that duty, and it becomes daily more and more difficult until that duty ends by seeming impossible to perform. . . . The only way I ever get out of difficult situations is through an explosion—but what I suffer in my existence is beyond expression, believe me!

At times, he clings to the idea of habit—the solution to his ills, if only he can attain it. On June 3, 1863: "Habit alone can offset all the vices of my temperament." Five months later: "The great aim, the only aim of my life now is to transform work, the hardest, most problematic thing in the world, into the thing I most enjoy, and that's a question of habit." But he never became a true creature of habit, or at least not of the good habits he wished so fervently to adopt. "I've acquired the detestable habit of putting off until the morrow all my duties, *even the most pleasant of them*," he wrote to his mother on December 31, 1863.

Reading his letters, you are rooting for Baudelaire to finally overcome his vices and achieve the equilibrium he so desperately craves, or at least that he claims to crave. He himself fantasized about this possibility, the tantalizing possibility of self-improvement. "Truly, I consider the man who succeeds in healing himself of a vice as infinitely braver than a soldier or a man who defends his honor in a duel," he wrote to his mother on July 31, 1864. "But how to heal myself?"

He never really figured it out, but it was in the midst of that struggle that his great poems were written, most famously *Les Fleurs du mal*, first published in 1857, but also his magnificent prose poems of the 1860s. The biographer Joanna Richardson writes that he "saw his poems as revenge for his destiny," and if that's true, then his revenge was astonishingly complete. (Even his mother, eventually, was impressed.) But he also recognized that the suffering, the poverty, the illness—it kept him from realizing all the projects he might have realized had he been able to achieve a more comfortable, steady existence. "I have in my head 20 novels and 2 plays," he wrote to his mother in February 1858, when he was almost thirty-seven. "I don't want an honest, commonplace reputation. I want to crush people, astonish them, like Byron, Balzac, or Chateaubriand. Is there still time? Oh, if only I'd known when I was young the value of time, health and money."

+ + +

For Virginia Woolf, her inheritance had been a means to an end; it enabled her to make her way as a writer, to slowly and painstakingly fulfill her potential as a novelist, to continue "eking out a delicate gift laboriously," as she once characterized another writer's project; she never could have done what she did without that £400 a year. For Baudelaire, did losing control of his money serve the same purpose? It gave him a condition to rebel against and an excuse for his inconsistent productivity; besides, his writing demanded that he be perpetually out of step with society. And also think of what he wrote about the sonnet, true perhaps of his life as well: "Because the form is constricting, the idea bursts forth all the more intensely."

And what happened to Fernando Pessoa after he exhausted his inheritance in less than a year's time? He found work writing business letters in English and French for Lisbon firms that did business abroad. It wasn't such a bad way to make a living; according to his biographer Richard Zenith, "he came and went pretty much as he wanted, never being obliged to work set hours." (He also borrowed large sums from his wealthy Aunt Lisbela that he never repaid.) This suited him. As an adult, Pessoa maintained a simple, ascetic lifestyle, living in rented rooms or with family, stopping every evening at a small corner store to buy two rolls, some ham and cheese, a pack of cigarettes, matches, and a pint and a half of cheap brandy. (He smoked and drank while he wrote in the evening; when the brandy ran out, at one, two, or three in the morning, he went to bed.) Losing his inheritance shrank his opportunities for action and engagement in the world, and at the end of the day that may have been what he preferred. For Pessoa, the ultimate measure of freedom was one's ability to do nothing much at all with it. As he wrote in *The Book of Disquiet*, his masterpiece, which he worked on for decades but never finished:

> Opportunity is like money, which, come to think of it, is nothing but an opportunity. For those who act, opportunity concerns the will, and the will doesn't interest me. For those like me who don't act, opportunity is the song of no sirens existing; it should be voluptuously spurned, stowed high and away for no use at all.

ALLOWANCE

Baudelaire embarked on adulthood with an inheritance, through his own improvidence saw it downgraded into an allowance, and then raged against this demotion for decades. But an allowance is nothing to be scoffed at! Indeed, is there any sweeter word in the English language? You are being *allowed* to do something—to continue to exist, at the very least, while you figure out your proper life trajectory. And it was familial allowances that enabled some of the greatest art of all time.

Paul Cézanne is a good example. Many artists' careers would have been difficult without parental support; Cézanne's would have been impossible. Though he is now celebrated as perhaps the pivotal figure in the transition from nineteenth-century impressionism and postimpressionism to twentieth-century modernism and abstraction, and though he was recognized as a pioneering genius by a small group of his fellow painters, Cézanne was snubbed by the art establishment of his time, ignored by collectors, and derided by the general public, earning essentially zero income from his painting for decades. He was thirty-five before he sold a painting to anyone other than friends and supporters, fifty-six when he had his first one-man show; before that point, according to his dealer Ambroise Vollard, Cézanne "had not made enough with his paintings after thirty-five years of unremitting toil, even to pay for his brushes and colors." He was able to continue painting for all those years only because of an allowance from his not-exactly-approving father, who for most of his life considered his adult son *sans profession*.

The painter's father, Louis-Auguste Cézanne, was the archetypal self-made man. Born in Aix-en-Provence in 1798, he apprenticed as a hat-maker and hat salesman in Paris in his early twenties, opened his own millinery business in Aix at age twenty-six, and from there expanded into money-lending, giving loans to local businessmen—and ruthlessly pursuing anyone who fell behind on their repayments. According to Cézanne biographer Alex Danchev, Louis-Auguste once "installed himself in the house of one spendthrift and proceeded to impose a regime more in keeping with their means, regulating all household expenditure, down to the amount of butter, meat, and potatoes to be consumed. After two years of enforced austerity, he recovered the full amount of his loan, with interest."

If such drastic tactics were not sufficient, and a businessman still could not repay his loan, no problem—Louis-Auguste would simply take over and liquidate the business, recouping his own investment and then some. This species of "moneylending bordering on usury," as Danchev describes it, proved highly profitable, and Louis-Auguste was eventually able to leave the hat trade for banking—he and his business partner literally bought the only bank in town—where he continued to specialize in short-term loans. Louis-Auguste had a gift for assessing the creditworthiness of potential borrowers, and between this gift and his relentless pragmatism, he raised himself from humble roots into wealth and status.

So what a delicious irony that Louis-Auguste's only son, Paul, born in Aix-en-Provence in 1839, would as a teenager fall in love with *painting*, perhaps the least pragmatic career imaginable, and would prove incapable of following any other path. As Cézanne's future dealer Ambroise Vollard put it years later:

> Monsieur Cézanne asked for nothing better than to see his son established some day in one of those honorable professions which are so abundantly lucrative and redound so creditably to the honor of a family. But, unfortunately, an irresistible leaning towards

painting, which was to become the despair of his parents, manifested itself very early in young Paul Cézanne.

Careful what you wish for, parents! This is not the only instance in art history when a parent's express disapproval of the arts seemed to practically guarantee a child's attachment to it. Not that Cézanne didn't try, reluctantly, to satisfy his father's wishes. After passing his baccalaureate at age nineteen (on his second attempt, three months after failing his first try), Cézanne did as Louis-Auguste wished: He registered with the Faculty of Law at the University of Aix-en-Provence and began attending the necessary courses, passing his first round of law exams in November 1859. The plan was that he would first become a lawyer and then join his father in working at the bank. But law school proved so odious to young Cézanne that, like Fernando Pessoa, he was moved to capture his distress in verse, with a poem beginning:

Alas, I took the torturous path of Law.
I took is not the word, I was forced to take
The Law, the horrible Law, with all equivocations
Will make my life a misery for three years!

Meanwhile, however, Cézanne had also begun taking evening classes at the local drawing school, where he excelled. In the spring of 1860, less than a year after embarking on his law studies, Cézanne refused to re-register at the university; "the horrible Law" could hold him no longer, and he was finally willing to endure his father's disappointment in exchange for turning his full attention to art. Even so, it took him another year to get himself from Aix to Paris, where his schoolboy friend Émile Zola had already established himself and was urging Cézanne to join him.

"Paul will be eaten up by painting," Louis-Auguste liked to predict. But at this point his disapproval couldn't have been *too* strong; he granted Cézanne an allowance of 125 francs a month, which, according to Zola, would be just enough to survive in the capital. In a letter, Zola—who at the time was making one hundred francs a month as a clerk for the publishing firm Hachette—laid out a painter's budget in Paris:

A room at twenty francs per month; *déjeuner* eighteen sous and dinner twenty-two sous, making two francs a day or sixty francs a month; adding the twenty francs for the room—that makes eighty all told. Besides that, you have your studio class to pay for; Suisse's, one of the cheapest, costs ten francs, I believe. Then I should say ten francs for canvas, brushes and paints, which makes one hundred francs. That leaves you twenty-five francs for your laundry, light, tobacco, pocket-money, and all the thousand and one little needs that come up from day to day.

In fact, Cézanne managed to spend a little less than two francs a day on food—not that he was keen on saving the excess. According to Vollard, "it was Cézanne's practice, when he had money in his pocket, to spend it before going to bed. '*Pardieu!*' he used to exclaim to Zola, who found him prodigal, 'if I should die tonight, would you want my family to inherit the money?'"

But Cézanne only lasted five months in Paris. He was not a natural city dweller, and he missed the countryside, whose beauty and mystery had always been integral to his painting. Now Louis-Auguste saw a fresh opportunity to alter his son's trajectory; if Paul could not stomach law school, he could simply start as a clerk in the family bank and work his way up from there. Cézanne did as his father asked. But this was an even worse fit than law school and resulted in another scrap of poetry by the stifled artist:

The banker Cézanne, with fear in his eyes,
Sees a painter-to-be from his counter arise.

At the same time, Cézanne resumed his studies at the local school of drawing, and after a year of lassitude and self-doubt in Aix he again gathered his resolve and mounted a fresh assault on Paris, returning in

November 1862. This time, it stuck. Though Cézanne was to move back and forth between Paris and the Provençal countryside throughout his life, he would never again waver in his choice of painting or entertain the possibility of a more practical occupation. This despite, as mentioned above, the rejection by virtually all art-world gatekeepers, not to mention all collectors of contemporary art. Of his paintings, Alex Danchev writes: "It would be an exaggeration to say that he could not give them away, but not much of an exaggeration—there were those who refused." He was refused, as well, at the École Nationale Supérieure des Beaux-Arts, the only school that mattered to him; it may have also mattered to Cézanne's father, who would have seen his son's acceptance as an official sanction on his talent that would somewhat justify his choice of profession. It wasn't to be—Cézanne applied twice and both times was rejected. That was just the beginning of his estrangement from the art establishment. Going forward, Cézanne annually submitted his work to the Salon de Paris, the most important art exhibition in France or, indeed, in the world at the time. Every year, beginning in 1864, he submitted his canvases; every year, with one exception, they were rejected. (The exception occurred in 1882, when Cézanne pretended to be the pupil of a painting teacher whose good friend was serving on the jury. This juror let Cézanne's work into the salon under the mistaken belief that he was doing his friend a favor.)

Why was Cézanne's work so universally derided, at least for the first thirty-five years of his career? From our current vantage point, it can be hard to comprehend what was so radical, even offensive about his still lifes, landscapes, and portraits. But Cézanne's willingness to leave forms abstracted and only partly defined, to retain blank patches of canvas in finished paintings, and just generally to eschew a strictly realistic depiction of his subjects in favor of a blocky, patchy, gauzy, or even borderline clumsy approximation of them—one that he felt *better* conveyed their essence, and one that he went to enormous lengths to realize (Cézanne was notorious was slashing works in progress to shreds, punching a hole through them in a fit of frustration, or, when painting outside, hurling a rock through the middle of a canvas)—well, it simply baffled contemporary viewers, who were quite certain that this rather brutish-seeming

Provençal lacked the talent to realize more conventionally pleasing compositions.

Fortunately, Cézanne's paternal allowance continued—and even increased, at some point, to two hundred francs a month. The extra funds soon proved necessary. In 1869, when he was thirty, Cézanne began a relationship with a nineteen-year-old artists' model named Marie-Hortense Fiquet. Fearing his father's disapproval, and the potential cessation of his allowance, Cézanne kept the relationship a secret from his parents, even after Hortense gave birth to a son, also named Paul, in 1872. Thereafter, Cézanne managed to keep both partner and child a secret from his father for another six years—until Louis-Auguste finally discovered the truth when he opened a letter addressed to his son, which mentioned "Madame Cézanne and little Paul." At this point, Cézanne was summoned to Aix for the father-son showdown he had long dreaded, and it is a testament to how bad their relationship was that the almost forty-year-old Cézanne could think of no course of action but to flatly deny the existence of Hortense and little Paul, despite the damning evidence to the contrary. Louis-Auguste, unconvinced, halved his son's allowance while he tried to decide what to do. The shrewd old banker regarded this Hortense as a gold digger and did not intend on supporting her and her child in addition to his impractical artist son. Cézanne feared that he would be cut off entirely—and then what? While he waited, he appealed to his old friend Zola to send sixty francs to Hortense, to make up the paternal shortfall. For the next five months, the father-son standoff continued; each month, Cézanne renewed his "monthly prayer" to Zola, who helped him without question.[*]

And then, suddenly, resolution. In September, Cézanne wrote to Zola, "*Nota-Bene*: Papa gave me 300 francs this month. Incredible." The reason for Louis-Auguste's change of heart is unknown, though there is some suggestion that he may have been distracted by a potential new mistress of his own. In any case, Cézanne had won; going forward, he would receive

---

[*] By this time, Zola was a successful novelist, having completed the first several volumes of his monumental Rougon-Macquart series. He had come a long way from his earliest days in Paris, when, legend has it, he would trap sparrows in his room and eat them to survive.

three hundred francs every month until his father's death, when he inherited his entire estate. He could continue painting in exactly the manner he pleased, which was really the only way he could ever do anything. In this sense, he wasn't so different from his father after all—he saw one way forward, the right way, and couldn't tolerate any deviation from that course. And when his father died in 1886, six months after Cézanne finally married Hortense and made little Paul his legitimate son, the painter was devastated. Louis-Auguste's lifelong resistance to his career was forgotten; now Cézanne recognized how much his support had enabled him. (It would still be almost another decade until Ambroise Vollard became Cézanne's dealer and finally brought him widespread recognition and financial success.) A friend who was with Cézanne while his late father's household was being cleared for auction reports the painter standing among Louis-Auguste's furniture, exclaiming:

> That armchair in which Papa had his nap. That table, at which he did his accounts all his life. Ah! He didn't miss a trick, not him, to provide me with an income. Tell me, what would have become of me, without that? You see what they do to me. Yes, yes . . . when you have a son who is an artist, you must provide him with an income.

+ + +

And what about when you have a daughter who is an artist? The Russian-born American sculptor Louise Nevelson said that she knew she was an artist from "earliest, earliest childhood." But after she graduated from high school in 1918, her parents certainly did not think of providing her with an income; in that era, it still wasn't common for young women to go to college, let alone follow their still-inchoate artistic dreams. Nevelson's father was a builder who ran a lumberyard in Rockland, Maine, where the family had emigrated from Russia in 1905 when Nevelson was six. Her mother admired her youthful creativity but didn't know the first thing about artists or the art world. So Nevelson had to figure out her own path toward her vocation. Wisely, she didn't have any expectations of making money *from* her art. "Who in this absurd world of ours becomes an artist with the expectation of making money?" she once asked. "Only the naïve. To survive, most need a job or private income or a rich lover or husband, or something." She wasn't too keen on getting a job—and, in 1918, there weren't a lot of employment opportunities for young women beyond teaching. A private income was not an option, alas. That left a rich husband.

As it happens, a candidate arrived the next year: a wealthy New York shipping executive named Charles Nevelson. Louise (born Leah Berliawsky) was nineteen; Charles was thirty-seven. He proposed after their first date. She was interested—provided he was willing to accept and support her as an artist. "I explained very carefully that I wanted to study art, that I was going to pursue a creative life," Nevelson said decades later, "and he said that was all right and there was no reason I couldn't continue. We could still get married."

They were married in 1920, and for a brief period the union worked. Nevelson didn't yet know exactly what kind of artist she wanted to be; she was interested in drawing and painting but also singing, acting, and dancing. Her new husband didn't complain when she wanted to take singing lessons for $50 a day, a phenomenal sum at the time (around $800 at present-day values). He also agreed with Nevelson that they would not have children, which she saw as an impediment to her creative ambitions. But his family was not so keen on this art-obsessed newcomer. Nevelson recalled:

> My husband's family was terribly refined. Within their circle you could know Beethoven, but God forbid if you were Beethoven. You were not allowed to be a creator, you were just supposed to be an audience. This empty appreciation didn't suit me, and from the beginning of my marriage I felt hemmed in. I was a creator and I had to make things.

Things got much worse when Nevelson accidentally got pregnant a year into their marriage, giving birth to a son in 1922. She did not adjust well to the demands of new motherhood. "I wasn't equipped, and

I've never been equipped [to be a mother]," she said many years later. As an adult, her son, Mike, remembered being three years old, clinging to his father's feet and pleading with him not to go to work, because he "dreaded" being home alone with his mother. "I don't think I gave him any particular attention," Nevelson admitted. "I don't even think I understood what being a mother meant, as such." She compared the combination of maternal guilt and frustrated ambition to a chronic toothache, and she began drinking too much to numb the pain. Finally, she saw no option but to break out. "I knew where my talents were and where I had to go," she wrote. She separated from her husband, put her son in the care of her parents in Maine, and sought out the legendary art teacher Hans Hofmann in Europe. By the early 1930s, she was back in New York with her son, living in primitive downtown studios, and working fiercely on her art.

Going forward, Nevelson's trajectory closely resembled Cézanne's: She exhibited her work for twenty-five years without making a single sale, didn't have her first solo exhibition until she was forty-two years old, and didn't get her big break until her work was included in a 1958 exhibition at the Museum of Modern Art, when Nevelson was almost sixty. Since then, she has been recognized as one of the most important sculptors of the twentieth century, who practically invented the field of environmental art with her large-scale monochromatic wooden sculptures—but getting there took decades of working with hardly any outside encouragement. Indeed, she saw Cézanne as a kindred spirit. "It is always amazing to me that in the nineteenth century when Cézanne lived, there really wasn't one person on earth who saw eye to eye with him," Nevelson said in one of the taped conversations that make up her 1976 autobiography, *Dawns + Dusks*. "This should be a lesson to the creative mind and give us courage. Just because there is no one on earth for the moment that sees it, that does not disturb a creative person." (It might have disturbed her more than she liked to admit. At another point in her autobiography she said, "For thirty years I wanted to jump out of every window.")

But of course Cézanne was able to persevere because of the allowance from his father. How did Nevelson do it? After her marriage dissolved, she was too proud to ask her ex-husband for alimony. Initially, she pawned the diamond jewelry he had given her to fund her studies; she may have also accepted money from some of the many lovers she took after the dissolution of their marriage. But her real solution ended up being the same as Cézanne's: a long-running allowance, in Nevelson's case not from her father but from her brother, Nate, who owned and operated a successful hotel in Maine. Starting in the mid-1940s, he gave her a monthly allowance of $225 (almost four grand at today's values), a practice he kept up for thirty years, by which time she finally no longer needed it. Even more crucially: In 1945, he helped her buy* a four-story town house on Manhattan's East Thirtieth Street near Second Avenue, where she would live and work for almost fifteen years, until the building was demolished in a redevelopment project. To pay to renovate the house, she also borrowed money from the art dealer Karl Nierendorf, who had given Nevelson her first solo show in 1941. By the time Nevelson settled into the town house, her son had left home to join the merchant marines, and he *also* started sending his mother regular checks, a practice he continued from the mid-1940s until the late 1950s. (He eventually became a sculptor himself.)

This town house became the site of Nevelson's proper maturation as an artist. Over the fifteen years she lived there, Nevelson filled almost every room with her sculptures and with the scraps of wood she used to construct them, many of which she scavenged from the street. And there were a lot of rooms to fill: In Nevelson's words, it was "an enormous, four-story brownstone house, including a cellar, which made it five stories. And a big backyard where I could work six to eight months a year." Oh, and it had seven marble fireplaces. To furnish it, Nevelson bought three identical sets of garden furniture and placed them on separate floors, "so there was a unity." She liked simplicity, order, and symmetry; later in life, she liked to start off her day by getting up at three in the morning and rearranging the furniture in her room before heading into her studio to work.

Despite the enviable live-work space—and contrary to the flamboy-

---

* Accounts differ as to whether the money for the town house was a gift from their parents, a portion of Nevelson and her siblings' inheritance after both parents died, a gift from her brother, or some combination.

ant outfits that she donned in public once she finally achieved art-world fame, with elaborate headscarves and thick eyelashes made from mink— Nevelson certainly did not live a luxurious lifestyle. She owned two sets of gray sweatshirts and sweatpants, which she slept and worked in; for food, she mainly subsisted on tinned fish, bread, and tea. She didn't cook, nor did she shop. According to the biographer Laurie Wilson, she "had an account at the corner restaurant and bar, from which she phoned in orders for whatever she needed, usually in quantity. That way she never had to go shopping, which she considered a waste of her energy." In her autobiography, Nevelson said:

> I trained myself not to waste. I feel that if you know you're going to live your life as an artist, you steel yourself daily. You don't develop fancy tastes, fancy appetites. An artist once said to me, "Well, it's all right, Mrs. Nevelson, but I have to eat." And it offended me. And I said, "Who said you have to eat?" You know you can eat bread or a cup of tea or a can of sardines when you're hungry. As a matter of fact, I prefer that to most of the fancy restaurants in New York. I couldn't afford to get caught in a lot of things on earth, because I had my sights in another place.

But—again—Nevelson could afford to keep her sights in another place for all those years because of her brother's hotel business. She wasn't exactly a hypocrite—for many years, she really did live on bread and tea and sardines. But she also never really had a day job[*] and never really concerned herself with anything but her work, and maybe wasn't able to do otherwise. A story related by Nevelson: Once, when she was feeling "a little sad," she walked up Fifth Avenue to do some window-shopping, admiring all the beautiful items in the department store displays. When she came to the luxury store Bonwit Teller, Nevelson ran a little thought

---

[*] The one exception was in the late 1930s, when she briefly taught at the Educational Alliance Art School, on New York's Lower East Side.

experiment for herself: "I'm not taken by 'beautiful things,'" she said, "but I was depressed and I said, Look, Louise, you don't feel so hot. If the president of Bonwit's came out and said, 'If you want to work for us two hours a day, from 12:00 to 2:00, we will give you half a million dollars for the year'—would you accept it? I said no."

+ + +

Cézanne's art career was enabled by a decades-long allowance from his father; Nevelson's was only possible thanks to a similarly long-running allowance from her brother (and the regular checks from her son didn't hurt, either). Both artists got their hands on said allowances not so much via any kind of clever maneuvering as through a monumental stubbornness, a persistent refusal to do anything other than what they had determined was their life's work, effectively forcing their families to support them or watch them starve.

But sometimes family money takes a little more coaxing. A good example is the English novelist and short story writer Christopher Isherwood, who was born to a family of landed gentry in Cheshire, in northwest England, in 1904. By this time, the family fortunes weren't quite what they had once been, his forebears having gradually depleted their wealth over the generations; Isherwood grew up among the shabby gentility of this decline. Still, from the moment of Isherwood's birth, his mother dearly hoped that he would one day inherit what was left and become the next steward of Marple and Wybersley Halls, the pair of ancient houses on the family estate. After Isherwood's father died fighting in World War I, in 1915, and then after his grandfather died nine years later, this seemed not only possible but likely. Only Isherwood's Uncle Henry, who had no children and was separated from his wife, stood in his way. Isherwood's mother urged her son to find a respectable middle-class career—she favored librarianship—create a solid footing for himself, and bide his time.

But Isherwood had his own plans. He intentionally failed his second-year exams at Cambridge and was asked to leave the university without a degree. This was phase one of disappointing his mother. Phase two was tinkering with the idea of going to medical school, but after six months abandoning that plan, and indeed abandoning England altogether in favor of Berlin, where Isherwood suspected he had a better shot of fully becoming himself as a writer and as a gay man. He departed on March 14, 1929, five months shy of his twenty-fifth birthday.

But how to pay for Berlin? The inheritance was a long way off, and he had no income in the meantime. But there was Uncle Henry. In the autobiography *Christopher and His Kind*, Isherwood wrote (referring to himself in the third person):

> Henry was the only member of the family who could be described as wealthy; he had inherited the Isherwood estates and money when his father died in 1924. Soon after this event, Christopher had decided to become Uncle Henry's favorite nephew; and he had done so instantaneously, by making it clear to Henry that they had the same sexual nature. Henry's brothers and sisters had always known about his homosexuality and had made unkind jokes behind his back, of which he was well aware. So Henry was delighted to discover a blood relative who shared his tastes—using the slang expressions of his generation, he referred to himself as being "musical" or "so."
>
> Once they had reached this understanding, it hadn't been hard for Christopher to introduce a benevolent idea into Henry's head. Since Henry was separated from his wife after a childless marriage; since, as a good Catholic, he couldn't remarry; since, being what he was, he didn't want to; since the estates were entailed and Christopher was the heir presumptive—why shouldn't Christopher be given a small allowance now, at a time of life when he really needed the money?

Well, why shouldn't he? Uncle Henry was convinced, promising to pay Isherwood an allowance every three months. But the money was not without strings attached.

> Christopher was expected to reciprocate by writing to him regularly and by dining with him when they were both in London.

Writing the letters was a weary task, because Henry had to be thanked for his bounty over and over again, and reassured that he was the Model Uncle. The dinners were more fun, because you could get drunk. Henry demanded to be told every detail of Christopher's sex life; Christopher obliged, exaggerating wildly.

After Isherwood shared all the details of his Berlin exploits, it was Henry's turn. Isherwood writes: "He had once paid a young man not to wash himself for a month. 'At the end of the month, he came to see me and he smelt exactly like a *fox*! Delicious!'" This mutual disclosure doesn't sound *too* onerous, and anyway it was unavoidable: Isherwood couldn't have afforded to live in Berlin without Henry's allowance. In fact, he could barely afford to live there with the allowance. Years later, his friend and fellow writer Stephen Spender recalled Isherwood's lifestyle in Berlin around 1930:

> During the years when I was often in Berlin, he lived in various poor parts of the town . . . the worst, that of the Hallesches Tor, an area of slum tenements. He lived very poorly, scarcely ever spending more than sixty pfennigs (about eightpence) on a meal. During this time, when I had meals almost every day with him, we ate food such as horse flesh and lung soup, which for some years ruined my digestion, and for all time my teeth, as they had long ago ruined his.

It wasn't that Isherwood and Spender were too lazy to work—at this moment in Berlin, making extra cash was no easy feat. "Sometimes [Isherwood] was broke and we would force ourselves to think up ways of earning money," Spender writes. "He gave English lessons, he translated, occasionally he even did a little journalism, but in Berlin in 1930 you not only had to work very hard to earn very little, you also had to be a financial genius to get paid."

So flattering Uncle Henry, and making him feel like they were in a league together, was easy work by comparison—though Isherwood was appalled by his uncle's snobbery and by his politics. (Henry spent winters in Rome and, Isherwood noted, "always approved of Mussolini, who had made the trains run on time.") The needy nephew made sure to "keep his mouth shut, project sparkling interest, and smile flatteringly at this aging beauty—it was as if he were a courtier of Queen Elizabeth I." And yet even with all this effort, Uncle Henry still sometimes failed to disburse the next allowance payment, to Isherwood's great dismay: "Thus Christopher was reminded that he wasn't a free spirit, as he liked to think, but a captive balloon."

It wasn't until a decade later that Isherwood was finally able to give up the allowance from his Model Uncle—and in a funny way, he was able to do so because of Henry's influence. It was 1940. By this time, Isherwood was living in Los Angeles, trying to break into Hollywood screenwriting—and quickly succeeding at doing so. In a letter to his mother, Isherwood explained that he no longer needed Henry's money, because he was receiving nearly one hundred pounds a week from Metro-Goldwyn-Mayer, a handsome sum. The studio was bankrolling him because of the success of his third novel, *Mr. Norris Changes Trains*; MGM wanted to make a picture with a character like Mr. Norris, the seedy double agent at the center of the novel. Mr. Norris has been commonly accepted as a fictionalized portrait of the British suspected spy Gerald Hamilton—"the wickedest man in England," as he was known—but, the biographer Katherine Bucknell writes, "the novel that made [Isherwood's] reputation and which gave him his first foothold in Hollywood . . . was inspired just as much by Uncle Henry."

Ultimately, this was the only family legacy that Isherwood would accept. When Henry died, shortly after the MGM money started flowing, Isherwood's mother's dream of her son becoming heir to the family fortune and steward of its ancient houses was at last possible—and, at last, decisively rejected. Isherwood declined his inheritance, letting everything pass along to his younger brother, Richard, instead. He wrote in his diary, "It is too late now . . . the absurd boyhood dream of riches is over forever."

As for the late uncle who had unreliably bankrolled him during those crucial early years, Isherwood wrote:

Poor Henry—he must be glad to get free of all this mess, at last. . . . I was fond of him, and he of me, in our different ways. No doubt he always thought of me as being after his money—as indeed I was. But this seemed to him perfectly natural and proper. He had the eighteenth-century conception of the relation between uncle and heir.

If Isherwood and his uncle had a kind of tacit understanding, the writer and his mother did not: She was devastated that her firstborn never shared her long-cherished dream of security and comfort in the ancestral family home; his rejection of his inheritance was the final blow. But then, as we've already seen with Cézanne and with Baudelaire—and as we will continue to see throughout these pages—disappointing one's parents is practically a prerequisite to becoming an artist.

THE ART OF MOOCHING

On October 26, 1911, a twenty-eight-year-old Franz Kafka made the following entry in his diary, reflecting on something he had read about the Irish playwright George Bernard Shaw's youthful strivings:

Because it consoles me I write down an autobiographical remark of Shaw's, although it actually is the opposite of consoling: As a boy he was apprentice in the office of an estate agent's in Dublin. He soon gave up this position, went to London, and became a writer. In the first nine years, from 1876 to 1885, he earned 140 kronen in all. "But although I was a strong young man and my family found itself in poor circumstances, I did not throw myself into the struggle for a livelihood; I threw my mother in and let her support me. I was no support for my old father; on the contrary, I hung on to his coat-tails."

Kafka found Shaw's example "the opposite of consoling" because he saw no similar path for himself; by this point, he had already gone to law school and found work in an insurance office, where he was miserable. (For more on Kafka's day job, see page 88.) His father, a Prague businessman, could have theoretically supported Kafka while he pursued his writing—but Kafka would never dare ask for such a dispensation. He was able to follow Shaw, he wrote, "only to the extent of having read the passage to my parents." In the diary, there is no mention of their reaction.

Would Kafka have been a little consoled, perhaps, to learn that Shaw's remark is exaggerated, or at least lacking crucial context? It's true that the Dublin-born Shaw did not, as a young man, rush to support his parents in poor circumstances. But you can hardly blame him. Shaw's father was an alcoholic with a gift for losing money. His mother, disappointed in marriage, fell under the spell of a musical impresario named George Vandeleur Lee—in Shaw's words, a "mesmeric conductor and daringly original teacher of singing," with a deformed foot, "pirate-black whiskers," and an air of mystery—and, when Shaw was seventeen, she moved to London with Lee, finding room there for Shaw's two sisters but leaving her son behind with a father who barely registered his existence. By this time, the teenage Shaw had already been put to work; after performing poorly at school, his family found him a job as an office boy at a land agent's firm, beginning when he was fifteen. More than three decades later, he would lend the experience to one of the characters in his play *Misalliance*, a nameless clerk who complains:

> Do you know what my life is? I spend my days from nine to six— nine hours of daylight and fresh air—in a stuffy little den counting another man's money. I've an intellect: a mind and a brain and a soul; and the use he makes of them is to fix them on his tuppences and his eighteenpences and his two pound seventeen and tenpences and see how much they come to at the end of the day and take care that no one steals them. I enter and enter, and add and add, and take money and give change, and fill cheques and stamp receipts; and not a penny of that money is my own: not one of those transactions has the smallest interest for me or anyone else in the world but him; and even he couldn't stand it if he had to do it all himself. . . . Of all the damnable waste of human life that ever was invented, clerking is the very worst.

But clerking taught Shaw an important lesson. He started at the land agent's with no intention of making a career there, only to find that his intentions made precious little difference: "I made good in spite of myself, and found, to my dismay, that Business, instead of expelling me as the worthless imposter I was, was fastening upon me with no intention of letting go."

So Shaw unfastened himself, lighting off for London in 1876, around the time of his twentieth birthday, joining his mother and sister and George Vandeleur Lee. (A family tragedy prompted the move—Shaw's sister Agnes was dying of tuberculosis, and he arrived in time to attend her funeral.) By this time, he had developed the ambition to become a writer and had also developed a nuanced appreciation of music; his first job in London was ghostwriting music criticism for Lee. But Lee and Shaw's mother soon had a falling-out. Abruptly, the mesmeric conductor was out of her life, though Shaw stayed in touch with him. Her music teacher and quasi partner gone, Shaw's mother was now forced to support herself by giving singing lessons—in Shaw's words, "drudging in her elder years at the art of music which she had followed in her prime freely for love"— and collecting a small monthly sum from her estranged husband back in Dublin.

This is the moment when Shaw said that he should have thrown himself into the struggle for a livelihood to spare his parents from paying his way. Years later, he called the fact that he failed to do so "monstrous." But perhaps they owed it to him. Shaw's parents had given him precious few opportunities in life, and yet somehow he had arrived at not only the ambition of becoming a writer but the enormous work ethic to match. In those early years in London, the twentysomething Shaw wrote and studied like a man possessed. He spent his afternoons in the British Museum's Reading Room, which became, one biographer has written:

his club, his university, a refuge, and the center of his life. He felt closer to strangers in this place than to his own family. He worked here daily for some eight years, applying for more than three hundred books each year, advancing through the *Encyclopedia Britannica*, medical and municipal statistics for future articles, writing lectures and letters to the press, adding to his musical knowledge and completing his long literary apprenticeship.

Shaw called his debt to the British Museum "inestimable." The work he did there did not pay off immediately; in his twenties, he wrote five novels in rapid succession, and all five were rejected by publishers. Still he persevered, turning from fiction to political writing, journalism, and eventually plays, where he finally broke through in 1892 with *Widowers' Houses*, the first of a string of increasingly sophisticated works for the stage. Over the ensuing decades, Shaw would go on to write an astonishing sixty plays, becoming the leading dramatist of his generation (and receiving the Nobel Prize in Literature in 1925). In his version of events, Shaw emphasized his tenacity and at the same time upbraided himself for depending on his parents—but it was his willingness to depend on his parents that allowed for his tenacity. Besides, Shaw was hardly the only artist whose career would not have been possible without some not-entirely-voluntary familial assistance.

+ + +

At the same time that George Bernard Shaw was becoming the most important playwright in London, a fellow Irishman twenty-six years his junior was preparing to become the most important English prose writer of the twentieth century. This was James Joyce, another Dublin native and another son of an alcoholic, spendthrift father who steered his family into financial ruin. Unlike Shaw, however, Joyce was a brilliant student. At age twelve, he won one of the top awards in Ireland's national preparatory school exams, which came with a twenty-pound prize, paid to the student's parents. Though by this time his family desperately needed the money, Joyce's father declared that young James should spend his prize however he liked. Joyce promptly bought presents for all ten of his siblings—carefully noting the expenditures in an account book, though he had no hope of ever being paid back—then used the remainder to treat his parents to the theater and restaurant meals.

It was the beginning of a lifelong habit: Whenever Joyce had money, he spent it rapidly, often extravagantly, insisting on footing the bill for taxis or restaurant meals he could scarcely afford—or else, like his father, drinking it away at the bars where he spent so many nights, belting out old Irish songs in his fine tenor voice or dancing a strange, loose-limbed jig that he perfected over many years of practice. He made up the financial gaps by borrowing relentlessly from anyone who would lend to him and then dodging relentlessly their attempts to recover their money. Needless to say, this pattern caused Joyce no end of troubles, though it's possible that the troubles that swirled about him all the time were in some way fruitful for him as a writer. He complained of the chaos, but it did not keep him from writing; in fact, during years that seem impossibly turbulent and unsettled, with mounting debts, frequent changes of address—and the frequent threat of eviction—the births of two children, and excruciating attacks of the eye disease that tormented Joyce throughout his adult life, he wrote a great deal and at an astonishingly high level. As the biographer Richard Ellmann has noted, "Underneath the excesses, [Joyce] was able to maintain a secret discipline about his work."

Joyce first set off from Dublin for the Continent in 1902, not long after graduating from the Royal University of Ireland. His destination was Paris, where he intended to study medicine at the Sorbonne. But Joyce was unprepared for medical school and soon dropped out in favor of a meager bohemian existence, spending his days reading in cafés and frequently going a day or two between meals—his was, he wrote, "a most villainous hunger." Before long, however, Joyce was recalled to Dublin by the news that his mother was gravely ill. She died several months later, and Joyce subsequently drifted around Dublin, succumbing to friends' entreaties that he embrace the comforts of drink—until this point, he had been a teetotaler; now he lunged in the opposite direction—while also writing a good deal and publishing some of what he wrote, placing poems and a few short stories in Irish periodicals.

He did some freelance journalism, too, but was not in a hurry to make it a profession, nor to pursue any other profession. He told his brother Stanislaus, "I should be supported at the expense of the state because I am capable of enjoying life."

In October 1904, Joyce tried to break free of Dublin again, and this time it stuck: He would live in self-imposed exile for the rest of his life, returning to his native city only a few times over the remaining decades. He left for mainland Europe with a plan for living and writing that was seemingly straightforward and pragmatic: He would teach English and write in his spare time. Departing Dublin, he already had a teaching job arranged at the Zurich branch of the Berlitz School. But nothing in Joyce's life was ever straightforward, and this trip would prove no exception. Upon arriving in Zurich, Joyce discovered that there was no job waiting for him after all. (It's not clear if the mix-up was on his part or the school's.) He was sent, instead, to the port city of Trieste, then part of the Austro-Hungarian Empire, and from there to another, smaller port city, Pola (now part of Croatia), where there was, at last, a job available teaching English to naval officers. To Joyce, it was "a naval Siberia," so he was relieved when, five months later, he was transferred back to the much more cosmopolitan Trieste, which would be his primary residence for the next decade.

With Joyce on this lurching journey was Nora Barnacle, the hotel chambermaid he had started wooing in Dublin the previous summer, who, only four months after their first date, agreed to leave Ireland with the peculiar young man. Despite Joyce's inability to provide a secure life, his staunch refusal to marry her—Joyce loathed organized religion and all its strictures, although he and Nora would finally be married in 1931 to secure their children's inheritances—and the fact that she did not particularly admire his early writing, Nora would remain loyal to him for the rest of his life, as would Joyce to her. Their relationship was one of the few anchors in a life of almost unrelenting turbulence. Nora was also a source of creative inspiration for Joyce: Her loving acceptance of him, her steadfastness, and the enduring erotic charge of their relationship helped enable his increasingly ambitious and unrestrained fiction. The character

Molly Bloom in *Ulysses* would be based on her, and the entire novel would take place on June 16, 1904—the day that Nora and Joyce went on their first date.*

The other anchor, during the first decade of Joyce's self-imposed exile, was his younger brother Stanislaus. If George Bernard Shaw could not have managed his long literary apprenticeship without his mother, Joyce could certainly not have managed his without reliable, beleaguered Stannie. He was summoned to Trieste in 1905, a few months after Joyce and Nora's first child, Giorgio, was born and the chaos of their lives reached a new crescendo. (Joyce's reaction to the heady responsibilities of fatherhood was to spend even more time drinking away his teaching salary at Trieste bars.) A couple of years earlier, Stanislaus—who also entertained literary ambitions, though his attempts always paled in comparison to his older brother's—had written in his diary a brief portrait of Joyce that is by turns admiring and incisive. He described Joyce as a genius and praised his "extraordinary moral courage," but he also noted the "meanness of whim and appetite" that characterized much of his behavior. "He has, above all, a proud willful vicious selfishness," Stanislaus wrote. He was now to find out how accurate this assessment was.

Stanislaus arrived in Trieste in October 1905 and began teaching alongside Joyce at the Berlitz School. The brothers' teaching styles reflected their opposing temperaments. Richard Ellmann writes, "Stanislaus was punctual and conscientious in his duties. James invariably arrived for his lessons late, and after a brief drill began to converse about all manner of subjects; the lesson would end with teacher and pupil singing an Irish song together, after which James would slide down the banister and leave, also very late." Joyce's English drills showed a similar mix of whimsy and rebellion; at one point, he had his pupils reciting and copying down the following passage:

---

* The date culminated in Nora giving Joyce a hand job in a deserted park near Dublin Harbor, an event that, years later, he lovingly recalled in a letter to her: "You who slid your hand down inside my trousers and pulled my shirt softly aside and touched my prick with your long tickling fingers and gradually took it all, fat and stiff as it was, into your hand and frigged me slowly until I came off through your fingers, all the time bending over me and gazing at me out of your quiet saintlike eyes." June 16 is now celebrated annually as Bloomsday.

The tax collector is an idiot who is always annoying me. He has filled my desk with little sheets marked "Warning," "Warning," "Warning." I told him that if he didn't stop it, I would send him to be f . . . ound out by that swindler, his master. Today, the swindler is the government of Vienna. Tomorrow it could be the one in Rome. But whether in Vienna or Rome or London, to me governments are all the same, pirates.

For the next decade, Stanislaus would all too often be the only thing that stood between Joyce and total dissolution. When Joyce stayed out too late drinking, Stannie went out to the bars and literally dragged him home. Eventually, he prevailed upon Joyce to stop drinking entirely—at least during the remainder of his time in Trieste—an intervention that proved crucial in his productivity. And he made up the shortfall in Joyce's household expenses, and settled Joyce's debts, countless times. Joyce took this all for granted. If he couldn't be supported at the expense of the state, his brother would have to step in. As Ellmann has written, "James saw no reason to limit his brother's sacrifices to genius, especially when genius had a family to support."

Joyce would rely on various additional saintlike patrons in the ensuing years—including Ezra Pound, who fiercely promoted Joyce's work and arranged for *Ulysses* to be serialized in the United States; the American expatriate bookseller Sylvia Beach, who published *Ulysses* in Paris when no one else would; and the English spinster Harriet Shaw Weaver, who subsidized Joyce while he wrote *Ulysses* and whose total donations to his upkeep over twenty years would amount to more than a million pounds at present-day values—but none of them would have entered his life without Stanislaus's support in these crucial early years. During his time in Trieste, Joyce completed the stories for *Dubliners*, wrote all of his first novel, *A Portrait of the Artist as a Young Man*, wrote his only play, *Exiles*, and drafted large sections of *Ulysses*. Sadly but perhaps inevitably, the brothers' relationship did not emerge from these years of lopsided support unscathed. When Joyce and his family left for Paris in 1920, Stanislaus stayed behind in Trieste, where he would continue teaching for the rest of his life (temporarily relocating to Zurich during Mussolini's reign). The brothers would meet only three times in the next two decades before Joyce's death, and Joyce would never really acknowledge his profound debt to Stannie. One depressing detail among many: When he was working to get *Dubliners* published, during the Trieste years, Joyce talked about dedicating the book to Stanislaus. By the time it was published, he had forgotten.

+ + +

Joyce's reliance on Stanislaus pales, however, in comparison to what must be the most famous case of sibling dependency in art or literary history: that of the Dutch painter Vincent van Gogh and his younger brother Theo. For years, Theo supplied Vincent with his only source of income, which Vincent extracted via an almost ceaseless epistolary campaign of begging, wheedling, proposing, scheming, lecturing, rationalizing, and otherwise contriving to gain just a few more guilders or francs—or at least this was my impression upon reading Steven Naifeh and Gregory White Smith's 953-page biography *Van Gogh: The Life*, published in 2011, a deeply researched and frequently brilliant book that made Vincent's never-ending campaign for Theo's money seem like the ultimate example of artist mooching. After spending some more time with Vincent's letters to Theo, however, I'm no longer sure I agree. Certainly Vincent was bad with money, and certainly he depended on Theo to keep working as a painter—but he did not evince the same kind of blithe entitlement that we just witnessed with Joyce. For Vincent, money, art, and family came together in an enormous emotional-logistical knot that he was always picking at but could never really untangle. And to think of him as a moocher is to miss his dedication and tenacity and also the beauty of Theo's support.

To appreciate the complexity of Vincent's situation, it helps to go back a generation to the dynamic between his father, Theodorus "Dorus" van Gogh, and Dorus's older brother Vincent "Cent" van Gogh. The brothers greatly resembled each other in looks, but in personality and trajectory they could hardly have been more different. Dorus was a stern, humorless soul who spent most of his life as a rector in the Dutch Reformed Church, ministering to the small Protestant population in the predominantly Catholic region of North Brabant, in the Netherlands near the border of Belgium, where Vincent, Theo, and their four siblings were born and raised. Cent, eight years older than Dorus, was one of the most successful art dealers of his era, a charming, sophisticated, and increasingly very wealthy entrepreneur who started selling art prints out of a paint shop in The Hague in the mid-1840s and eventually joined the Paris-based art dealership Goupil & Cie, which was making fortunes for its partners selling art prints to the burgeoning European middle class. Vincent grew up hearing Uncle Cent's letters read aloud to the family, and he must have wondered how brothers who looked so alike—and who, further, married a pair of sisters, Anna and Cornelia Carbentus, daughters of a prosperous Hague merchant—could be so different in outlook and lifestyle.

Vincent and his father were very different, too—Dorus was pious and stolid, Vincent a moody and combative soul almost from the moment of his birth, in 1853—and they frequently butted heads, especially after Vincent dropped out of boarding school at age fourteen. So he seized the opportunity, two years later, to follow in Uncle Cent's footsteps, starting in 1869 as the youngest employee of Goupil & Cie's branch in The Hague, packing and unpacking artwork and performing other junior assistant duties. Though Vincent was eager to learn and willing to work hard, he had trouble making friends in the city, and his rough, unpolished demeanor attracted the ire of his supervisor, who also resented his family connections. Then, according to Naifeh and Smith, things got much worse: Vincent seems to have become embroiled in a scandal, possibly involving a prostitute, though the exact details are unknown, which caused the firm to consider him a liability. He was transferred to Goupil's London branch, where he was happy for a time but then became involved in new difficulties when he fell in love with his landlady's daughter, who did not return his affections. (Vincent's young adulthood was studded with obsessive, mostly inappropriate romantic entanglements, causing considerable consternation among his family.) Next he was brought to the firm's Paris headquarters; then, in 1876, he was dismissed entirely. Meanwhile, Theo—four years Vincent's junior—had also started at Goupil and was succeeding where Vincent had failed, moving rapidly up the ranks and winning praise from all he encountered. He would work there for the entirety of his career and become a significant force in introducing contemporary Dutch and French art to the public.

After his expulsion from Goupil, Vincent swerved toward the other family business, making a short-lived effort to study theology and, when that didn't work out, becoming a kind of itinerant preacher among the coal miners working in the Belgian Borinage. But he flamed out there as well, landing back at home and into worse-than-ever tensions with his father. After a brief but unsuccessful stint as a teacher, art was his next and final career choice, and in a weird way it made perfect sense: Vincent would take his years of exposure to historical and contemporary European painting at Goupil, weld it to his missionary zeal and his passion for the downtrodden and the beauty of God's creation, and reinvent himself as a painter of landscapes, portraits, and still lifes. Of course, he had received no formal art education at this point, though he had learned to draw as a child and had kept it up somewhat over the years. Now, with Theo's encouragement, he declared his intentions: He would be an artist. He was twenty-seven and would live for only another decade.

Initially, Dorus provided a monthly allowance; then Theo took over, at first giving Vincent informal payments, then assenting to his demand of a 100-franc monthly allowance, and later agreeing to raise the amount to 150 francs—this at a time when a teacher earned around 75 francs a month. Yet Vincent was still always complaining of low funds; even his expressions of gratitude have an undertone of neediness. "Thank you for your letter, but I was really kicking my heels this time; my money ran out on *Thursday*, so until midday on Monday it was *damned long*," he wrote in one example from October 1888, thanking Theo for sending money and in practically the same breath trying to impress upon him how desperate things got before it arrived, as if to warn against future delays. "Throughout those 4 days I lived mainly on 23 coffees, with bread, and for which I still have to pay. It's not your fault, it's mine, if fault there is."

Well, Vincent was right about that. The reason that he was always low on money is that he was always spending it, on paints and canvases and frames, on models to pose for him, and on alcohol and prostitutes (not so much on food, the one area where he consistently economized). In Naifeh and Smith's eyes, Vincent's "plaintive, coercive arguments for further subsidies" became "the corrosive hallmark" of his correspondence with Theo, and ushered in a "world of suspicion and reserve" between the brothers, condemning them to "an unending cycle of resentful pleading and guilty scheming." But the reason he spent so much on paints, canvases, frames, and models was that he was producing a tremendous amount of work in his bid to transform himself from a late-blooming, mostly self-taught outsider into a major painter. And the editors of the Van Gogh Letters Project, who in 2009 published the definitive edition of the artist's correspondence, point out that Theo was in a good position to help. Theo was quite successful as an art dealer, making a base salary of 4,000 francs a year plus 7.5 percent of the net profit of the Goupil branch he managed, a significant bonus. In fact, Theo's average annual bonus came out to double his base salary, with the result that he earned on average 12,000 francs a year between 1882 and 1890, the years when he was giving Vincent a monthly stipend. That stipend averaged 1,750 francs a year, meaning that Theo spent roughly 14.5 percent of his income on Vincent—a significant sum, certainly, but not a ruinous one. (He kept this up even after getting married, in 1889; his wife, Johanna, would become Vincent's next most important supporter—more on that below.) Moreover, starting in June 1882, Theo generally sent Vincent his money in thrice-monthly installments, around the first, the tenth, and the twentieth of the month, rather than in a lump sum, no doubt to prevent Vincent from spending it all at once. So a great deal of what seems like begging for more money in Vincent's letters is in fact urging Theo to send the next installment right on time, or perhaps a little early.

So, yes, Vincent was bad with money, just as he was bad with school, with jobs, with appropriate love interests, with taking care of his health—in short, with living in any kind of rational, dependable, and orderly way. At the same time, it's hard to overemphasize what a funny, frustrating position he was in as an artist. His Uncle Cent was one of the era's great art dealers, and in fact two of Vincent's other uncles were also successful in the art trade. And Theo, who had encouraged Vincent to become an artist, was intimately acquainted with the painting avant-garde and was one of the few dealers with enough foresight to champion the Impressionists in Paris. Yet Uncle Cent was only really interested in art as a commodity (his motto as a dealer: "Everything gets sold"), and after Vincent's expulsion from Goupil he showed no interest in his nephew's art career and certainly no interest in funding it. As for Theo: As much as he empathized with Vincent's struggles and supported him emotionally and financially, he didn't think there was a market for Vincent's work, especially his early drawings and paintings of laborers in the fields around Nuenen, where Vincent stopped for a couple of years during a period of frequent relocations in the Netherlands and Belgium. The culmination of this period was 1885's *The Potato Eaters*, a relentlessly murky and hypnotically strange group portrait of poor laborers huddled around a peasant meal. It was Vincent's personal favorite of his paintings and now an acknowledged masterwork. Theo regarded it as unsellable and was probably right.

This is the real tension in Vincent's letters: between his gratitude for Theo's support and his deep frustration that no one else seemed to believe what he believed—that this money was not mere charity but an investment in the future promise, both artistic and financial, of his work. And this is what makes Vincent's letters to Theo so irresistibly compelling and frequently touching, and not merely pathetic. His pleas were like an externalization of his internal struggle: In trying to convince Theo that he deserved the money and was putting it to good use, he seemed to be trying to convince himself of those same arguments, to reassure himself that he was indeed on the right track, that all his striving was part of a trajectory toward something meaningful and original. He wrote to Theo in November 1882:

> One can't present oneself as somebody who can be of benefit to others or who has an idea for a business that's bound to be profitable—no, on the contrary, it's to be expected that it will end with a deficit and yet, yet, one feels a power seething inside one, one has a task to do and it must be done.

That feeling of "a power seething inside" is itself something precious and enormously valuable, I would argue, but because it so often does not have immediate income-generating potential, it gets neglected or diminished, when what it really needs is to be indulged. Vincent would pay a steep price for indulging his own power, and Theo would, too, but even so I can't help but see them both as figures to admire and emulate. As much as any artist in history, Vincent knew, intimately, how much *effort* it takes to realize one's talent, how gradually progress accrues, and to what an extent money is a determining factor in this accrual, even if one doesn't particularly care about money—perhaps especially then. In relying on his younger and more levelheaded brother for financial support, Vincent was of course grateful—but more than that, he was hungry for Theo's understanding; he saw Theo as a collaborator, and he wanted Theo to see their relationship in the same light. In a letter to Theo from October 1888, Vincent mused about the idea of success—was his heart set on achieving it?

> *No*, and a thousand times *no*. I'd like to succeed in making you clearly feel this truth, that in giving money to artists you yourself are doing an artist's work, and that I'd wish only that my canvases might become of such a kind that you aren't too unhappy with *your* work.

The great irony of Vincent's pleas with Theo is that he was right, of course: Theo was making a winning investment, perhaps the most profitable investment in the history of art, though neither of them would live to see it mature. Just as Vincent was starting to get some critical notice for his painting, he died from a self-inflicted gunshot wound to the chest; and Theo died just six months after Vincent, from grief coupled with the effects of the syphilis he had contracted years earlier. It was left up to his widow, Jo van Gogh–Bonger, to preserve the hundreds of Vincent's paintings, and the hundreds of his letters, that ended up in her possession. Ultimately, it was her decades-long advocacy for Vincent's work that allowed it to be recognized as one of the greatest artistic achievements in human history. "I have high hopes," she wrote in her diary in February 1892, as this process was just beginning. "I have a feeling of indescribable triumph when I think that it's finally arrived—the appreciation—the liking—I must go to hear what people are saying—what their attitude is. The ones who used to ridicule Vincent and call him a fool."

JOBS

ODD JOBS

When you have a son who is an artist," Cézanne said, "you must provide him with an income." But when no such parental income is available, what then? Cézanne couldn't bear working as a clerk in his father's bank; plenty of other artists have managed to do as much or have endured far worse impositions on their time and energy, though rarely without a measure of angst about the bind this put them in, over and over.

One of the best records of this bind can be found in the journals of the American artist Grace Hartigan, who with great effort made herself into one of the foremost painters of the second-generation abstract expressionists, those mostly New York artists who followed in the footsteps of Willem de Kooning and Jackson Pollock in the 1950s and '60s. Of that group, Hartigan would have the most rapid and unlikely ascent: from a suburban New Jersey housewife with no formal art education to one of the most important artists of her generation, and one of the very few women artists to break through with collectors, curators, and the wider public. Hartigan was the only woman featured in the two groundbreaking 1950s exhibitions of American painting at the Museum of Modern Art, and in 1957 *Life* magazine called her the "most celebrated of the young American women painters."*

---

* Hartigan always chafed at this kind of praise. "To be truthful I didn't think much about being a woman [artist]," she said. "I thought about how difficult it was to paint."

Born in Newark in 1922, Hartigan grew up the oldest of four children in a New Jersey family that was hit hard by the Great Depression. According to her biographer, Cathy Curtis, "the family often lived on cornflakes or boiled potatoes. . . . When bill collectors knocked on the door, everyone hid and kept quiet to preserve the illusion that no one was home." The family's precarious finances spoiled Hartigan's plans for attending college; instead, after high school, she went directly to work in a clerical position at the Prudential Insurance Company in Newark. There she met a twenty-year-old accountant, Bob Jachens, who felt similarly stymied: His family's finances had forced him to drop out of Columbia and go to work. They began to date, and in May 1941, shortly after Hartigan turned nineteen, they tied the knot. "I married the first boy that read poetry to me," Hartigan said. He was also the first person to take her to the Metropolitan Museum of Art, in New York, which she said was the first time she was really "conscious of art."

After marriage: escape. Inspired by the 1935 movie version of Jack London's *The Call of the Wild*, Hartigan and Jachens quit their jobs and traveled across the country by bus, intending to become pioneers in what was then the Alaska Territory. But they ran out of money in Los Angeles, where Hartigan also discovered that she was pregnant, to her dismay; the life of adventure and creativity that she was seeking seemed to be over before it had even begun. Pretending that he knew how to ski, Jachens found a job selling ski equipment at a department store; at night, he and Hartigan took classes in drawing and painting at a local high school. The Japanese attack on Pearl Harbor—followed by the birth of their son, Jeffrey, in February 1942—prompted the couple's return to New Jersey, where they moved in with Jachens's parents. A year later, Jachens was drafted and sent to Europe, and Hartigan found herself living with her young son in her in-laws' house in Bloomfield. Feeling more stifled than ever, she decided to look for work and ended up becoming a "woman draftsman" at the Wright Aeronautical factory just north of Newark, moving with Jeffrey to an apartment nearby.

A book of Matisse reproductions, which a factory coworker showed her at lunch one day, changed her trajectory. "It was love at first sight, mostly, I must confess, because it looked so easy, I thought I could do it, too," Hartigan said. On the colleague's recommendation, she began taking night classes from a local art teacher and painter with the improbable name of Ike Muse, and before long they began an affair. Around the same time, Jachens confessed to his own wartime affair by letter: He had fallen in love with a Dutch woman and intended to stay with her in the Netherlands after the war. So when Muse decided, in 1945, that he needed to move to Manhattan to further his art career, Hartigan went with him, bringing her son along to their new home on Seventh Avenue and Nineteenth Street. Five-year-old Jeffrey went to the Grace Church School while Hartigan commuted to a new drafting job at the Diamond Match Company in White Plains. Muse stayed home and painted all day, which grated on Hartigan, who was footing the bills for them both. She soon discovered that this was a common arrangement among the downtown artist couples they were getting to know: The painters Mark Rothko, Milton Avery, and Adolph Gottlieb were all supported by their wives. (Rothko's second wife, Mary Alice, was a commercial artist; Avery's wife, Sally Michel, worked full-time as a freelance illustrator; and Gottlieb's wife, Esther, was a teacher.)

And yet, even with much less time to pursue her own painting—and with just a small corner of the bedroom curtained off as her "studio"— over the next few years Hartigan began to outgrow her mentor. Once, when Muse had a group of artist friends over to see his latest work, he let Hartigan hang one of her paintings among his own without telling any of the guests that it was hers. Everyone agreed that it was his best piece by far, to his fury. In January 1948, the couple went to see an exhibition of Jackson Pollock's paintings at the Betty Parsons Gallery on Fifty-Seventh Street. Hartigan was bowled over, Muse unimpressed; it was the beginning of the end. After three years trying to care for her son and her partner, work full-time, and develop as a painter, Hartigan needed to make a drastic break. Cathy Curtis writes:

During one whirlwind week in April [1948], she asked her boss to fire her (so that she'd receive a year's unemployment compensation), deposited Jeffrey with his father's parents, and moved out. Her new digs, at 330 East 33rd Street—an apartment on the seventh floor of a cold-water walk-up near the East River—were cramped and inconvenient. But no longer would she be beholden to anyone else's beliefs or schedules or needs, not even her son's. Instead, she vowed, "I was going to paint every day of my life."

She kept her vow, over the next several years progressing rapidly on her painting and at the same time finding her way into a tight-knit circle of downtown painters and poets that became known as the New York School. (She mainly saw her son on weekends and holidays—until Jeffrey was a teenager, when she sent him to California to live with his father and stepmother, who had by this time settled in Los Angeles. After this point, Hartigan didn't see her son for thirty years.*) She briefly married another painter, Harry Jackson, whose GI Bill benefits kept them both afloat while they painted away in the Thirty-Third Street apartment. When that relationship ended, Hartigan moved in with a new artist boyfriend, Al Leslie, on Essex Street, in a fourth-floor loft without electricity or heat, working as a nude model at the Art Students League, eavesdropping on the teachers as they went from student to student offering instruction, picking up whatever lessons she could use in her own work. She had her first one-person show in January 1951. Only one painting sold (for fifty dollars, to a young man whose mother later made him return it), but the reviews were positive: A critic for *Art News* wrote that Hartigan's paintings showed "such vitality that they seemed to give off sparks."

As a painter, she had come a tremendous distance in just a few years—but her financial situation was murkier than ever. "Getting enough money for materials is a constant worry," Hartigan wrote in her journal on April 17, 1951, a few weeks after her twenty-ninth birthday, in one of numerous entries that lay out the essential conundrum of so many artists, then and now: She wasn't making enough money from the sales of her paintings

---

* Depressingly, the history of art is also often a history of truly terrible parenting, by fathers and mothers alike, though of course the mothers' neglect tends to receive more scrutiny.

to make art full-time, but working a full-time job prevented her from making substantial progress on her artwork. "I think I'm incapable of sustaining a painting mood while working 8 hours a day," she wrote, "and if I must do it I shouldn't even try to paint at the same time."

The best compromise she could come up with was temping, and through a temp agency Hartigan cycled through a variety of short-term gigs as needed. She was always trying to work just enough to get through the next month without a job, to "live & paint until the money runs out again." In mid-May 1951, she started "working as a file clerk all day and painting each evening," but she quit when her art dealer promised to send her a few hundred dollars. The money never materialized, and Hartigan got a new temp position working from 3:00 to 11:00 PM at a travel bureau. This time, she didn't get any painting done. "The last month and a half has been almost artistically sterile," she wrote on October 3, 1951. "I feel terribly pent-up and unrealized." This pattern continued into the next year; on March 5, 1952, she wrote: "A whole month gone and I haven't even lifted a brush. Worked three weeks at a clerical job that was a miracle of stupidity, all the time low, really despairing. And now we're more broke than ever."

"We" referred to her and Walter Silver, the photographer she was living with by this time. He wasn't making much money, either. Not long after the above journal entry, Hartigan noted that together they owed $400–$500 (around $5,000 at present-day values), a debt that weighed on them both and required her to find yet another day job. Meanwhile, the dream of making money *from* her art was still painfully elusive: "Any kind of 'success' as far especially as sales are concerned seems farther away than ever," she wrote on March 29, 1952, a week after her thirtieth birthday. By mid-April, she was back to temping again: "Tuesday I begin work at a drafting job for about two months," she wrote. "It means giving up painting entirely for that period, but I hope to save enough money to paint without interruption thru the whole summer."

If this sounds fairly manageable to the contemporary reader—working a drafting job for two months in the spring to spend the entire summer painting probably sounds like an impossible fairy tale to an artist in today's exorbitantly expensive New York—it's important to remember just how austere Hartigan's lifestyle was. Especially during her first years on Essex Street, Hartigan endured "steady, endless poverty, when I felt bloated with bad food" that she purchased from "the stale bread store and the little stands that sell penny tomatoes, that foul market that has meat for 15¢ a pound." Her first winter there, it was so cold in the unheated loft that she reported in her journal: "I'm working in ski clothes." When Hartigan was living with Al Leslie, their fellow painter Helen Frankenthaler observed that they seemed to live entirely on cereal. "They used to eat Wheatena, at periods three times a day," Frankenthaler said. "I mean they had nothing." Cohabiting with Walter Silver was a little better; he was happy to cover their joint expenses when his freelance photography work brought in sufficient income. But that wasn't steady or predictable, either. Often, they couldn't afford to pay the phone or gas bills and risked having service shut off. "It takes more than a lifetime to paint," Hartigan complained in her journal, "and then all these added anxieties!"

Granted, some of Hartigan's chronic anxiety was temperamental; she was not and would never be an easygoing painter, nor an easygoing person. This is also amply documented in her journals: "My God how hard it is to paint" (November 28, 1951); "Everything coming with the greatest amount of difficulty and confusion" (January 11, 1952); "Back to work, with fresh doubts" (March 31, 1952); "The weather is singing to-day, while I drink iced coffee and stew and fret over money and painting" (August 18, 1952). "Of course I doubt myself all the time," she reaffirmed in another entry, "but I must obey my instincts, they are the only things I can trust." Periodically, she experienced surges of belief in herself, in what she *could* do if she just had the time and the materials and an uncluttered mind. "I believe I am the first woman of major stature in painting," she wrote in one of these surges, "and I feel that given a long life and sufficient courage and energy, I may become a great artist."

In the same entry, Hartigan noted that she had "worked at a job at the Medical Society for four days filling envelopes with pamphlets" and used the money to restock her paint supply. "I hated giving up those few days, but now with the paint here I think it was worth it." Five months later, a glimmer of hope: Hartigan's dealer called to tell her that a collector was strongly considering one of her paintings. In her journal, she resolved to quit the "tabulating job for morons" she was then working, writing: "I refuse to submit myself to such degradation." Two days after that, the sale fell through and Hartigan—who had apparently made good on her promise to quit the tabulating job—had to find yet another temporary gig. "In a terrible state of melancholy," she wrote in her journal.

+ + +

Is it worth pausing here for a moment to survey, briefly, the great variety of artist day jobs through the ages, and to acknowledge that every one of these artists probably felt the same as Grace Hartigan did at one point or another?

A partial list of some of my favorite examples would have to include the Chilean poet and novelist Roberto Bolaño, who, according to the translator Natasha Wimmer, worked as "a dishwasher, waiter, longshoreman, garbageman, seasonal laborer, and receptionist," though his favorite job was as a night watchman at a campground outside Barcelona; the Argentinian writer Jorge Luis Borges, who didn't have his first full-time job until he was thirty-eight (his parents paid his way until then), and who, as a library assistant in a working-class district in Buenos Aires, found "nine years of solid unhappiness"; the English novelist Charlotte Brontë, who endured miserable stints as a teacher and a governess before an inheritance from her aunt allowed her and her sisters to write full-time ("A private governess has no existence, is not considered as a living and rational being except as connected with the wearisome duties she has to fulfill," she wrote to her sister Emily); the American science-fiction author Octavia Butler, who worked a series of "horrible little jobs"—as a dishwasher, a telemarketer, a warehouse worker, and a potato-chip inspector—and wrote in the early mornings before work, sometimes starting as early as 2:00 AM; the artist Joseph Cornell, who for years worked nine to five in the home-furnishings division of a Manhattan textile studio and, at night, sorted and assembled material for the shadow boxes that would become his artistic legacy, working at the kitchen table while his mother and brother slept upstairs; the sculptor Petah Coyne, who as a young artist in New York in the 1970s worked in advertising during the day and made her sculptures at night, twice a week pulling an all-nighter and returning to the office the next morning without having slept, a grueling schedule she kept up for almost a decade ("That was the hardest time in my life, to work that hard," she said); the novelist and poet James Dickey, who worked at an Atlanta advertising office writing radio commercials for Coca-Cola bottlers while at the same time working in secret on his poetry ("Every time I had a minute to spare, which was not often, I would stick a poem in the typewriter where I had been typing Coca-Cola ads," he said); the composer Philip Glass, who, in the 1960s and '70s, in between short tours with his music ensemble, ran a moving company with his cousin and worked as a plumber and a New York taxi driver ("I expected to have a day job for the rest of my life," he said); the abolitionist and writer Harriet Jacobs, who was born a slave in North Carolina in 1813 and who, after having her freedom purchased for her by her employer, worked as the family housemaid caring for five children seven days a week, writing her book *Incidents in the Life of a Slave Girl* at night while the children slept ("I have not yet written a single page by daylight," she confided in a letter); the Hungarian writer László Krasznahorkai, who, in 2018, told *The Paris Review* that his favorite job was as a "night watchman for three hundred cows," though he also worked as a miner for a time ("That was almost comical—the real miners had to cover for me," he said); the artist Agnes Martin, who worked as a waitress, a dishwasher, a janitor, a cashier, a receptionist, a playground director, and a tennis coach, as well as jobs for a mining company, in country schools, in a factory, in a hamburger stand, in a butcher shop, in a nursery, in a cafeteria, and as a baker's helper ("Also raised rabbits and ducks," she noted in a handwritten list of all the jobs she ever had); the poet Lorine Niedecker, who worked as a library assistant, a writer and research editor for a Wisconsin guidebook, a scriptwriter for a Madison radio station, a stenographer and proofreader for the journal *Hoard's Dairyman*, and, from 1957 to 1963, a cleaner at the Fort Atkinson Memorial Hospital in southern Wisconsin—her final day job before her retirement at age sixty—during which time she adopted a unique haiku-like form that became a signature of her late style; the painter Henry Taylor, whose earliest artwork included drawings of patients at the Camarillo State Mental Hospital in Southern California, where he worked the night shift as a "psychiatric technician" for eleven years, from 1984 to 1996; the Victorian novelist Anthony Trollope, who produced more than two dozen books during the thirty-three years he worked as a civil servant at the General Post Office, writing for three hours every morning before he dressed for breakfast; the author Kurt Vonnegut, who at various points worked in public relations for General Electric, tried to invent a board game, lasted one day as a writer for *Sports Illustrated*, and managed a Saab dealership on Cape Cod (his son later called him "the world's worst car salesman"); the Swiss writer Robert Walser, who worked as a journalist, a bank clerk, an inventor's assistant, and, for six months, a butler for a count who lived in a castle in Upper Silesia* (Walser's time at a Berlin school for domestic servants inspired his 1909 novel *Jakob von Gunten*, now considered his finest work and a masterpiece of early-twentieth-century fiction); and the playwright Tennessee Williams, who as an aspiring young writer worked at the International Shoe Company factory in St. Louis and hated it so much that he set himself the goal of writing one short story per week, working late into the night at his parents' house. After work, Williams "would go to his room with black coffee and cigarettes and I would hear the typewriter clicking away at night in the silent house," his mother recalled. "Some mornings when I walked in to wake him for work, I would find him sprawled fully dressed across the bed, too tired to remove his clothes."

+ + +

Last we left Grace Hartigan, she was in "a terrible state of melancholy" after a painting sale evaporated, forcing her to look for yet another temporary job to pay the bills. In fact, though she couldn't know it, Hartigan

---

* Walser's approach to day jobs was similar to Grace Hartigan's. He said: "I was often unemployed, which is to say that as soon [as] I had rustled together a bit of money, I handed in my notice so that I could write undisturbed. Anyone who wants to do something properly must give himself to it fully, in my experience. Writing, too, requires all of one's strength. Yes, it downright bleeds one dry. Writing on the side, as an arabesque, so to speak, rarely yields anything lasting."

was on the verge of a commercial breakthrough. In 1953, the Museum of Modern Art purchased her painting *The Persian Jacket* for $400, and the thirty-one-year-old Hartigan no longer had to live on "oatmeal and bacon ends." A year later, the museum purchased another painting, *River Bathers*, for $1,000. She was on the ascent. In the coming months, the Whitney Museum and the Art Institute of Chicago purchased paintings; so did Nelson Rockefeller and the playwright William Inge. In 1957, Hartigan sold everything she painted. Cathy Curtis writes: "Her prices remained low. . . . Yet she was finally able to devote her full attention to the one thing in the world she really cared about; her long string of hated temporary jobs was over." After the Museum of Modern Art purchased *River Bathers*, Hartigan wrote in her journal:

> It would be impossible to describe my feelings, so I won't even try. All I can think of is the time it gives me, freedom to work without the pressures of financial worry. Since I'll have $1,000 for myself,* I could go to Europe, but I feel at this time I'd rather stretch it out and just live and work. I think I have some good pictures in me. I'm going to get a roll of linen! And a *lot* of paint!

This is a frequent trajectory in artists' biographies: years of struggle and uncertainty, often alongside miserable attempts to pay the bills through jobs that continually impinge on their time, energy, and optimism—until, finally, commercial success, and with it, at last, money and the opportunity to make art full-time.

But many brilliantly talented and hardworking artists never reach that point. The Canadian painter Emily Carr is a good example. Though she has become a national icon in the decades since her death in 1945—beloved for her postimpressionistic depictions of the forests and landscapes of British Columbia, and of the First Nations villages and monuments she sought out on her frequent painting expeditions—in her own lifetime

---

* To be clear: Hartigan received two-thirds of the proceeds of her sales, and her art dealer kept the other third. In this instance, sales totaling $1,500 were about to go through, so Hartigan would receive $1,000. (Nowadays, art galleries typically take a 50 percent commission on the sale of two-dimensional works like paintings.)

Carr's paintings received a mixed reception at best, and they never earned enough money for her to live comfortably. Fortunately, Carr did have one major financial asset: a plot of land in Victoria, on the southern tip of Vancouver Island, where Carr was born and raised, which she and her sisters inherited after their father's death in 1888, when Carr was sixteen. After years of study abroad—at the California School of Design in San Francisco, the Westminster School of Art in London, and an art colony in St. Ives—plus years of honing her craft as a painter in London, Paris, and Vancouver, Carr decided to resettle in Victoria and make use of her parcel. It was 1913, and she had recently turned forty-one; previously, she had been working as an art teacher in Vancouver, where Carr's bold, experimental canvases invited scorn from the local Ladies' Art Club (in Carr's words, "a cluster of society women who intermittently packed themselves and their admirers into a small rented studio to drink tea and jabber art jargon"). Struggling to sell enough paintings or find enough pupils to fund her art practice, Carr borrowed money to build a small apartment house on her inherited land, reasoning that she could have a light-filled painting studio, a large garden, and living quarters for herself, and fund this pleasant arrangement by renting out two suites on the main floor. This would be her day job: a landlady who painted. Surely there are worse arrangements.

Carr embarked on the project with great optimism but terrible timing, putting her plan into motion just as World War I broke out, which severely depressed the Canadian economy and caused unemployment to skyrocket. Suddenly, the respectable, reasonably well-to-do tenants she had envisioned were in short supply. To keep Hill House (as it was named) afloat, Carr was forced, after a year, to divide her own living quarters, creating an additional rental unit. When that wasn't sufficient, she moved into the attic and converted the entire second floor into a ladies' boardinghouse, transforming what had been her painting studio into a dining room and common area. At one point, Carr even had to move out of the house entirely, setting up a primitive camp for herself in the backyard, where she slept in a tent and cooked meals in a lean-to. (Drying her laundry over the campfire, Carr noted, "made my undies look and smell like smoked fish.") Not surprisingly, this series of demotions made painting increasingly difficult and then outright impossible (though she did, eventually, reclaim her studio space in the house). "I never painted now—had neither time nor wanting," Carr wrote. "For about fifteen years I did not paint."

Carr ran the apartment house for twenty-two years. And even with all her sacrifices, she barely made ends meet. "No matter how I pinched, the rentals would not stretch over mortgage, taxes, and living," she wrote. "I tried in every way to augment my income. Small fruit, hens, rabbits, dogs— pottery. With the help of a chimney sweep I built a brick kiln in my back yard, firing my own pots. . . . I made hundreds and hundreds of stupid objects, the kind that tourists pick up." She bred dogs, too, establishing a kennel of Old English bobtail sheepdogs in her backyard, selling the puppies to men returning from war. The bobtails were companionable working dogs and proved to be in high demand; Carr ultimately raised some 350 of them. The money helped her pay the taxes she owed on Hill House—but selling the house, unfortunately, wasn't an option; the housing market was too depressed. Carr was trapped. She felt, she wrote:

> *screwed* into the house . . . twist by twist. Every circumstance, financial, public, personal, artistic, had taken a hand in that cruel twisting of the driver. My screws were down to their heads. Each twist had demanded—"Forget that you ever wanted to be an artist. Nobody wanted your art. Buckle down to being a landlady."

Carr's initial entrepreneurial zeal soon curdled into bitterness and resentment, often directed at her tenants. According to the biographer Maria Tippett, "she performed the apartment chores grudgingly, taunted her tenants, and abused anyone who crossed her." Carr herself wrote, "I loathed being a landlady." Even decades later, she still blamed "those filthy tenants" for "sapping the joy out of everything."

The following passage from Carr's journals catches the artist at one of these low points—and it may feel familiar to anyone who's tried to balance ambitious creative work with a dismal and time-consuming side gig:

Oh dear, oh dear, all the wickedness in me rebels at the beastly, rotting house. I know it is crumbling up, I know it needs repairs, I know it is not modern, I know I am not a real downright good landlady, willing to grovel before my tenants, to lick their dirt and grab their cheques. It crushes the life out of me, this weight of horrid things waiting to be done because my back hurts so I can't do them myself and have no money to pay someone to do them. And then maybe I go into the beautiful studio and see some sketches about and feel my skin bursting with things I want to say, with things the place said to me that I want to express and dive into, to live—and there's that filthy furnace to clean out and wood to chop and sweeping and dusting and scrubbing and gardening, just to keep up a respectable appearance for the damn tenants so as to squeeze out a pittance of rent to exist on.

But even during her worst years of being a landlady, Carr wasn't entirely hopeless—even the long, bitter journal entry above ends with a glimmer of resolve, maybe more than a glimmer. After venting her complaints at length, Carr writes:

Now go out, old girl, and split bark and empty ashes and rake and mend the fence. Yet—should I? Or should I climb higher, shut my eyes to these things and paint? Rise above the material? No—I think you've got to climb through these things to the other.

+ + +

Is there another path for the artist who needs a job and really, truly can't bear to "climb through these things to the other"? One model, for those willing to entertain all options, might be Kathy Acker, who as a young writer in the early 1970s loathed the idea of normal, nine-to-five employment—"A straight job would lobotomize me," she said—and opted for sex work instead: acting in porn films with her then-boyfriend; performing live sex shows at Fun City in Times Square with the same boyfriend (they had a Santa Claus routine; the sex was simulated); and stripping in sailor bars in San Diego. These gigs paid better and took up less time than "straight" jobs—at Fun City, Acker only had to work one day a week; she wrote the other six days—and they gave Acker a new perspective on society and relationships that proved fruitful for her writing. "You see people from the bottom up," she said.

Of course, Acker was drawn to acts of transgression, in life and in literature. Her first breakthrough as a writer occurred thanks to the poet David Antin, whose seminars at the University of California San Diego Acker attended in the late 1960s. (She was born Karen Alexander in 1947, to a prosperous but emotionally—and financially—withholding Upper East Side family.) In class, Antin instructed students to make poems out of snippets of text they copied from library books; subsequently, Acker began making longer prose works with this same method. She would lift passages from existing books, make some small changes as she felt like it (or not), and insert excerpts from her own real-life diaries and letters alongside the "plagiarized" passages to create something bracingly original, though not everyone agreed about the readability of the final results. Asked how she made things hold together without a proper narrative, Acker said, "I couldn't have cared less in those days. I wrote so many pages a day and that was that." She set up "guidelines" for each piece, and then simply executed the work according to the rules she had established. "It was task work," she said. "I really didn't want any creativity, so I set up this task, this nutty task basically, and I'd do it!"

"I'm trying to get away from self-expression but not from personal life," one of Acker's narrators says in *The Childlike Life of the Black Tarantula*, one of her earliest works, originally published as a series of self-produced pamphlets that Acker mailed to a small subscriber list. "I hate creativity. I'm simply exploring other ways of dealing with events than ways my lousy habits—mainly instilled by parents and institutions—have forced me to act." Acker's parents especially had let her down: Her father left her mother when she was three months pregnant; Acker never met him. Her mother was a stingy and self-centered woman who never gave Acker the love and approval she craved, or the cash to fund her writing aspirations. (In the most extreme rejection imaginable, Acker's mother killed herself on Christmas Eve 1978, just as she and her daughter were starting to reconcile after years of estrangement.)

Acker's writing was a plea for something *more* from life: a wider range of experience, deeper connections, less self-editing, and fewer pointless hang-ups. She dreamed of a society that allowed for "a whole range of feelings—really, a fuller life," she said in a 1991 interview. "I keep thinking: what we know of as 'life' is so thin and juiceless and boring, frankly—we're ground into nothing before we even start out!"

So sex work was an antidote to the thin and juiceless and boring task of earning a living—and it gave her literary material, too. She said in another interview:

> I was working as a stripper to earn money and I would spend most of my time hanging out in the dressing room with all the other strippers hearing stories. It was the days of a lot of drugs, especially hallucinogens, so the girls just got totally wacked out of their minds and would tell great stories. I started writing the stories down, but I didn't want to be a sociologist. The stories were very immediate to me, so I put everything in the first person, plus some of my dreams.

Acker's forays into sex work have become a part of her legend as a radical underground writer, but she didn't actually do this work for very long: She worked at the Times Square sex shows for six months, as a stripper for somewhat longer. Later, violating her prohibition against "straight" jobs, she worked briefly as a secretary for a Riverdale publishing services company, took tickets at the downtown art space the Kitchen (the only job she ever enjoyed), and worked for an organic bakery in the East Village. "My last job was selling cookies," she said. "It was so bad. I was 31 and said, I can't do this anymore. Sentences out of my mouth for hours: 'What cookie would you like?'" In her next novel, 1984's *Blood and Guts in High School*, Acker would lend this experience to a narrator named Lousy Mindless Salesgirl, who gripes: "As soon as I dare to take the time to think a thought, to watch a feeling, usually hatred, develop, to rest my aching body, a customer enters."

All this time, Acker was writing furiously, routinely completing three or four thousand words a day, but she never really made any money from her writing, which was too experimental and abrasive to sell in any kind of quantity. So how did Acker afford her life? For a long time, she just squeaked by, on money from the aforementioned odd jobs, a 1976 CAPS grant for $7,000—the first and only grant she ever received—and occasional loans from friends and lovers. Then, in 1981, a more durable solution, and a depressingly familiar one: Acker's grandmother Florrie died at age eighty-seven, and her scrappy proto-punk writer and former sex worker and organic-cookie salesgirl granddaughter was soon collecting $40,000 a year (around $128,000 at today's values), disbursed in quarterly installments from a trust fund. She never had a day job again.

DOUBLE LIVES

One approach to the problem of making art and making a living is to work a series of "horrible little jobs," as Octavia Butler called them, and do your *real* work in your own time. This is the classic day-job strategy: to sell your time but not your mind, to give as little of yourself as you have to give to your employer and save as much of yourself as you can for your art. But the trade-offs, as we've seen, are low pay, exhausting work, lack of stability, and a different kind of brain drain, the kind that comes from continually performing labor that does not draw upon your intellectual capacity or in any way validate your existence as a person of creativity, judgment, and skill. ("What cookie would you like?")

Is there another way? When I was a young aspiring writer trying to decide what kind of job to get after college, for some reason the example that was repeatedly cited to me was that of Wallace Stevens, the American modernist poet who worked as an insurance executive for decades while at the same time writing some of the most important verse of the twentieth century. (Stevens worked for the Hartford Accident and Indemnity Company, in Connecticut, for thirty-nine years, from 1916 until his death in 1955, the same year that he received the Pulitzer Prize for his *Collected Poems*.) Here was a different model: Find a steady, predictable, well-paying professional career, carve out some time on the side for your creative work, dismiss any thought of making money *from* said work, and settle in for the long haul.

Born in Reading, Pennsylvania, in 1879, Stevens first began to publish poetry as a student at Harvard, where he was the editor of *The Harvard Advocate*. From there, it was not much of a leap to trying out a career in journalism in New York, though this proved a bad match, temperamentally and financially—Stevens thought that what he was writing was trash, and he was barely scraping by. He considered a switch to publishing but was dissuaded by a book publisher he met with who told him, Stevens recalled, that "the business was chiefly clerical—unpleasant fact—& that I could hardly expect to live on my wages." At that point, he gave in to pressure from his father and enrolled at New York Law School.

Stevens's father was a lawyer himself and prosperous enough to pay for his three sons' educations. But not long after Stevens enrolled in law school, in 1901, his father suffered a devastating financial reversal due to bad real estate investments; he ended up having a nervous breakdown and spent six months at a rest cure in Saranac, New York. According to the biographer Paul Mariani, Stevens's father returned home a changed man: "He was only fifty-four, but his shoulders stooped, haggard lines etched his face, and his earlier buoyancy was gone." When we look at Stevens's lifelong preference for financial stability over a riskier life as a man of letters, it's hard not to see his father's breakdown looming in the background.

Stevens passed the bar in 1904 and worked for a series of law firms in New York, not entirely successfully; after four years, he decided to make the switch to insurance, a growing industry with better opportunities. In 1909, he married a fellow Reading native, Elsie Kachel, and began to build his twin existences as poet and businessman. He wasn't sure the two could be reconciled. "I wish that I could give all my time to the thing, instead of a few hours each evening when I am often physically and mentally dull," he complained in a 1915 letter. "It takes me so long to get the day out of my mind and to focus myself on what I am eager to do."

Even so, these years in New York became the scene of Stevens's proper "awakening" as a poet, largely thanks to his association with a loose literary circle that included the poet William Carlos Williams, the writer and photographer Carl Van Vechten, and the wealthy arts patron Walter Arensberg. In 1914, Stevens began to publish poetry again for the first time since his student days at Harvard. According to the biographer Peter Brazeau, these poems "quickly established his reputation as one of the most accomplished poets of the younger generation."

So the move to Connecticut, in 1916, was a blow, even though Hartford offered undeniably better career prospects. "I miss New-York abominably," Stevens wrote shortly after arriving. Worse, his new job initially required a lot of travel, which hopelessly disrupted his writing. "I have not had a poem in my head for a month, poor Yorick," he wrote to Elsie from a business trip in 1920.

But the traveling eventually ceased, the poems gradually returned, and Stevens's first book, *Harmonium*, came out in 1923, when he was forty-four years old. It contains some of Stevens's most anthologized poems—including "Sunday Morning," "The Emperor of Ice-Cream," and "Peter Quince at the Clavier"—but it did not overly impress critics at the time and sold poorly. (Stevens complained in a letter that his "royalties for the first half of 1924 amounted to $6.70.") He didn't publish a second volume, *Ideas of Order*, for another thirteen years. One factor in the delay was the muted response to his first book, which demoralized him; another was the birth of Stevens's only child, a daughter named Holly, in 1924. In a letter to Harriet Monroe, the editor of *Poetry* magazine, Stevens wrote that the responsibilities of parenthood were a "terrible blow to poor literature" (even though, naturally, he left the bulk of the caregiving duties to his wife). On top of that was the problem of Stevens's health. In 1926, doctors told him that he was severely overweight and had high blood pressure; a strict new regime of diet and exercise was prescribed. The following year, Stevens described his daily routine in a letter to Williams:

I rise at day-break, shave etc.; at six I start to exercise; at seven I massage and bathe; at eight I dabble with a therapeutic breakfast; from eight-thirty to nine-thirty I walk down-town; work all day [and] go to bed at nine. How should I write poetry, think it, feel it?

He did it, finally, by incorporating the writing into his workday routine. After Stevens's death, Peter Brazeau interviewed a number of his associates at the Hartford Accident and Indemnity Company for an oral biography of the poet; their recollections make for fascinating reading. For the most part, his colleagues knew of his poetry. One of his secretaries, Marguerite Flynn, recalled:

> He arrived at the office punctually at nine o'clock and left again at four-thirty, never leaving things to be done after closing. When he was in good health he walked to and from the office to his home, a distance of three or four miles. It was on these long walks that he jotted down lines for his poetry, polishing it up later.

Richard Sunbury, who worked as a mail boy in the office from 1931 to 1934, added that Stevens normally didn't eat lunch but would go for an hour-long walk instead: "He most always had some envelopes stuffed in his pocket, and he'd just pull them out and write on the back," Sunbury said. "Just walking, he'd say, 'Wait just a minute, please.' He'd pull out an envelope. He always had about a half-dozen in his pocket."

Returning to the office from his walks, Stevens would hand any poetic notes he'd made to his secretary to type up. "They're pretty indecipherable when she gets them," he admitted. After the secretary had deciphered and typed up these scraps, the drafts went into the file cabinet of Stevens's desk. According to Sunbury:

> He had a peculiar filing system. He always filed his poetry notes in his lower right corner of his desk, which was open most of the time to a degree. It seemed to me there were sheaves and sheaves. And sometimes he would reach down, and he'd shuffle through three or four. He'd scratch out something or put something in. Or he might take the top one and just add a line or two.

That image of the insurance executive reaching into his bulging drawer of poetic drafts, to "scratch something out or put something in," seems a wonderful justification of Stevens's career: His desk was the home base to which he returned from his poetic rambles. And after *Ideas of Order* appeared in 1936, Stevens published more steadily, with new books appearing every few years. He had found his rhythm; in a 1952 letter, he wrote, "I find that having a job is one of the best things in the world that could happen to me. It introduces discipline and regularity into one's life. I am just as free as I want to be and of course I have nothing to worry about about money." He even claimed to have found some affinity between poetry and the surety and fidelity bonds he specialized in at Hartford. "Poetry and surety claims aren't as unlikely a combination as they may seem," Stevens said in a 1954 interview. "There is nothing perfunctory about them, for each case is different."

In fact, Stevens still harbored plenty of doubts about the path he'd chosen. In a 1950 letter, he lamented that he had "not even begun to touch spheres within spheres that might have been possible if, instead of devoting the principal amount of my time to making a living, I had devoted it to thought and poetry." Several years before that, he had sounded even more regretful in a letter to his daughter, who had decided to drop out of Vassar, to Stevens's great disapproval. He wrote hoping to dissuade her:

> Please don't allow yourself to come to a final decision about college and I beg you not to do this. . . . You don't find yourself or your way through life by getting a job, except for a very brief period of time. . . . Take my word for it that making your living is a waste of time. None of the great things in life have anything to do with making your living.

+ + +

William Carlos Williams would have disagreed with this sentiment, though his own trajectory was in many ways similar to his friend's. As Stevens was settling down to work in insurance, in Hartford, Williams was establishing his practice as a family physician in his native Rutherford, New Jersey; between 1912 and 1955, he would deliver approximately three thousand babies while also writing such masterpieces of imagist poetry as "The Red Wheelbarrow" and "This Is Just to Say." But Williams always said medicine was a boon to his writing, and it seems worth unpacking why.

It was his parents who pushed him toward medicine; if he had selected his own path, Williams said, he would have gone into forestry. But he wasn't the type to resist his parents' wishes, and thus he went straight from high school at Horace Mann, in Manhattan, to medical school at the University of Pennsylvania. (At the time, the university allowed graduates of elite private schools to bypass undergraduate studies and enroll directly in its medical school.) Williams realized that he wanted to be a writer after he'd already begun studying medicine. He considered dropping out but thought, *Well, why?* He asked himself, "Would it add anything to give it up?" To the contrary, he concluded, practicing medicine would put him in an enviable position for a poet, in short: "No one was ever going to be in a position to tell me what to write. . . . That was number one."

So "it was money that finally decided me," Williams wrote in his autobiography.

I would continue medicine, for I was determined to be a poet; only medicine, a job I enjoyed, would make it possible for me to live and write as I wanted to. I would live: that first, and write, by God, as *I* wanted to if it took me all eternity to accomplish my design. My furious wish was to be normal, undrunk, balanced in everything. I would marry (but not yet!) have children and still write, in fact, therefore to write. I would not court disease, live in the slums for the sake of art, give lice a holiday. I would not "die for art," but live for it, grimly! and work, work, work (like Pop), beat the game and be free (like Mom, poor soul!) to write, write as I alone should write, for the sheer drunkenness of it, I might have added. And complete defiance of the world or what might come after it, if anything.

Am I alone in detecting a perhaps too emphatic insistence on this point, that only medicine could have made it possible for him to live and write as he wished? The mention of his mom and pop seems significant: Williams wanted utter freedom as an artist without having to defy his parents or shock the neighbors. If he felt a tad defensive on this point, he might have been thinking of two of the writer friends he made at the University of Pennsylvania, Ezra Pound and Hilda Doolittle, future poets who were not nearly as concerned with conventional respectability. (In his autobiography, Williams recalled that, while writing, Doolittle liked to splash ink over her clothes, "to give her a feeling of freedom and indifference toward the mere means of the writing.")

In any case, medicine didn't only provide Williams with an income and all the artistic freedom that came with it;* it acquainted him intimately with his fellow humans, and that up-close exposure proved indispensable to the poet he became. As his poetry matured, Williams found that he wanted to "elucidate" the interior lives of the everyday New Jerseyans whom he served—and, he wrote, "my 'medicine' was the thing which gained me entrance to these secret gardens of the self. . . . In illness, in the permission I as a physician have had to be present at deaths and births . . . just there—for a split second—from one side or the other, it has fluttered before me for a moment, a phrase which I quickly write down on anything at hand, any piece of paper I can grab."

It wasn't just his patients' lives that inspired him—it was their speech, the language they used and the rhythms of that language, that Williams pulled into his verse. "The sheer sense of what is spoken seemed to me all important," he wrote. Famously, he would jot down scraps of verse between house calls, on prescription blanks, or he would type them between patient consultations in his office. "Five minutes, ten minutes, can always be found," he wrote in his autobiography.

> I had my typewriter in my office desk. All I needed to do was to pull up the leaf to which it was fastened and I was ready to go. I

---

* And let's not underemphasize how important this was. In a 1938 letter to another poet, Williams complained, "Meanwhile I receive in royalties for my last two books the munificent sum of one hundred and thirty dollars—covering the work of a ten or fifteen year period, about twelve dollars a year. One must be a hard worker to be able to stand up under the luxury of those proportions. Nothing but the best for me!"

worked at top speed. If a patient came in at the door while I was in the middle of a sentence, bang would go the machine—I was a physician. When the patient left, up would come the machine. My head developed a technique: something growing inside me demanded reaping. It had to be attended to.

That passage hints at an additional advantage of Williams's career: Practicing medicine gave him a feeling of absorption that proved essential for his writing. Working with patients demanded his full concentration, but when he stepped away and came back to himself, there would be a line or a phrase waiting. Exhaustion wasn't a problem; in fact, it was almost an advantage. "In my case it's not in a dreamy, relaxed state whatever, but in a tense state, that the best work occurs," Williams said. "It might be when you're fatigued. Perhaps fatigue is an anesthetic, lets the body go to some unimportant place, lets the faculties come out sharply and dominate the whole psychosomatic picture."

At the same time, Williams said that pursuing two very different occupations protected against fatigue. Responding to people who wondered how he had the energy to work as a doctor and as a writer, he said, "They do not grasp that one occupation complements the other, that they are two parts of a whole, that it is not two jobs at all, that one rests the man when the other fatigues him." He continued:

As far as the writing itself is concerned it takes next to no time at all. . . . When by chance we penetrate to some moving detail of a life, there is always time to bang out a few pages. The thing isn't to find the time for it—we waste hours every day doing absolutely nothing at all—the difficulty is to catch the evasive life of the thing, to phrase the words in such a way that stereotype will yield a moment of insight. That is where the difficulty lies. We are lucky when that underground current can be tapped and the secret spring of all our lives will send up its pure water. It seldom happens.

+ + +

For a time, Williams hired a young patient, a Vassar student named Katherine Johns, to type his manuscripts for him. Johns's mother was an Ives, related to Charles Ives, the pioneering modernist composer and another "funny money-man"—how the poet John Berryman once described Wallace Stevens—worth considering here.

Ives was born in Danbury, Connecticut, in 1874. Like Stevens, his artistic career was powerfully influenced by his father. George Ives was a Civil War bandleader who taught music in Danbury, led the local marching band when Charles was a child, and had his teenage son practicing piano for four hours a day. He was apparently seen as a bit of an oddball in Danbury, and that part of the musician's life did not appeal to young Charlie. In later life, Ives would say that he was "partially ashamed" of playing music as a child. "When other boys . . . were out driving grocery carts, or doing chores, or playing ball, I felt all wrong to stay in and play piano. And there may be something in it. Hasn't music always been too much an emasculated art?"

Ives proved his masculinity on the baseball diamond—he was team captain at his New Haven prep school—and at Yale, where he studied music under the noted composer Horatio Parker but also played football, embraced Greek life, and was an energetic, gregarious presence on campus. After graduation, he settled with some of his former classmates at the affectionately named Poverty Flat, a pair of apartments on Manhattan's West Fifty-Eighth Street occupied by a rotating cast of Yale grads busy establishing themselves in law, medicine, and business. Ives, meanwhile, found work as a church organist; in fact, according to his biographer Jan Swafford, he was "one of the finest American organists of his generation" and could have pursued a career as a professional musician, playing organ, teaching, composing—his father's path but on a bigger stage. Instead, he signed on as a clerk with the Mutual Life Insurance Company.

Swafford explains the move, in part, as a product of Ives's love of

American transcendentalist thought, especially Thoreau and Emerson, and his desire to "continue groping in his own direction" as an utterly independent, self-reliant figure. His undergraduate compositions, already pushing toward unfamiliar and sometimes jarring musical juxtapositions, had been met mostly with bafflement; Ives didn't see the appeal of forcing his ideas on an unwilling American public, or in scraping by to do so, or forcing the wife and children he hoped for to scrape by alongside him. As he put it, he did not intend "to let the children starve on his dissonances."

So Ives applied himself to the actuarial tables, and he soon met Julian Myrick, with whom he would go on to found Ives & Co.—later Ives & Myrick—and thereby make his fortune as a pioneer in the art of life insurance sales. His timing was excellent: At the turn of the century, the American economy was booming, and life insurance was becoming a necessary safety net for middle-class earners who had left behind the farms and small towns of their youth for increasingly crowded cities, and whose young families would be in a disastrous position should the worst occur. Ives proved a master at pitching life insurance to this new urban breadwinner, perhaps because he saw himself in his target customers: These were independent men who put duty to their families first and wholeheartedly embraced the American gospel of self-reliance.

Unlike Wallace Stevens, Ives did not delve into the finer points of insurance claims but instead took charge of training his company's sales force, and he proved something of a genius at it. In 1920, he published an elaborate book, based on his earlier how-to-sell pamphlets, titled *The Amount to Carry: Measuring the Prospect*. According to Swafford, "It is still read in the industry as one of the first studies of what came to be called 'programming' or 'estate planning,'" a practice that would become fundamental to the insurance industry.

Meanwhile, Ives composed music that was decades ahead of its time, taking the marching band and church music of his youth, along with popular songs and dance tunes, and combining them all into something new and strange and at times chaotic. His compositions celebrated and mourned the bustling musical life of his New England childhood at the close of the century, and they dared that music to compete with the European classical tradition.

While he lived at Poverty Flat, Ives would race home from work each evening and compose at the piano in the living room (this was an era when a bachelor apartment had a piano in the living room) until the cook announced it was time for dinner (this was also an era when a group of recent college grads employed a cook to prepare their meals). Later, after getting married, moving to the suburbs, and adopting a daughter, Ives carried on with more or less the same routine. According to a personal secretary employed by the Ives family for a time, "Mr. Ives would come home from a strenuous day in the insurance business, have his meal, and then go [to] the piano and forget all about time until the wee small hours. He would be completely absorbed in his music."*

Like Stevens, Ives also allowed for inspiration during the nine-to-five workday. His secretary recalled, "At work sometimes Mr. Ives would be dictating a letter, and all of a sudden something in the music line would come up in his head, and he'd cut off the letter and go into the music. I think that music was on his mind all the time." Unlike Stevens, whose colleagues described him as distant and aloof, Ives was a well-loved figure in his business life, remembered as a soft-spoken but warm presence in the office. If one of Ives's salesmen was having a bad month, the boss was known to pull cash out of his own wallet and press it upon him, no need for repayment later.

If this sounds like the perfect marriage of art and business, creative experimentation and upper-middle-class prosperity—unfortunately, the marriage did not last. The strain of pursuing both paths proved immense. In 1918, Ives suffered a heart attack, thought to be brought on by overwork, followed by a string of health ailments. He continued going into the office for a time but finally had to retire, against his will.

---

* This secretary added that Ives's daughter, Edith, "had learned to adjust. He couldn't take any interruptions because he was listening to what was inside him. He'd play, and the little girl was allowed to sit there underneath the piano and play with her dolls, but she must not make a sound."

Financially, he was set—Ives & Myrick had made him a millionaire. Musically, he was done—he stopped composing new work and used his dwindling energy to organize his existing compositions for posterity. Looking at the full sweep of his life, it's hard not to read it as a cautionary tale. This, at least, was how the younger composer Bernard Herrmann, who discovered Ives's music as a teenager, saw it. "Any artist who can make up his mind to spend three-quarters of his life being an insurance man and another quarter being an artist is a pretty unique compromise," Herrmann said. "It is not often done. It is a very difficult thing to maintain the equilibrium, and I think that he fell off it. He couldn't maintain it after a while."

+ + +

We can hardly talk about twentieth-century modernist pioneers who worked in the insurance business without leaping from New York and Hartford to Prague, where, in 1907, a twenty-four-year-old writer and recent law-school graduate named Franz Kafka began working in the city's branch of the Assicurazioni Generali, an insurance company based in Trieste. Neither insurance nor law held any great interest for Kafka; he had studied law purely because he thought it would afford him the best chance of being able to write fiction in his free time. As Louis Begley* has written, "Kafka's plan for his career had quickly boiled down to finding a dignified and secure occupation that would leave him enough time for his writing, and not be so arduous as to drain him of intellectual and psychic energy." His options were limited by antisemitism; at the time, Prague Jews could not expect to work at the university for a living wage, so an academic career was out of the question. Law, medicine, and business were the viable choices. Kafka had shown no aptitude at science, so medicine was out. His father was a businessman, and Kafka had a deeply troubled relationship with his father, so that was out as well. As he wrote later, "Law was the obvious choice."

---

* Begley's 2008 "biographical essay" on Kafka, *The Tremendous World I Have Inside My Head*, is one of the most perceptive things I have read on the writer—perhaps because Begley himself combined a prestigious law career with the writing of ten novels and several other books.

But Kafka was an undistinguished law student and barely graduated. Afterward, he did an unpaid year in the court system, required for lawyers who intended to sit for the bar, though Kafka had no such intention and used the year more as a buffer period to recover from the stress of exams and to begin looking for work. His sole ambition was to secure a job on the "single-shift" system, an enviable schedule offered only by the state bureaucracy and a few private companies, with hours from 8:00 or 9:00 in the morning until 2:00 or 3:00 in the afternoon—perfect for a writer. Unfortunately, because of his lackluster law school record, Kafka had to take what he could get, and he landed at the Assicurazioni Generali only thanks to the intervention of a well-connected uncle. The job was on the "double shift": 8:00 AM–6:00 PM, with two hours off for lunch, which still sounds pretty forgiving by contemporary standards. However, the office also demanded frequent overtime, and, Begley writes, "supervisors were in the habit of brutalizing junior employees." As a result, Kafka wrote little while he worked there, though he did publish his first short prose pieces in the magazine *Hyperion* in March of that year. He also began, almost immediately, to look for another job.

He found it several months later, this time thanks to the help of a university friend's father. His new employer was the Workers' Accident Insurance Institute, a semigovernmental agency that insured workers against industrial accidents and performed factory safety inspections, and that was on the coveted single-shift schedule. Kafka's ideal writer's day was now possible, at least in theory. A diary entry he made in early 1911, a few years after he started at the institute, describes how it went:

19 February. When I wanted to get out of bed this morning I simply folded up. This has a very simple cause, I am completely overworked. Not by the office but by my other work. The office has an innocent share in it only to the extent that, if I did not have to go there, I could live calmly for my own work and should not have to waste these six hours a day which has tormented me to a degree that you cannot imagine, especially on Friday and Saturday, because I was full of my own things. In the final analysis, I know,

that is just talk, the fault is mine and the office has a right to make the most definite and justified demands on me. But for me in particular it is a horrible double life from which there is probably no escape but insanity.

Kafka didn't feel this way all the time; there are moments in his diary when he seems to be on the verge of achieving some equilibrium between his work at the institute and his real work as a writer. On October 4, 1911, he writes, "most of the time in the office I do what I am supposed to, am quite calm when I can be sure that my boss is satisfied, and do not feel that my condition is dreadful." But the mood doesn't last; by October 17, he's back to despair: "I finish nothing because I have no time and it presses so within me." On November 5 of the same year, feeling dissatisfied about a story that he gave to his friend and eventual biographer Max Brod to read, Kafka writes, again in the diary: "I explain it to myself by saying that I have too little time and quiet to draw out of me all the possibilities of my talent."

Kafka wasn't wrong about this, or he wasn't entirely wrong. Certainly he lacked quiet. After completing law school and beginning his career, Kafka did not seek out lodgings of his own but continued to live with his parents and his three sisters in the family apartment in Prague. He had his own room, but it was, Begley writes, "a room more like a passageway, leading from the parents' bedroom to the living room and the communal bathroom"—hardly the zone of quiet contemplation that he sought for his writing, especially when Kafka's father was home. Hermann Kafka was the physical and temperamental opposite of his son: A large, loud man, supremely self-confident and assertive, he was not the type to tiptoe around his delicate firstborn's literary efforts. In his diary, Kafka describes his room as "the very headquarters of the uproar in the entire house" and complains of how his father "bursts through the door of my room and passes through in his dragging dressing gown," followed quickly by the voice of his sister, "shouting through the anteroom as though through a Paris street, whether Father's hat has been brushed yet."

The result was that Kafka felt he had no choice but to wait until everyone was asleep at night to attempt his writing. In November 1912, he described his daily schedule in a letter to his on-again, off-again fiancée, Felice Bauer:

> For the past six weeks, with some interruptions in the last few days, due to unbearable weakness, my timetable has been as follows: from 8 to 2 or 2:30 in the office, then lunch till 3 or 3:30, after that sleep in bed (usually only attempts . . .) till 7:30, then ten minutes of exercise, naked at the open window, then an hour's walk—alone, with Max, or with another friend, then dinner with my family . . . then at 10:30 (but often not till 11:30) I sit down to write, and I go on, depending on my strength, inclination, and luck, until 1, 2, or 3 o'clock, once even till 6 in the morning.* Then again exercises, as above, but of course avoiding all exertions, a wash, and then, usually with a slight pain in my heart and twitching stomach muscles, to bed.

As is often the case with Kafka's writing, there is a touch of comedy in this bleak scenario. The timetable he describes was drawn up by a bachelor with a six-hour workday, who had no dependents and whose meals were prepared for him by the family's live-in cook. Between leaving the office at 2:30 and beginning writing at 10:30, eight hours elapsed. It's hard to imagine that he couldn't have found some way to write during these hours, perhaps by going to a library or a café, renting a small office, or using the apartment of a friend who worked in the afternoon. As Begley has written, "The truth was that he wasted time."

In fairness, Kafka's chronic insomnia was a real obstacle here. Very often he couldn't get to sleep after his late-night writing sessions, and thus he began work the next morning with the feeblest reserves. "In one

---

* This singular occasion was the night of September 22–23, 1912, when Kafka wrote his breakthrough story "The Judgment" in one sitting, from 10:00 PM until 6:00 the next morning. He then called in sick to the office—and he was so elated by the successful effort that he attempted, the very next night, to replicate it. "Only *in this way* can writing be done, only with such coherence, with such a complete opening out of the body and soul," he wrote in his diary. Alas, Kafka wasn't able to repeat the experience the following night or any other night.

of the corridors along which I always walk to reach my typist," he wrote to Felice, "there used to be a coffinlike trolley for the moving of files and documents, and each time I passed it I felt as though it had been made for me, and was waiting for me." An afternoon nap must have seemed like a nonnegotiable necessity, even if it reinforced this unhappy cycle. Also, it seems likely that Kafka simply wrote best late at night, because of his need for quiet but also because this was just how his internal clock operated.

Starting in 1911, there was an additional obstacle that contributed to Kafka's difficulty writing. In October of that year, his family decided to open an asbestos factory as a side business—his father's primary business was running a haberdashery shop—and Kafka was expected to take part in the venture on top of his job at the Workers' Accident Insurance Institute. At one point, in 1912, as he was trying to make progress on the draft of his first novel, *Amerika* (which, like all his novels, ultimately remained unfinished), Kafka had to supervise the factory every afternoon for two weeks straight, depriving him of his all-important nap. This stint made him so miserable that he confessed in a letter to Brod that he had contemplated suicide: "I stood at the window a long time, and pressed my face against the glass, and I more than once felt like frightening the toll collector on the bridge by my fall." He ultimately concluded, however, that "by staying alive I should interrupt my writing less . . . than by dying."

Reading this and similar passages, you may find yourself wanting Kafka to make a more decisive break with his family—to give up the stupid factory work, move out of the family apartment, perhaps move away from Prague altogether. Could he not have secured an office job in another city? Or found work writing in some capacity so that he could be professionally engaged in the world of literature that was, as he said, the only thing that mattered to him?

Kafka did entertain the idea of quitting the Workers' Accident Insurance Institute and finding work as a writer. In a March 1914 diary entry, he considers what would happen if he were to leave his job and leave Prague. Berlin would be his best option, for there he could earn a living in journalism, he thinks, "and so find a means of livelihood at least partially suited to me." He continues: "Whether in addition I shall be capable of inspired work, that I cannot say at present with any degree of certainty." He never tested this proposition, and it's hard to imagine him actually doing so. As much as he complained about his work at the institute, he was able to find a weird kind of equilibrium there, and after all he *was* getting writing done, even if it took every ounce of his strength to do so. The bind he found himself in—prevented by circumstances from drawing out all the possibilities of his talent, yet unable or unwilling to change those circumstances—was itself generative in a way and is part of what has made his work so compelling to generations of readers. His fiction is full of people—and animals, in the several stories that feature nonhuman narrators—who are part of the stream of normal everyday life and also separate from it; who yearn for freedom from the mysterious and complicated forces that ensnare them, and who sometimes find that this freedom is, in fact, available to them if only they choose it—but who do not choose it, either because they doubt its reality or because they ultimately prefer their constrained position, which offers its own subtle advantages. As the canine narrator of Kafka's late story "Investigations of a Dog" thinks at one point, reflecting on the unspoken laws of dog life: "I shall never actually overstep their laws, but content myself with wriggling out through the gaps, for which I have a particularly good nose."

CULTURE WORKERS

So far, we've looked at a variety of day jobs in which the artist was laboring in fields quite outside his or her creative passion: as an office temp, a stripper, an insurance executive, a family doctor, a groveling landlady, or some other decidedly unartistic job or career. And there is a long tradition of advice for artists that recommends just this course. In a 1958 interview, for instance, the playwright Thornton Wilder told would-be writers: "Do not aspire to earn your living by your pen—get some job to support you while you write at midnight, and take a job as little connected with writing as possible—teaching mathematics, I think, would be splendid. Having a gas station on the New Mexican desert would be wonderful." Or here's the English literary critic Cyril Connolly in his 1938 book *Enemies of Promise*: "An outside job is harmful to a writer in proportion as it approximates his vocation. Thus reviewing poetry is the worst profession for a poet, while broadcasting, advertising, journalism or lecturing all pluck feathers from the blue bird of inspiration and cast them on the wind."

This idea that artists should find a job doing anything but their art—so as not to squander their creative brainpower on money-earning work—is compelling. But is it wise counsel? In the biography of Franz Kafka that he wrote more than a decade after Kafka's death, at age forty, from tuberculosis, his friend and fellow writer Max Brod took a more nuanced view of the question. As a young writer, Kafka had insisted that money-earning work and literary work be kept strictly separate, and Brod had adopted this same stance, to his later regret.

When it came to the point of choosing a profession, Franz postulated his job should have nothing to do with literature. That he would have regarded as a debasing of literary creation. Bread-winning and the art of writing must be kept absolutely apart, a "mixture" of the two, such as journalism, for example, represents, Kafka rejected—although at the same time he never laid down dogmas, but merely withdrew, as it were, with a smile, explaining that "I just can't do it." He influenced me and my choice of a profession for years with these views of his and, like himself, out of respect for art, I went through agonies, in the most hideous, prosaic, dry, profession of the law and didn't find the road to theatrical and musical criticism until years later. Today I regard Kafka's severity on this point a noble error, and regret the hundreds of joyless hours I let slip by in a mood almost of despair, wasting God's high creation, time, in offices just like those in which Kafka now set out on his martyr's way.

Brod found theatrical and musical criticism a far more congenial way of earning a living than the law—and doesn't what he writes here make a lot of sense? *Wouldn't* it be better for the artist who needs a job to work in the vicinity of the art or literary or music world, so as to at least be laboring in service of the culture you hope to eventually contribute to, and with any luck enriching your own work along the way?

This was the approach of the poet Frank O'Hara, to my mind one of the great day job–holders in literary history. Indeed, O'Hara's legacy rests largely on poems that he composed on his lunch breaks from his job at the Museum of Modern Art, as laid out in the promotional copy that he wrote for the back cover of his *Lunch Poems*, published in 1964:

Often this poet, strolling through the noisy splintered glare of a
Manhattan noon, has paused at a sample Olivetti to type up thirty
or forty lines of ruminations, or pondering more deeply has with-
drawn to a darkened ware- or firehouse to limn his computed mis-
understandings of the eternal questions of life, co-existence and
depth, while never forgetting to eat Lunch his favorite meal.

The "sample Olivetti" O'Hara mentions would have been found at the
Italian typewriter manufacturer's Fifth Avenue showroom, eight blocks
south of the Museum of Modern Art, where O'Hara started working at
the front desk in December 1951. "It seemed like Frank could write under
almost any conditions," his friend and fellow poet James Schuyler said.
"The first time I ever saw him working at the museum—I was working for
a bookstore and I came over to meet him for lunch—he was in the ticket
booth with a yellow legal pad writing a poem in the intervals between
selling tickets."

Raised in Grafton, Massachusetts, O'Hara had enlisted in the navy at
seventeen and used the GI Bill to study English at Harvard, where he also
fell in love with modern art. In August 1951, when he was twenty-five, he
moved to New York. He got the idea of working at the Museum of Modern
Art because he wanted to be able to see the Matisse exhibition that was
then on display multiple times for free. He stayed at the front desk for
the next few years, selling tickets, postcards, and publications to visitors
entering the stark International Style building at 11 West Fifty-Third Street.
He could not have found a better perch. In his biography of O'Hara, Brad
Gooch writes, "Stationed at one end of the counter, O'Hara continually
ran over to the other side to chat with friends or painters who had stopped
by to see the show, or simply to visit him." Gooch continues: "Within three
months of his arrival [in New York], O'Hara had figured out a clever way
to combine his need for art, money, friendship, and poetry. He needed a
job, and he found one that exposed him to painting and painters while still
allowing him time to write poems."

In January 1955, O'Hara was hired by the museum's International
Program as a special assistant to help prepare an exhibition of French

masterpieces. It was a temporary assignment, but O'Hara proved efficient enough at dealing with the mountains of exhibition paperwork to be promoted in April to a permanent position as an administrative assistant in the International Program. He eventually worked his way up to curator there; as Gooch writes, this was an era when "it was still possible for a clever, though academically untrained and curatorially uncredited young man such as O'Hara to make his way up through the ranks." Even as O'Hara's museum duties grew exponentially, he never had trouble pursuing his poetry on the side. "As far as I could tell, writing poetry was something Frank did in his spare time," his friend, longtime roommate, and sometime lover Joe LeSueur recalled. "He didn't make a big deal about it, he just sat down and wrote when the spirit moved him."*

How convenient! But this approach wasn't incidental to O'Hara's aesthetic goals—it was integral to a poetry that he wanted to feel casual and tossed-off, and no less profound for it. As he wrote in his tongue-in-cheek manifesto for "Personism," the poetic philosophy he invented, also on a whim: "I'm not saying I don't have practically the most lofty ideas of anyone writing today, but what difference does that make? They're just ideas. The only good thing about it is that when I get lofty enough I've stopped thinking and that's when refreshment arrives."

+ + +

O'Hara was hardly the only notable cultural figure to work at the Museum of Modern Art. Others included the photographer Edward Steichen, who served as the director of the museum's photography department from 1947 to 1961; the filmmaker Luis Buñuel, who worked on the museum's Latin American Project in the early 1940s; and the artist Sol LeWitt, who in 1960 got a job at the museum's book counter through his cousin (who worked in the publicity department) and later worked evenings at one of the museum's entrance desks. During his time at the museum, LeWitt

---

* LeSueur also claimed that O'Hara's description of writing poems on "a sample Olivetti" was a piece of invention, to provide "an irreverent, tongue-in-cheek" blurb for the back cover of *Lunch Poems*. LeSueur wrote that O'Hara's blurb "led later commentators to assert that he sometimes wrote his poems on an Olivetti showroom typewriter. The dumbbells—didn't they know when they were being kidded?"

met the artists Dan Flavin and Robert Ryman, both of whom worked as security guards; the artist Scott Burton, who worked at the membership desk; and the writer and art historian Lucy Lippard, who worked in the library. Lippard's duties included indexing magazines and filing material on artists. Thinking back on her time at the museum years later, she said: "I looked at every single thing that went under my nose and I got an incredible education."

LeWitt found the job similarly formative. "If I hadn't been working [at the museum] and if I hadn't known Flavin and Ryman and Lippard and some other people, it may not have clicked," he said. "You never know; it may have or it may not. But it did. So that was crucial. The policy that they had of employing artists as guards and as people doing lesser jobs was, I think, a very good policy."

In 1977, a twenty-two-year-old aspiring artist named Jeff Koons began working at the Museum of Modern Art's ticket booth, later transferring to the membership desk. Koons had just arrived in New York from Chicago, where he was working as an artist's assistant after finishing his studies at the School of the Art Institute of Chicago. (He had studied for three years at the Maryland Institute College of Art, in Baltimore, before transferring to Chicago for his final year.) One day in 1977, Koons heard Patti Smith on the radio talking about the downtown club scene in New York; he hitchhiked there the next day and never left.

The MoMA job was a perfect fit for Koons, who was a natural salesman. To start, he knew how to dress the part. It "was a little bit like a performance for me," Koons said later. "I would wear inflatable flowers and paper vests. I would wear things that people, when they were speaking to me, would get a little distracted by, and just kind of caught up a little bit in the event and hopefully that would help me get them to a higher membership level, just by getting a little lost in the cufflink, the way it was glittering." According to Koons, the number of memberships doubled during the time that he worked there. The journalist Ingrid Sischy worked at MoMA at the same time as Koons, and she vividly remembered his presence: "I often spied him in the lobby in his eye-catching outfits and attention-getting accessories, such as paper bibs, double ties, and store-bought inflatable flowers around his neck," she recalled. In an interview for a documentary about Koons, Sischy added that he was "like part clown, part performance art. . . . Now, when you look back at it, I would call that a breakthrough work."

A few museum visitors were so charmed by the young artist that they offered him a job on the spot. "They'd come up and say: 'Jeff, you should work for me,'" Koons recalled. Eventually, he accepted: He took a job selling mutual funds door-to-door—not a far cry from his very first job, as a schoolchild in York, Pennsylvania. "After school, I would go door-to-door, and I would sell products," Koons said in an interview for a documentary about his work. "I'd sell candies, I would sell gift-wrapping paper. I liked almost being anybody that the person wanted me to be when they answered the door."

From mutual funds, Koons moved on to selling commodities on Wall Street, getting himself a broker's license and working at First Investors Corporation. If the Museum of Modern Art was a natural fit for aspiring artists, Wall Street was not; especially among the late-1970s downtown art scene, the idea of working in the city's finance sector was outlandish, almost horrifying. In 2019, a journalist asked Koons if he regretted the move. "No!" he said. "I was always an artist, and everyone around me knew that. But I needed a higher income to make the work I wanted to make, and I couldn't do that by selling memberships at MoMA."

On Wall Street, Koons made enough to fund the production of his first exhibition, *The New*, in 1980, for which he filled the window of the New Museum of Contemporary Art with brand-new Hoover vacuum cleaners arrayed in Plexiglas boxes lit by fluorescent tubes—the start of a long career repurposing everyday consumer objects for artwork that could seem joyful, creepy, and ironic all at once. The work wasn't cheap to produce: According to Koons, a two- or four-vacuum assemblage cost him up to $3,000 to make (more than $10,000 at present-day values), and there were numerous such pieces in the exhibition. Subsequently, an art dealer managed to sell one of them for $5,000, but it was too little, too late: Koons was broke and had to move into his retired parents' apartment in Florida for six months. Then it was back to selling commodities on Wall

Street, and back to buying the freedom to make the kind of art he wanted to make. Over the next five years, Koons saved up enough to finance his next series of work, titled *Equilibrium*, which featured, among other objects, basketballs suspended in clear liquid inside Plexiglas vitrines.

When *Equilibrium* was shown at an East Village gallery in the spring of 1985, the art world took notice, and the now thirty-year-old Koons quit selling commodities to make art full-time. He followed *Equilibrium* the next year with *Statuary*, a series of consumer objects recast in stainless steel. After *Equilibrium*, Koons had begun to sell some of his sculptures—at a loss, he said—but *Statuary* launched him to a whole new level. One of the most memorable works, a mirrored-stainless-steel re-creation of an inflatable rabbit toy, titled *Rabbit*, was made in an edition of three. Koons's gallerist kept one; the other two sold for $40,000 each (more than $100,000 at today's values), and Koons never again had to sell MoMA memberships, mutual funds, or anything else other than his own art.

+ + +

Of course, not all artists lucky enough to work at a major museum have found it a perfect springboard for their own careers. A less sunny story of museum employment, also set at the Museum of Modern Art, involves the painter and curator Howardena Pindell, who started at MoMA in 1967 as an exhibition assistant and gradually worked her way up to associate curator, becoming the museum's first Black woman curator. It was a familiar position for Pindell: Born in Philadelphia in 1943, she was the only Black student in her class at the Yale School of Art, where she studied color theory and began experimenting with abstract painting. Upon graduating, Pindell moved to New York and stayed on friends' couches while looking for work, getting rejected by around fifty jobs before landing the entry-level position at MoMA. There, she tried to strike the balance that so many artists with day jobs have sought, and for the most part succeeded. "I would say I lived two lives," Pindell said in 2022. "I was an artist at night, and I was a museum worker during the day."

But being the museum's first female curator of color put Pindell in an awkward position. The other Black artists she knew in the city wanted her to use her role to advocate for greater diversity in the museum's exhibitions and collection; meanwhile, Pindell found that she was often ignored or excluded by her fellow curators in the museum. "Everyone was mad at me: the artists on the outside who wanted me to help them get into the museum, and the people on the inside who were mistrustful of artists and me in particular," she said. Her situation also posed a dilemma for her own art-making: Pindell was acutely aware of racial injustice in the art world, but the abstract paintings she was making at night didn't seem to say anything about that injustice. "I wanted to be playful, and at the same time I had a lot of anger at the art world," Pindell said. She didn't know how to reconcile the two things.

Gradually, however, Pindell's work began to mature, and she found a way for abstract paintings to subtly reflect the larger issues of her life. In the early 1970s, Pindell started incorporating the hole punch into her process, punching out innumerable small circles in sheets of paper and affixing the leftover chads to canvases, creating a unique textured surface that sometimes resembled confetti. Circles had a special resonance for her, though she didn't realize why until later: They were tied to a childhood memory of going on a family road trip to Ohio in the 1950s and stopping at a root beer stand in northern Kentucky. Drinking root beer with her father, Pindell noticed a large red circle on the underside of her mug and wondered aloud about its significance; her father explained that it was there to indicate which glassware was to be reserved for non-whites only. Circles have remained fundamental to her work to this day.

But as her painting was progressing, Pindell finally reached her limit with the art world's racism. In 1979, a white artist staged an exhibition of charcoal drawings at the nonprofit art gallery Artists Space, which was (and still is) funded by the New York State Council on the Arts. The exhibition title used a racial slur, in what struck many as a gratuitous effort to shock; Pindell thought that it was an empty provocation, deeply insensitive, and hardly worthy of public funding. She and other artists wrote an anonymous letter of complaint to the gallery, which prompted a different faction of artists to come out and vocally defend the artist's right to free speech. The exhibition stayed open. Pindell was so disappointed in the

New York art world that she decided she could no longer be part of one of its major institutions, resigning her position at MoMA. "The racism in the art world drove me out, as I did not want to remain silent," she said.

It was a year later that Pindell made her most explicitly political work, a twelve-minute video titled *Free, White and 21*, for which she staged a dialogue between two women. One was Pindell herself, vocalizing some of the many instances of discrimination she had encountered throughout her life and career. The other was Pindell in whiteface and a blond wig, reacting to this litany in the way that so many white curators, artists, museum administrators, and others had reacted to her over the years. "You know, you really must be paranoid," the white character says at one point. "Those things never happened to me. I don't know anyone who's had those things happen to them." At another point, she says: "You won't exist until we validate you. And if you don't want to do what we tell you to do, then we'll find other tokens."

When *Free, White and 21* was first shown, in 1980, "the whites freaked out," Pindell said. "They went wild. They were not happy with it." But in the years since—as Pindell has received late-life renown and, in her seventies and eighties, seen her work enter the collections of the Brooklyn Museum, the Metropolitan Museum of Art, and the Whitney Museum—it has become her best-known and most celebrated piece, exhibited around the world. "And the Modern had it for a while," Pindell said, "which is kind of ironic."

+ + +

After Howardena Pindell left MoMA, in 1979, she was invited to join the faculty at Stony Brook University, on Long Island, where she has been an art professor for more than five decades. The university proved to be a mostly friendly environment for her, as it has been for so many writers, artists, and intellectuals through the centuries—though not always as friendly as expected. Here, for instance, is Kurt Vonnegut, reflecting on his time at the Iowa Writers' Workshop, perhaps the most prestigious writing program in the United States, where he taught for two years beginning in 1965: "It is spiritually pooping to care desperately about student work that probably isn't worth caring about." Or here is the Russian American novelist Vladimir Nabokov writing to his friend Edmund Wilson from Cornell University in January 1952: "I am sick of teaching, I am sick of teaching, I am sick of teaching." Okay—but didn't Nabokov famously pre-write his lectures and simply read them aloud from the lectern? That barely seems to qualify as teaching at all—and by all accounts, Nabokov certainly did not fuss too much over his students' intellectual development or their potential as future writers. Professors who *do* care about their students—who don't find it "spiritually pooping" to care about their work and their potential—aren't they the ones who should be complaining? After all, it's no easy thing to care deeply about others' works in progress and your own simultaneously. As the novelist Elizabeth McCracken (a graduate of the Iowa Writers' Workshop and the daughter of academics) said in a 2022 interview:

> The sad truth is, when teaching goes badly, you go home and you can't write. When teaching goes well, you go home and you can't write. I'm not sure if teaching plays with the same part of the brain, but it certainly plays with the same part of the soul that feeds your writing.

McCracken's solution was to reject the classroom in favor of the library, which, like the museum, may provide the perfect mix of cultural relevance and duties that don't draw *too* much on the part of the brain that feeds one's art. She said:

> I wanted a job that I could leave at the office. Library work is like that. People kept saying to me, "You probably write when you're at the library," and I'd say "No, I have to work. That's why I'm there." I didn't write when I was working, but when I returned home, I could do it. People would ask me questions during the day, but by the end of the day they were all answered. Writing is such solitary work, but it is also good to go out into the world and serve people. I don't mean that in some sort of "Mother Teresa washing the feet

of the lepers" way. It is good to stand behind a desk and have people ask you to do things, and you do them.

More recently, I was intrigued to read about the musician Daniel Lopatin, who releases experimental ambient music under the name Oneohtrix Point Never. After college, Lopatin moved to Brooklyn and enrolled in the library science program at Pratt Institute. "The plan was to become a librarian and do music at the same time," he told *The New Yorker* in 2023. "I thought that would be a perfect life." As it happens, this was my thinking right after college, too. After graduating with an English degree in 2002, I got a job at a university medical library in Nashville, Tennessee, and settled down to write fiction in my spare time. I found an affordable apartment near the library and could walk to and from work; my duties were engaging but not too demanding; my co-workers were pleasant and kind. And yet in my three years at the library, I wrote virtually nothing. I'm not sure the *job* was to blame, but even so I can't help but wonder if sometimes the "perfect life" is no good for your art, as much as you wish it would be.

+ + +

Let's conclude these ruminations with the poet John Berryman, who, in 1943, found himself in a familiar predicament: He wanted to write poetry, but he needed, rather urgently, to pay the bills. To do the latter, he had previously secured teaching positions at Wayne State University and then at Harvard—but the Harvard appointment was now ending, and as the spring of 1943 rolled around and no other positions had materialized, the twenty-eight-year-old Berryman began to feel desperate. In April, he wrote to his mother:

> We have nothing in the bank and live with difficulty from week to week, although neither of us eats enough, we entertain very little, we go nowhere, and we spend on non-essentials practically nothing, on essentials less than we must (clothes for instance both of us need badly))))) UGH

"We" referred to Berryman and his first wife, Eileen, whom he had married the previous fall. In June, the couple decided to embark on "a plan of prudent desperation," relocating from Boston to New York so that Berryman could search for work at the city colleges there, staying first with Eileen's aunt and then with her sister. But nothing turned up. According to Eileen, Berryman sent out at least fifty letters of application—not only to colleges but to publishing houses, magazines, tutoring schools, night schools, libraries. Still nothing. ("Every day I'm made to peel off my skin—to no purpose," he complained.) Finally, he took out a classified ad in *The New York Times*:

> POET, 28, married, 4F, educated here and abroad, critic, editor, and experienced and competent university instructor, would like to continue living and writing if possible.

Was it possible? For a while there, in the summer of 1943, it seemed like it might not be. The classified ad, not surprisingly, did not turn up anything. After that, Berryman resorted to an even less likely plan: selling encyclopedias door-to-door in Harlem, a job so unsuited to his temperament that he only lasted two days; "trembling & half-mad," he quit in disgust without making a single sale.

Teaching was a better fit—Berryman possessed a fearsome intellect and was an inspiring and often funny presence in the classroom—but as the summer neared an end, still no university offers had arrived. (The war was partly to blame; universities were emptied of male students, and programs were being retooled to accommodate military officers in training.) In mid-August, a Catholic boys' high school in New Rochelle, New York, offered Berryman a job teaching Latin and English to two hundred students; he had no choice but to accept. "This is not a subject for congratulation," he wrote to his mother, "but presumably we will be able to live through the year." Berryman's mother and stepfather had sent him to boarding school in his own youth, and these had been years of pure misery for the gawky, nearsighted adolescent; he did not think teaching at a similar institution would be much of an improvement, and he was right.

Eileen remembers: "The headmaster reprimanded him for being a poor disciplinarian; his colleagues were almost as immature as the students; his office was in the men's room; he had to stay up half the night reviewing Latin and correcting papers."

Five weeks later, however, Berryman was rescued from "Hell-in-New Rochelle" with an offer to teach at Princeton University for a four-month term beginning November 1. It wasn't a glamorous position: Berryman would be teaching 110 navy personnel in the wartime Armed Services Training Program, Monday through Saturday from 8:00 AM until 6:00 PM. But Princeton was a congenial atmosphere for a poet, and Berryman found friendly colleagues and began working on his own poetry again. (He had written nothing during the previous five months.) He ended up working at Princeton, in various positions, for much of the next decade, and he would never again face a stretch of unemployment as harrowing as the one he'd endured in the spring and summer of 1943. Even so, financial security remained elusive—in November 1961, when he was forty-seven, he complained to his mother, "I have *no* savings, and yesterday I had 12.50 in my checking acc't"—and anytime Berryman *was* making a decent salary, the money-earning work inevitably took away from his poetry, creating an intolerable tension. He wrote to one of his mentors, the poet and professor Mark Van Doren: "Each year it is more plain to me that probably there exists no way of making a living (available to me) which will be either agreeable to my sensibility or convenient to what I pretend is my work."

Things finally took a decisive turn toward prosperity after the publication, in 1964, of *77 Dream Songs*, Berryman's fourth book of verse, which won the Pulitzer Prize for poetry the next year. "So easy:—only 8 years' work," he joked after delivering the manuscript. It was more like thirty years' work—all Berryman's ambitions, all his humiliations, all his guilt and humor and love of literature had found its way into these strange, beguiling, multivoiced poems, by turns funny, despairing, beautiful, and baffling. Even when he resolved to move on to new forms, after publishing a second volume of the *Songs* in 1968, he kept writing them, telling a visiting interviewer that he just couldn't bear "to be rid of that admirable outlet, that marvelous way of making your mind known to many other people."

Does this mean that all the years of insecurity were finally justified, in a way—that what hadn't killed him had made him stronger, as the saying goes? Not exactly. Eileen wrote, "He might say in conversation that it was necessary for a poet to suffer, and even believe it, but no one was more eager to be relieved of suffering than John." The arrival of money and fame did not cure Berryman of his depressions; he died of suicide in 1972, when he was fifty-seven years old. Still, achieving recognition, and the easing of his financial burdens, had meant something to him, had meant a lot. As he wrote in the opening lines of "Dream Song 340":

The secret is not praise. It's just being accepted
at something like the figure where you put your worth
anywhere on the bloody earth

PATRONS

ELITE STATUS

I don't really care about money," the painter Grace Hartigan wrote in her journal on October 8, 1953, "but I need time desperately. I don't want to give up my solitude for the nightmarish intrusion of a job. What I really need is a patron."

Many artists have shared Hartigan's dream, and many artists' careers would have been impossible without the well-timed appearance of a wealthy supporter—though often these supporters had to be chased, courted, or coaxed into offering meaningful funding, and often artists had to exhibit a range of skills beyond sheer talent: for self-promotion, flattery, and diplomacy, and for making their funders look good (or feel important) while satisfying their own creative ambitions.

For a foundational example, let's leap from Grace Hartigan's unheated Lower East Side studio to Rome on the morning of April 8, 1341. It is Easter Sunday and a crowd has gathered on the Capitoline Hill for a spectacle: A senator is about to crown Rome's first poet laureate in more than twelve hundred years. But first the poet himself—thirty-six years old; a native of Arezzo, some twenty miles south of Florence; educated as a lawyer, though he abandoned his legal studies as soon as he could—steps forward to address the assembly. He quotes Virgil, "the greatest and most illustrious of all poets," and speaks of the difficulty of their shared profession, "in which nothing can be accomplished unless a certain inner and divinely given energy is infused in the poet's spirit." And this energy, though divinely given, needs some bolstering by the poet's friends and supporters—a point the soon-to-be laureate drives home by quoting the ancient Roman satirist Juvenal:

> But the good poet, whose line is not commonplace . . . must have a spirit free from anxiety, untouched by any bitterness, eager for the woods, and ready to drink at the fountain of the Muses. For none can sing in the Pierian cave or wield the thyrsus who is oppressed by sad poverty and lacks the coin to meet the body's daily and nightly needs.

In other words: Minutes before kneeling to receive the crown of laurel, our poet took a moment to remind everyone present, and anyone who would read the text of his oration in the centuries to come, of an important fact: Poets gotta eat! The Muses do not invite to their fountain the anxious, the bitter, or the impoverished.

Granted, this new poet laureate—his name was Francesco Petrarca, known to English speakers as Petrarch—had never experienced real poverty himself, though he had certainly risked it by pursuing an independent literary career at a time when there really was no such thing. That he avoided destitution and ultimately flourished was thanks to his undeniable talent as a poet and a scholar, as well as his lifelong charm and tenacity, and also a gnawing hunger for fame. The coronation itself is a perfect example. Many years later, Petrarch wrote that he had "blushed to accept . . . the verdict" of the men who summoned him for the ceremony, stressing his "unworthiness" for such a great honor. In fact, the entire event had been orchestrated by Petrarch himself and only took place thanks to a behind-the-scenes influence campaign spanning months. Petrarch's coronation was therefore not just the revival of an ancient literary pedigree but a brazen act of self-promotion and a canny guarantee of future income.

In his coronation speech, Petrarch emphasized the difficulties he had borne to reach that exalted moment: "How hard and inexorable fortune has been to me, with what labors she has oppressed me from my youth up, how many blows I have endured from her, God knows, and they also know who have been my close companions." In truth, Petrarch's luck hadn't been all bad. He was fortunate to be born the son of a notary—a respected professional who dealt in contracts, wills, statutes, and other official proceedings—which meant he was raised in an environment where reading and writing were valued. Petrarch's father, Ser Petracco, even nurtured a love of Cicero, which he passed on to his son. But young Petrarch's love proved immoderate. "I gave myself wholly to Cicero," he recalled. "That love . . . increased day by day, and my father, amazed, encouraged my immature propensity through paternal affection. And I, dodging no labor that might aid my purpose, breaking the rind began to savor the taste of the fruit, and couldn't be restrained from my study."

Meanwhile, Ser Petracco was making his own plans for his son's studies, intending that he become a lawyer, a step up from a notary in prestige and economic opportunity. At age twelve, Petrarch was sent with his brother to the first of two universities to study civil law, beginning in Montpellier and later transferring to Bologna. (Though Petrarch was born in Arezzo, he spent much of his early life in Avignon, France, where Pope Clement V had moved his court in 1309; the papal enclave provided ample work for notaries like Petracco.) But Petrarch's studies did not translate into a love of the law: "In my law studies I spent, or rather entirely wasted, seven years," he recalled. In secret, Petrarch continued to savor the fruit of Cicero and other ancient writers, stashing the books he was able to collect in a hiding place in his room. Famously, Petracco discovered this cache on a visit to Montpellier and, condemning the books as an impediment to Petrarch's law studies, cast them all into the fire, causing Petrarch to "burst out in cries of woe." At this, Petracco relented a little, pulling out of the fire "two volumes already scorched"—a book of Virgil and Cicero's *Rhetoric*—and telling his son, "Take this one as an occasional recreation for your mind and the other to comfort and aid you in your law studies."

So Petrarch soldiered on, though never with any enthusiasm. "I couldn't reconcile myself to make a merchandise of my mind," he said. Then, in 1326, Petrarch's father died, and the twenty-two-year-old law student was suddenly free to pursue his own path. (Petrarch's mother had died several years earlier, and he wrote his first extant poem out of grief at the loss.) Unfortunately, the funds he received from his father's estate were quickly depleted—according to one biographer, they were "either mismanaged or embezzled or a bit of both"—and Petrarch was forced to find ways to fund the life of the mind he sought.

Luckily for him, the twentysomething Petrarch was no brooding bookworm: He was a young man of immense natural charisma, with a genius for friendship as well as scholarship. (The writer Boccaccio, who was nine years Petrarch's junior, wrote that his "affability is so exceptional that, whereas many illustrious men disappoint in the encounter, he surpasses all expectations.") In Bologna, he met and formed a deep friendship with a young Italian bishop named Giacomo Colonna—Petrarch called the summer they met "the happiest summer of my life"—and, through him, began a lifelong association with Giacomo's older brother, Cardinal Giovanni Colonna, who became his first and longest-lasting patron. The Colonnas were a powerful and wealthy family with close ties to the papal court, and their palatial Avignon home—it comprised fifteen adjoining houses—was a gathering place for eminent visitors. Petrarch became a fixture there and, in 1330, officially entered the service of Cardinal Colonna, a position he would hold for the next seven years. "Serving him was better than living independent," Petrarch said, "for without him I could never have enjoyed a really free and tranquil life."

So here, at the dawn of the Italian Renaissance, we have an example of artistic patronage at its most ideal: a kind of socioeconomic symbiosis, with each party gaining something it needs and neither party losing anything it can't easily spare. In this case, Petrarch needed a steady income and all the other perks of a court appointment: the time and space to read and write and think; opportunities to travel (during which he scoured monastic libraries for classical manuscripts that he later edited and disseminated); exposure to a variety of individuals of intellect and renown. Cardinal Colonna needed witty and learned members of his household to impress visitors. Petrarch, though still a budding poet, qualified, and as his literary fame increased—through his revival of ancient texts as well as his sonnets dedicated to the woman he called Laura, whom he first encountered in 1327 and loved from afar for the rest of his life—so did his utility as a resident celebrity; in addition, he performed secretarial duties, tutored the cardinal's nephew for a time, and went on diplomatic missions as the cardinal's ambassador. He lived in Colonna's home and served him as needed, and apparently the cardinal did not need his services so often as to sour Petrarch on the arrangement.

Petrarch would live on patronage of one variety or another for the rest of his life, eventually becoming quite well off in the process, though he always claimed to be on the edge of poverty. Wisely, he didn't rely solely on individual favors. A crucial component of Petrarch's long-term financial success was his decision, in his early twenties, to take minor ecclesiastical orders, becoming a low-ranking member of the clergy. This meant that he was eligible to receive church benefices, permanent appointments in which property and income are provided to church officers. (It also meant a vow of celibacy, though it seems Petrarch didn't take this too seriously; he eventually fathered two children from unknown women.) In Petrarch's time, certain of these appointments were essentially sinecures; the duties were light or nonexistent, and the revenues could be handsome. Cardinal Colonna recommended Petrarch for the first of these, a canonry in the cathedral of Lombez, and Petrarch was later granted additional benefices through his continued association with Colonna and other powerful patrons. By the end of his life, one historian has written, "Petrarch's benefices and the favors of the great permitted him to live very much at his ease and free from any tiresome obligations."

Just as important to Petrarch, it was Colonna who proved a receptive audience to his cherished scheme of reviving the poet laureateship, who put the idea in the heads of Rome's rulers, and who ultimately proved decisive in making the coronation happen (though he wasn't the only powerful person Petrarch lobbied in his quest for the crown). Without their successful partnership—*almost* a friendship, though not quite, and maybe that's impossible in any relationship between patron and artist—we might not have more than a dozen nations appointing poets laureate today, though these appointments do not carry quite the same weight as in Petrarch's vision. In the United States, we get a new poet laureate every year; each receives a $35,000 annual stipend, an amount that has not been adjusted for inflation since 1986.

+ + +

Petrarch was lucky: Cardinal Colonna treated him like a privileged member of his household rather than a mere servant, and he allowed him opportunities to read, write, study, and travel. Alas, few artists have enjoyed such consistently preferential treatment from their patrons. The Austrian composer Joseph Haydn is a good example. Though he blossomed as an artist under the patronage of the two Hungarian princes he served for almost thirty years starting in 1761, he had to manage an enormous workload of official duties, and he was rarely permitted to leave the royal residences where he labored; even as his fame grew throughout Europe, Haydn was only dimly aware of his public reputation and had the barest contact with the world of music beyond his tightly limited sphere.

Of course, simply finding his way to making a living as a musician, let alone enjoying comfortable royal patronage, was something of a miracle for Haydn. Now considered the father of the symphony and of the string quartet, he was born into a family with zero musical lineage; the biographer Karl Geiringer writes that Haydn was "one of the most independent spirits in musical history. . . . Going back to his great-grandfathers on both sides, we fail to find among them a single musician or even a man who pursued any kind of intellectual occupation. They all toiled with their hands as vinegrowers, farmers, wheelwrights, or millers." Haydn's mother was a cook for the Austrian nobility; at twenty-one, she left their employ to marry Mathias Haydn, a wagonmaker, who built them a small, thatch-covered hut in the village of Rohrau, where Joseph and his eleven siblings were born (only five made it past infancy). Decades later, when Beethoven was shown a picture of the Haydn residence, he exclaimed: "Strange that so great a man should have been born in so poor a home!"

Though there were no professional musicians in Haydn's family, his father had, during his journeyman years, taught himself to play the harp, and Haydn grew up hearing his parents sing Austrian folk tunes to his father's harp playing. As a young child, Haydn proved so gifted at singing along to these folk tunes—and also keeping time with a make-believe violin he fashioned out of a pair of sticks—that his talent was recognized by a visiting relative who was a headmaster and church choir director in nearby Hainburg. This cousin offered to bring Haydn back to Hainburg for a proper musical education; Haydn's parents, wanting a better life for their eldest son, agreed. Joseph was just five and a half. Thereafter, he would only return to Rohrau for occasional brief visits.

In Hainburg, young Haydn received extensive musical instruction, as promised, but also "more floggings than food" and few material comforts. "I could not help perceiving," Haydn recalled decades later, "much to my distress, that I was gradually getting very dirty, and though I thought rather highly of my little person, I was not always able to avoid stains on my clothes, of which I was dreadfully ashamed—in fact, I was a regular little ragamuffin." After a few years, another chance discovery allowed him to improve his station: A visiting court composer named Reutter was sufficiently impressed by Haydn's singing that he offered to bring him to Vienna as a chorister at the famous Cathedral of Saint Stephen, where Reutter was the newly appointed chapel master. With Haydn's parents' assent, he made the trip to Vienna upon his eighth birthday.

Materially, Saint Stephen was not as much of an improvement as Haydn must have hoped; under Reutter's care, one early biographer has written, "Joseph's stomach had to get accustomed to continuous fasting." Musically, it was only partway satisfying. All of Reutter's pupils learned to become expert singers and sight readers, and also to play the clavier, the violin, and the organ. As Haydn got older, however, he yearned to begin composing his own music, an inclination that Reutter did nothing to encourage and at one point openly mocked.

Eventually, as he approached his sixteenth year, Haydn's tenure at Saint Stephen was endangered by the deterioration of his voice due to puberty; none other than the Empress Maria Theresa complained of the teenage Haydn "crowing like a cock." Not long after this, Haydn made the terrible choice of playing a practical joke on one of his fellow choristers, cutting off his pigtail with a pair of scissors. Reutter seized the opportunity to get rid of Haydn, ordering that he be caned and dismissed. Now seventeen,

Haydn found himself cast out on his own in Vienna with no money, no singing voice, and no connections to speak of; his only possessions were three shirts and a worn coat. His parents, distraught, urged him to enter the priesthood. Haydn refused, determined to still somehow make his way as a composer.

A singer Haydn knew slightly took him in for a time, and Haydn began to cobble together income from a variety of small jobs. Geiringer writes: "He played at dances, he arranged compositions for various instruments, he took pupils for miserably small fees." He also earned money playing open-air serenades, a popular custom in Vienna at the time. Eventually he could just afford a shabby sixth-floor garret without a stove for heat or even a window for light, but with an "old worm-eaten clavier" on which Haydn taught himself music theory at night, after long days giving lessons and hustling assorted jobs. (Of teaching, he said: "Many a genius is ruined by this miserable mode of earning daily bread, as it leaves no time for study.") Though evidence of his progression was slim, Haydn was blessed with a potent combination of optimism and stubbornness, always maintaining confidence that he was "making something out of nothing."

He absorbed knowledge from wherever he could. "Proper teachers I have never had," Haydn once remarked—but he heard much great music in Vienna and, he said, "listened attentively and tried to turn to good account what most impressed me." He also acquired the scores for six keyboard sonatas by Carl Philipp Emanuel Bach, which he studied obsessively; later, a tutoring position brought him into the orbit of a famous Italian composer and singing teacher named Nicola Porpora. Haydn offered to work as Porpora's menial servant—cleaning his shoes, beating his coat, attending to his wig—in exchange for the opportunity to act as his accompanist and study his method, an arrangement he kept up for three months. At the end, Haydn felt that he had finally mastered "the genuine fundamentals of composition."

By this point, Haydn's makeshift apprenticeship had lasted far longer than he could have imagined when he was turned out of Saint Stephen with just the clothes on his back; in his own words, Haydn "had to eke out a wretched existence for eight whole years" before he finally began to make inroads with the aristocracy, which at this time was really the only means of making a comfortable living as a composer. One of Haydn's sonatas impressed a Viennese countess, who—despite her initial shock at Haydn's shabby clothes and awkward manners—hired him for singing and clavier lessons. On her recommendation, Haydn received a series of more prestigious appointments—and as his fortunes rose, so did his artistic ambitions; Haydn composed his first string quartet for one of these new patrons, and his first symphony for a later one, Court Morzin. When Morzin ran into financial difficulties and had to give up his orchestra, Haydn was hired for the position he would keep for the next three decades: as Vice-Kapellmeister (later promoted to full Kapellmeister) for Prince Paul Anton Esterházy and his successor, Prince Nicolaus, whose family were the largest landowners in Hungary and who stood at the very top of the country's nobility.

Haydn's employment contract has survived, and it provides a fascinating glimpse of the day-to-day expectations of an eighteenth-century court composer. The new Vice-Kapellmeister was obliged to "appear daily . . . in the [prince's] antechamber before and after midday, and inquire whether His Highness is pleased to order a performance of the Orchestra." In addition, he was "under obligation to compose such music as His Serene Highness may command, and neither to communicate such compositions to any other person, nor to allow them to be copied," retaining them for "the exclusive use of His Highness" (though this prohibition was later lifted, permitting Haydn's compositions to be disseminated across Europe). On top of composing new works and arranging for frequent orchestra performances, Haydn had to "take careful charge of all music and musical instruments, and be responsible for any injury that may occur to them from carelessness and neglect"; to "instruct the female vocalists, in order that they may not forget in the country what they have been taught with much trouble and expense in Vienna"; to "take care himself to practice" all the musical instruments on which he was proficient; to ensure that the orchestra always appear before company in a uniform of "white stockings, white linen, powdered, and either with pigtail or hairbag, all, however, of identical appearance"—in short, to "place the orchestra on such a footing, and in such good order, that he may bring honor upon himself and deserve the further favor of the Prince his master."

If this sounds like a lot—yes, that was the nature of these appointments. Karl Geiringer writes, "The number and variety of duties expected from Haydn are staggering. . . . Three different spheres of activity were entrusted to him. He was conductor, which meant daily practice with the orchestra and very frequent performances; he had to compose a great part of the enormous amount of music performed; finally, he was an important officer of administration, uniting in his person the positions of music librarian, supervisor of instruments, and chief of the musical personnel." And throughout it all, he had to maintain an attitude of extreme humility befitting a member of the royal household. Here, for instance, is the beginning of a letter from Haydn to Prince Nicolaus dating from late 1766:

The most welcome arrival of my patron's name day (which may Divine Grace let Your Serene Highness spend in perfect well-being and happiness) causes me not only to offer to Your Serenity in dutiful submission six new divertimenti, but also to kiss the hem of your robe for graciously presenting us with our new winter clothes, which a few days ago were handed to us.

Sheesh. In the letter, Haydn goes on to "submissively inquire" about some issues with alterations to an earlier disbursement of official clothes; to "also submissively inquire" about the binding of a previous batch of his compositions; and to very carefully explain that a pair of oboes "are deteriorating because of old age" and need to be replaced, explaining what this should cost and wishing, in closing, for "Your Serene Highness' gracious consent to acquire the two urgently needed oboes at the above-mentioned price."

By all accounts, Prince Nicolaus was a genuine music lover who savored and encouraged his Kapellmeister's growing artistry. And under his patronage Haydn composed a remarkable array of works: 108 symphonies, 68 string quartets, 47 piano sonatas, 26 operas, 4 oratorios, and hundreds of smaller pieces. (The historian Jan Swafford writes, "He entered the employ of the Esterházys a conventional minor composer; thirty years later, he emerged a world-famous genius who had changed the face of music.") But Nicolaus was also a busy and sometimes forgetful nobleman who didn't like to be bothered with unnecessary matters and who entrusted much of the day-to-day palace administration to an army of subordinates, who were not always as friendly toward Haydn and his musicians. As Haydn put it, "I had a gracious Prince, but sometimes I was forced to be dependent on base souls."

A larger problem for Haydn was the location of Prince Nicolaus's court: The castle of Eszterháza, which the prince had built deep in the countryside of western Hungary, was called the "Hungarian Versailles," but it was in an isolated and frankly miserable location. Geiringer writes, "It was a desolate place, filled with mud as far as the eye could see. Every sort of insect abounded there, and fever was a popular guest." (It was also subject to, in Haydn's words, a "vexatious, penetrating north wind.") And Nicolaus did not like to be without his esteemed Kapellmeister, politely yet firmly denying Haydn's requests for leave. Haydn wrote, "It is scarcely credible, and yet the refusal is always couched in such polite terms as to render it utterly impossible for me to urge my request."

In many ways, Haydn's isolation was an advantage, or at least that's how he framed it to himself. He said:

> My prince was always satisfied with my works. Not only did I have the encouragement of constant approval, but as conductor of an orchestra I could make experiments, observe what produced an effect and what weakened it, and was thus in a position to improve, to alter, make additions or omissions, and be as bold as I pleased. I was cut off from the world; there was no one to confuse or torment me, and I was forced to become *original*.

It's true. In his three decades working for the Esterházy princes, Haydn became one of the most groundbreaking and original composers in music history; Geiringer writes, "It cannot be denied that Haydn's life in the service of Prince Nicolaus gave him just the opportunities he needed for his artistic growth." But Haydn didn't always feel so reconciled to his seclusion. In January 1790, on returning to Eszterháza after a rare and wonderfully stimulating visit to Vienna, the fifty-seven-year-old Haydn wrote to his host in the city: "Well here I sit in my wilderness; forsaken, like some poor orphan, almost without human society, melancholy, dwelling on the memory of past glory days." And in another letter a few months later, he lamented, even more pitifully, "It is indeed sad to always be a slave."

+ + +

Haydn contorted himself to the demands of his patrons and ultimately flourished creatively, even if it meant decades-long isolation, chronic overwork, and periodic obstruction from royal lackeys. (Fortunately, his isolation was not indefinite; just months after complaining of being forsaken and melancholy at Eszterháza, Prince Nicolaus died, and Haydn was finally free to travel and choose his own projects, funded by a generous royal stipend.) Other artists have been considerably less compliant. Perhaps the supreme example is the American expatriate painter James Abbott McNeill Whistler, who from a young age demonstrated an immense natural charisma and an equally immense antiauthoritarian streak. Not surprisingly, these traits created constant tension. Throughout his life, Whistler hustled his way into remarkable opportunities and then blew them to smithereens.

Whistler's Peacock Room was ground zero for one of these spectacular detonations. This was a commission begun in the summer of 1876 and completed in February of the following year—though even calling it a commission is somewhat misleading. The funder was a Liverpool shipping magnate named Frederick Leyland, who was an enthusiastic collector of Renaissance bronzes, Chinese rugs and porcelain, Chippendale and Louis XVI furniture, and much else, as well as a patron of the Pre-Raphaelite poet and painter Dante Gabriel Rossetti. Starting in 1866, thanks to Rossetti's influence, he had become Whistler's patron as well.

Leyland was in many ways a dream patron—he was quick to write a check and loath to question what exactly his funds had produced, even when commissions were slow to materialize or never materialized at all— and by this point Whistler had completed some of his most ambitious paintings with Leyland's support. But the Peacock Room ignited Whistler's worst tendencies: his monomania, his grandiosity, and his willingness, even eagerness, to shoulder aside friends and collaborators in his quest for public recognition, which was never as plentiful or as worshipful as he thought he deserved.

The project began at Rossetti's urging. "Why don't you give yourself the delight in life of building a fine gallery for big pictures?" he asked Leyland just after Christmas in 1871. "What a jolly thing it would be!" Rossetti was surely thinking it would be a jolly thing for his own career; all that gallery space would need large new paintings from Leyland's favored artists. The words Rossetti whispered in Leyland's ear are almost a parody of the hungry artist's message to the wealthy patron: "I know I'd do it I were you," Rossetti told him, "for what is life worth if one doesn't get the most of such indulgences as one most enjoys?"

Leyland saw his point. In 1876, he purchased a new London residence at 49 Prince's Gate, in Kensington, a twenty-two-year-old town house with three connected living rooms; when the walnut-and-brass folding screens that separated these rooms were opened, it became a salon ninety-four feet long. What better setting for the fine gallery of Rossetti's dreams?

Leyland embraced the dream, hiring interior designer Thomas Jeckyll to transform the central of the three rooms into a magnificent dining room that would showcase some of Leyland's favorite objects. Jeckyll was given three tasks: He had to find a way to display Leyland's sizable collection of blue-and-white porcelain; he had to direct guests' attention to Whistler's *Princess from the Land of Porcelain*, a large canvas that Leyland had commissioned in 1864; and, on the walls, he had to employ a stock of floral-embossed Cordovan leather that Leyland had already acquired and was eager to put to good use.

Combining Leyland's Chinese porcelain and Spanish leather would have been a challenge for any designer, but Jeckyll's addition of carved walnut shelving and an elaborate Jacobean pendant ceiling—with each pendant holding a gas lamp—did not help. A visiting architect generously described the result as "at the best a trifle mixed." Sensing the failure, Leyland and wife, Florence, decided to ask for outside help.

At this point, Whistler had designed several interiors, including the inside of the Leylands' previous London home, which they were preparing to vacate for Prince's Gate. Since that collaboration had gone well, and since Whistler's *Princess* was already hanging in Jeckyll's "a trifle mixed" dining room, it's not surprising that Florence Leyland reached out to the artist for his thoughts about improving on Jeckyll's work. Specifically, she asked him for help with the colors in the room—they weren't working. In response, Whistler suggested trimming off the red border of the carpet and touching up the embossed flowers on the leather walls, adding yellow and gold paint. But these modest interventions made no improvement—in fact, painting on top of the embossed leather was something of a disaster—and Frederick Leyland, distracted by business concerns, eager to return to his permanent residence in Liverpool, and just wanting the room finished, decided to let Whistler take over and do whatever he deemed necessary. Whistler biographer Stanley Weintraub writes:

> Concluding a hasty gentleman's agreement about remuneration, mentioning, he thought, a figure of about £500, he left for Liverpool. Not only was the London season over, and his wife eager to return to Speke Hall [their permanent residence] for the summer, but he was busy arranging for the launching of the Leyland Line into the increasingly profitable North Atlantic shipping routes, a task which, fortunately for Whistler, kept Leyland away for months.

Whistler kept the couple updated on his progress via post, in a series of letters that, to my eye, have an unmistakably unhinged quality. (Weintraub describes Whistler's tone as a "*mélange* of cockiness and magnanimity.") As summer turned to fall, he wrote:

> *Mon cher Baron—Je suis content de moi!* The dining room is really alive with beauty—brilliant and gorgeous while at the same time delicate and refined to the last degree—
> I have *enfin* managed to carry out thoroughly the plan of

decoration I had formed—and I assure you, you can have no more idea of the ensemble in its perfection, gathered from what you last saw on the walls, than you could have of a complete opera judging from a third finger exercise!—*Voila*—But don't come up yet—I have not yet quite done—and you mustn't see it til the last touch is on.

Reading this, I'm reminded of those Hollywood coming-of-age comedies where the teenage protagonists have thrown an enormous, destructive house party while their parents are out of town, only to learn that the parents are thinking of coming home early. "Oh, no, not yet—please enjoy your vacation, we're doing just fine here—" Indeed, this is not far from the truth of the situation. As Frederick Leyland was busy running his North Atlantic shipping line from Liverpool, Whistler was letting himself get completely carried away by a project that he had decided (without telling the Leylands) would be his greatest artistic triumph yet. It would be organized, he determined, by an elaborate peacock motif. Peacocks were a favorite of the Pre-Raphaelites—Rossetti even kept real ones in his Chelsea residence—and they seemed to Whistler just the thing to tie together the dining room's disparate decorations with his own *Princess from the Land of Porcelain*. He would make a pattern, adapted from the "eye" of the peacock feather, and use it to create a "harmony in blue and gold" across the entire room. This pattern, and another devised from the bird's breast feathers, would appear on the ceiling, the walls, the shelves, and even the floor, and peacocks would appear, in blue, on the gold shutters and, in gold, on an expanse of blue wall. "It is a *noble* work," Whistler wrote to his mother.

As for the problem of applying color to leather walls that did not want to take that color, Whistler had a simple solution: just add more. Pail after pail of Antwerp blue were brought in, along with book after book of expensive gold leaf, all charged to Leyland's account, naturally. One of the workers Whistler hired recalled applying gold leaf, Weintraub writes, "until their hair and faces were gilded, and they and the room were a shimmer of gold and blue." Meanwhile, Whistler canceled his other engagements and spent virtually all his time on the increasingly elaborate interior design, sometimes arriving at seven in the morning and not leaving until midnight.

Even as Whistler was freely spending the Leylands' money, and treating the Leylands' salon as a playground for his heretofore underrecognized genius, he had the gall to disparage his patron behind his back. Writing to the critic J. Comyns Carr, Whistler scoffed:

> Leyland, you see, Carr, is utterly ignorant of art. He's only a millionaire, and that a thing should be costly is the only proof that he has of its value. Well, let him spend his money on doing the thing as I tell him it has got to be done. I'll see that it doesn't cost too little!

Meanwhile, the Leylands were exhibiting an impressive degree of patience. The work on their new home, which Frederick had envisioned taking a month or two, had instead stretched through the summer and fall. Just before Christmas, Whistler informed Florence Leyland that it would be finished "this week" and instructed her: "Tell Freddie that I think it will be a large sum but even then [it] barely pays for the work." If that sounds presumptuous, his message to Frederick Leyland himself, upon the project's completion, was even worse. Whistler had planned a viewing for critics on February 9, 1877—he was practically vibrating with anticipation of their praise—but he instructed his patron to stay in Liverpool, writing: "These people are coming not to see you or your house: they are coming to see the work of the Master, and you, being a sensitive man, may naturally feel a little out in the cold."

Leyland, apparently, could stomach Whistler's imperiousness. But one individual did not come out of the affair unscathed, and this was Thomas Jeckyll, the interior designer whom Leyland had originally hired to create his magnificent dining room—and whom Whistler had promised to consult as he made his emendations, though he never did. Jeckyll attended the critics' opening on February 9, and according to Weintraub, he stumbled home in grief and was found later babbling incoherently of fruit and flowers and peacocks while feverishly working at gilding the floor of his bedroom. He was taken to an asylum, where he died four years later without recovering his reason.

When Whistler learned of Jeckyll's breakdown, he was unconcerned, reportedly saying, "To be sure, that is the effect I have upon people."

As for the effect that the Peacock Room had on its owner and funder when he was finally permitted to see it—Frederick Leyland was furious. He considered the room ruined without his consent and at tremendous cost in gold leaf, which he was expected to cover. Plus, there was the matter of Whistler's fee. Though they had initially discussed five hundred pounds, the artist now asked for two thousand guineas. (A guinea was equal to one pound and one shilling; a shilling was worth one-twentieth of a pound.) Rossetti advised Leyland not to pay at all. But the Liverpool shipbuilder was not the type to stint on debts, and he came back to Whistler with a very reasonable counteroffer of one thousand pounds.

Whistler accepted the lower fee, but not happily. He was particularly rankled to be paid in pounds rather than guineas. Professionals were typically paid in guineas—the extra shillings amounted to a sort of tip. Tradesmen were paid in pounds, and Whistler considered Leyland's offer an insult, which he stewed over as he finished the last remaining work on his Peacock Room. One of its central features was a large panel depicting two peacocks fighting, and at the last moment Whistler retouched this panel, surrounding one peacock with gold coins and placing a pile of silver coins under its feet. This was Leyland, and the silver coins that he straddled were the extra shillings that Whistler should have received. He titled it *Art and Money; or, the Story of the Room.*

The panel depicts a grand clash between patron and artist, and you almost wish that were the case. In truth, Whistler was always spoiling for a fight. He needed to feel that his work had been realized, heroically, against almost impossible odds; otherwise, one senses, the whole thing would be a little dull. Leyland just wanted to be able to entertain guests in his new London town house and get back to work. What Whistler depicted as a cockfight was really a cold shoulder: Leyland paid Whistler his fee and instructed his servants to refuse the artist future entrance to his home at Prince's Gate. Whistler never saw his glorious Peacock Room again.

GOVERNMENT CHECKS

I f aristocratic patronage is difficult to arrange, and pretty fraught even then, and if few can count on a Stanislaus Joyce or a Theo van Gogh to continually bail them out of financial straits, and if getting a day job is a profoundly problematic exercise that may well exhaust all one's energies, creative and otherwise—well, how about just getting some money from the government?

At this moment, in the United States, this idea may attract at best a wan smile from anyone who has tried to compete for the National Endowment for the Arts' ever-dwindling funds—indeed, as I write this, it is unclear if the NEA will even exist in another year or two—but such stinginess has not always been the case. In fact, the art world as we know it may not even exist if it weren't for a robust federal funding program implemented in the depths of the Great Depression. In this chapter, I want to unpack that moment and the artistic scene that sprang out of it—with its interaction of government money, one-on-one patronage, and the commercial marketplace—to show what an infusion of federal money *can* do, in a country not accustomed to it, even if there's little hope of the stars aligning in this way ever again.

The stars aligned in 1935. President Franklin Delano Roosevelt's newly launched Works Progress Administration was putting the first of an eventual eight and a half million Americans to work building roads, highways, dams, airports, schools, firehouses, and other essential infrastructure. Artists weren't part of Roosevelt's original vision for the WPA, but it didn't take much to convince him to bring them on board. The art historian Mary Gabriel explains how it happened: "When told that painters were starving and needed federal help, [Roosevelt] said, 'Why not? . . . I guess the only thing they can do is paint and surely there must be some public place where paintings are wanted.'"

With that offhand act of presidential generosity, the Federal Art Project was born. It was the country's first major attempt at government patronage of the visual arts, and it was an immediate sensation. Five thousand American artists signed up in the first year alone. In New York—then as now the nation's art capital, and my focus in this micro-history—artists practically raced to join: "They were shouting with the excitement of children at a zoo," one observer wrote. The Project got off the ground in August 1935. By November, more than a thousand New York artists were on its payroll, making easel paintings, sculptures, or works of graphic design at home or in their studios; or researching, planning, and executing public murals and posters at locations throughout the city. For their efforts, they collected checks for $23.86 a week. This was a decent wage; according to US Bureau of Labor statistics, it was on par with the average starting salary of a worker in automobile manufacturing. For artists who had barely been scraping by, standing in breadlines for their only meal of the day—and in a New York City where, since the 1929 stock market crash, one million adults had lost their jobs and two hundred thousand were being thrown out of their homes each year—it was a life-changing windfall. Before the Project, the illustrator Bob Jonas recalled, desperate New York artists would frequent McFadden's restaurant, where they could get a bowl of hot water that they dressed up with "ketchup, salt, pepper, anything that was around." After the Project, they could not only afford rent and proper meals but studio space, painting supplies, whiskey. "I can't begin to tell you how rich everybody was," said the paintmaker Leonard Bocour, who saw artists' spending habits up close.*

---

* If Project artists suddenly felt rich, it was partly a result of past deprivations, but also because of the genuinely low cost of living in New York City at the time: In 1935, twenty-four dollars a week was more than enough to live on. Subway fare cost a nickel, as did a cup of coffee at a diner. At that same diner, a sandwich might run fifteen

For Project artists, the fact that they were not only receiving a decent salary but receiving it to *make art* nearly defied belief. Even before the crash, virtually no one made a living from their art, certainly not the downtown New York artists who were then abandoning traditional representation in their work and pioneering new modes of abstraction. The American art market was, at the time, incredibly narrow. In New York, a handful of galleries on the Upper East Side sold paintings by one of two categories of artists: Europeans and deceased members of the Hudson River School. "If you happened to be concerned at all about the contemporary movements in art at the time . . . why there was absolutely no place to show your work," the abstract painter Burgoyne Diller* recalled.

Without galleries, sales were exceedingly rare, and artists' income came instead via a patchwork of odd jobs: for men, laborer gigs like carpentry, house painting, and interior remodeling; for women, waiting tables or modeling for art classes (often in the nude). Hunger was a daily reality. "You learned to eat practically nothing so you could buy a tube of paint," Diller said. "You went through such a variety of funny, ingenious ways of trying to live." So the change to a steady, predictable salary was dramatic. "You can't imagine how wonderful it was to get that money just to paint," the artist Mercedes Matter said. "It was the most important thing that ever happened to me or this country as far as art was concerned."

This isn't an exaggeration. In the 1920s and early '30s, New York artists had worked largely in isolation, without any institutional support and frequently without more than a few contacts among their fellow artists. The Project transformed this scattering of art-obsessed loners into a true community. Artists saw each other regularly at the Project headquarters uptown,

---

cents, a plate of pork chops or a steak twice that—though you could always eat for a bit less at an automat, where most dishes cost five or ten cents. The cheapest available housing option in the city was a tenement, where the typical rent for a three-room, 350-square-foot apartment was eighteen dollars, often shared between five or six people. Artist lofts—raw live-work spaces in industrial buildings that lacked many creature comforts—could be found for a bit more, maybe twenty to twenty-five dollars a month; similarly, these were typically shared between two or three people.

* In 1935, Diller became a Federal Art Project supervisor in New York, overseeing the execution of more than two hundred public murals across the city. His dogged work identifying potential mural sites and convincing the site's owners that they not only wanted a mural but that they were comfortable with a "decorative" direction—the term Diller used instead of "abstract" in order not to frighten people off—made him one of the era's unsung heroes.

and after cashing their checks on Fridays, they would often gather at one of the bars nearby. The Unemployed Artists Group, established in 1933, changed its name to the Artists Union and became a powerful advocate for its new constituency, fighting to keep Project artists employed in the face of frequent attempts by conservative lawmakers to cut the program's funding. "For the first time there was an association of artists," Diller said, "and by that I mean mutual association because of mutual needs. For the first time artists were talking together in large groups so that there was a possibility for arriving at opinions that were mutually heard. And God knows there are differences of opinion, but on the whole they were united by one very simple, basic thing. They needed to eat."

The Project and the union gave New York artists a taste for each other's company. In the late 1930s, a small handful began gathering at the Jumble Shop on Eighth Street in Greenwich Village, to drink beer and talk art. In the early 1940s, a larger crowd adopted the Waldorf Cafeteria on Sixth Avenue and Eighth Street; six nights a week, ten to eighteen artists met in the back, nursing five-cent cups of coffee for hours. In 1949, the Waldorf crowd decided to pool its money to rent a nearby loft for more organized discussions at what became known as the Club.* Around the same time, members of the Club and their extended circle began hanging out at the Cedar Street Tavern—more often called the Cedar Bar or just the Cedar—where painters, poets, composers, critics, curators, and art dealers all mingled over fifteen-cent beers, fifty-cent whiskeys, and plates of "hamburger steak."† On a busy night in the mid-1950s, a visitor to the Cedar might not only run into Frank O'Hara and Grace Hartigan, whispering conspiratorially in a booth, but Willem de Kooning, drinking beer by himself at the bar; the painters Helen Frankenthaler, Joan Mitchell, and Larry Rivers; the poets Kenneth Koch and John Ashbery; and the composers John Cage

---

* Another factor in the Club's founding was the fact that the always-seedy Waldorf Cafeteria had become even more so, with fights regularly breaking out among its late-night crowd of toughs, driving its artist clientele out onto the sidewalk to continue talking Picasso and Matisse until order was restored inside. But the last straw was when the Waldorf raised the price of a cup of coffee from five to ten cents, spurring outraged artists to take their late-night conversations elsewhere.

† This was a euphemism for what one Cedar regular remembered as "a big, flat pancake of low-grade chopped meat. Its price of sixty-five cents included French fries and one cup of coffee."

and Morton Feldman, who after meeting in 1950 began a daily dialogue that they carried on for years. "John and I would drop in at the Cedar Bar at six in the afternoon and talk with artist friends until three in the morning, when it closed," Feldman wrote later. "I can say without exaggeration that we did this every day for five years of our lives."

+ + +

Willem de Kooning—drinking beer by himself at the bar—is one of those artists who probably never would have broken through without the Federal Art Project. The Rotterdam-born painter had arrived in New York in 1926 as a twenty-two-year-old stowaway aboard the SS *Shelley* and had made a living first as a housepainter in New Jersey and later as a commercial artist for the firm Eastman Brothers, in Manhattan. After the stock market crash, freelance commercial work kept him afloat for a while; when that dried up, the Project provided a lifeline. De Kooning only worked for the Project for a year and a half; having arrived in the country illegally, he was always fearful of deportation, and in 1937 he chose to resign rather than have his citizenship status questioned. Nevertheless, it was a decisive turning point for him. "The Project was terribly important," he said. "It gave us enough to live on and we could paint what we wanted. . . . Even in that short time, I changed my attitude toward being an artist. Instead of doing odd jobs and painting on the side, I painted and did odd jobs on the side. My life was the same, but I had a different view of it."

When De Kooning resigned from the Project, he was in the midst of a four-by-six-foot sketch for an abstract mural. One of the artists hired to take it over was Lee Krasner, a Brooklyn-born painter four years his junior. If De Kooning would go on to become abstract expressionism's founding father, Krasner was its godmother—or, in the critic Robert Hughes's formulation, "the Mother Courage of Abstract Expressionism." Though she would become better known for her marriage to a scowling alcoholic painter named Jackson Pollock, she was a working artist long before he was, and she would continue to make influential and groundbreaking paintings for decades after most of her fellow ab-ex pioneers had burned themselves out.

Krasner was born in 1908, to a family of Russian immigrants who ran a fish, vegetable, and fruit stand in Brownsville, Brooklyn. "We were very poor," she recalled later. "Everyone had to work. Every penny had to be dealt with." As a result, Krasner was, in her words, "brought up to be independent." Her parents were too busy making ends meet to micromanage their children's aspirations. "They didn't encourage me," Krasner said, "but as long as I didn't present them with any particular problems, neither did they interfere. If I wanted to study art, it was all right with them."

Krasner did want to study art, starting at Washington Irving High School, an all-girls public school in Manhattan that allowed students to choose between an academic curriculum and technical training; the technical courses of study included drawing, illustration, printmaking, and photography. To get to the school from Brooklyn, Krasner "earned my own car fare. . . . I had all kinds of jobs. I painted lamp shades. I put vertical stripes on felt hats." At seventeen, she moved on to Cooper Union, a tuition-free college in the East Village, where she quickly distinguished herself as a young painter of promise. She continued to commute from home, and she shared a painting studio with friends, paying her portion of the rent by modeling nude for another artist in the building. She never received any material help from her parents or anyone else. "I came out of nowhere," she said.

Before the Federal Art Project materialized, Krasner worked at a basement nightclub in Greenwich Village called Sam Johnson's, waiting tables in Chinese silk "hostess" pajamas in exchange for dinner and tips. In 1936, now on the Project payroll, she and her first serious boyfriend, a Russian émigré artist named Ivan Pantuhoff, rented an eight-room cold-water flat on West Fourteenth Street for $23 a month; they shared it with another artist couple and a bachelor friend, bringing the rent down to $4.60 each.

As it did for so many, the Project carried Krasner through the Depression, allowed her to continue developing as an artist while earning a living, and introduced her to a new community of her peers, including De Kooning and his fellow abstract painters Stuart Davis and Arshile Gorky. Through Davis, in 1941, she met an art dealer named John Graham, who invited Krasner to show one of her paintings in an international group exhibition he was arranging uptown. She was one of several Americans in the show, including a name she didn't recognize: Jackson Pollock. It turned out that he lived around the corner from her apartment, and Krasner—now single following Pantuhoff's abrupt abandonment of New York for Florida—soon dropped by to "make his acquaintance."

Pollock was born in 1912 in Cody, Wyoming, but before he reached his first birthday, his parents had moved the family to California, where they shuffled from town to town in search of economic security. After being expelled from Manual Arts High School in Los Angeles, Pollock followed his eldest brother, Charles, to New York to study at the Art Students League, under the muralist Thomas Hart Benton. By the time Krasner met Pollock, he had begun to develop a rhythmic, energetic approach to abstract painting that was distinctly his own. Krasner recognized his talent at once. Over the next few years, she became his life partner as well as his biggest promoter, a role that would have dramatic unforeseen consequences for them both.

+ + +

Jackson Pollock had worked for the Project, too, both on murals and in the easel division. But by the early 1940s, the Project was dropping artists from its payroll and reducing the salaries of those who managed to hang on. After it was dissolved entirely in 1943, Pollock found a job as a custodian and handyman at the Museum of Non-Objective Painting, a relatively new institution opened on East Fifty-Fourth Street by the scion of a wealthy mining family named Solomon R. Guggenheim. (It later changed its name to the Solomon R. Guggenheim Museum and moved to its famous Frank Lloyd Wright–designed building uptown.) Two years earlier, another Guggenheim—Solomon's forty-three-year-old niece, Peggy—had arrived in New York from Europe, looking to make her own mark on the city's art scene. She came at an auspicious moment. Thanks to the Project, the city now had a community of artists who for several years had been working *as* artists, meeting regularly to discuss art history and recent developments in European painting, and finding growing confidence in their uniquely American response to the European avant-garde and the horrors of World War II. This group of artists was beginning to have places to show its work, even if some of these shows had to be self-organized. What it needed was a patron.

In his introduction to Peggy Guggenheim's 1946 autobiography, Alfred H. Barr Jr. "used the threadbare and somewhat pompous word 'patron' with some misgivings," he wrote. Barr—who was an art historian and the first director of the Museum of Modern Art—continued:

> For a patron is not simply a collector who gathers works of art for his own pleasure or a philanthropist who helps artists or founds a public museum, but a person who feels a responsibility towards both art and the artist together and has the means and will to act upon this feeling.

Guggenheim fit this description exactly. Born in Manhattan in 1898, she certainly had the means, though they were not as extensive as most people assumed. Her paternal grandfather, Meyer Guggenheim, had made his fortune in mining and smelting, becoming patriarch to one of the world's wealthiest families. But when Peggy was a child, her father, Benjamin Guggenheim, decided to exit the family business and pursue his own investments; he also largely exited life with his wife and daughters in New York, spending much of his time with a mistress in Paris (and pouring much of his fortune into a company that proposed to install elevators in the Eiffel Tower). In 1912, when Peggy was thirteen, he booked his return passage from Europe to New York on the RMS *Titanic*; his body was never recovered. When his brothers went to assess his estate, they found that it had been badly depleted; together, they set up a system of family trusts to provide for his wife and daughters, albeit at a humbler standard than they had been accustomed to.

So when Guggenheim turned twenty-one, she inherited $450,000, or around $8 million at present-day values; almost two decades later, she would receive another inheritance upon the death of her mother, the daughter of a wealthy banking family. But most of her fortune was always tied up in trusts, putting distinct limits on how much cash she could access at any given time. In her biography of Guggenheim, Francine Prose writes, "She was rich compared to most people, but in fact *not* wealthy by Guggenheim standards, and her resources were meager compared to the fortune her family had enjoyed and spent freely when she was a child." The historians Charlotte Gere and Marina Vaizey write: "In millionaire terms, Peggy made one of the most outstanding collections in the world on a shoestring."

That came later—first, Guggenheim left New York for Europe and fell into a series of troubled relationships, starting with her first husband, the emotionally and physically abusive Laurence Vail, a writer and Dada artist who "was considered," she wrote, "the King of Bohemia." Guggenheim supported him financially and began supporting several other writers and artists in their circle, helping Mina Loy open a shop in Paris where she sold lamps fashioned out of antique bottles to support her poetry writing, and, starting in the 1920s, giving the novelist Djuna Barnes a monthly stipend, which Guggenheim kept up, with a few interruptions, for the rest of her life. (Guggenheim died in 1979, Barnes in 1982.) In addition, in the summers of 1932 and '33, Guggenheim and her lover at the time hosted Barnes and two other writers at Hayford Hall, an English country manor where Barnes found the perfect conditions to write and revise much of her 1936 novel *Nightwood*, the only novel she ever completed and a masterpiece of the era. Even so, Barnes's biographer Phillip Herring writes: "Barnes seemed to take for granted that the wealthy naturally owed a debt to artistic genius, which would be paid indefinitely and without resentment at bohemian irresponsibility."

This was a problem for Guggenheim throughout her life. Everyone assumed she had far more money than she did, and they interpreted her attempts to economize as evidence of a selfish, miserly nature. In return, Guggenheim resented that her generosity was taken for granted, that the writers and artists she associated with invariably expected her to pay the rent and pick up the check, gossiping about her stinginess if she even dared to scrutinize the bill at the end of a lavish meal. At the same time, Guggenheim *could* be genuinely stingy (perhaps in retaliation), choosing to economize on expenses that would hardly make or break her budget— for instance, hosting artist parties in her apartment in which she served only whiskey and potato chips, and for which she had secretly decanted cheap whiskey into the bottles of single-malt Scotch that were supposedly on offer.

In any case, the transition from ad hoc individual support to something larger and more impactful didn't happen until around Guggenheim's fortieth birthday, when she received the money from her mother's estate and a friend made the fateful suggestion that she open an art gallery. Guggenheim liked the idea, and in 1938 she opened Guggenheim Jeune in London. "Little did I dream of the thousands of dollars I was about to sink into art," she wrote. Part of what made the enterprise so expensive, from the outset, was Guggenheim's feeling of responsibility toward the artists she represented. As she wrote: "This was before I was thinking of collecting. But gradually I bought one work of art from every show I gave, so as not to disappoint the artists if I were unsuccessful in selling anything. In those days, as I had no idea how to sell and had never bought pictures, this seemed to be the best solution and the least I could do to please the artists."

After a year and a half, the gallery was losing so much money—about six grand a year—that Guggenheim resolved to open a museum of modern art instead, reasoning that she "might as well spend a lot more and do something worthwhile." But while she was in Paris borrowing paintings for the museum, World War II broke out. With London terrorized by German bombers, Guggenheim pivoted to collecting, putting herself on "a regime to buy a picture a day." She kept this up until the Germans neared Paris, when she had her collection shipped to a friend's château near Vichy, where it was stored in a barn for the duration of the war.

+ + +

Two days before the Germans arrived in Paris, Guggenheim escaped to Marseille and eventually New York, arriving on July 14, 1941. By the fall of 1942, she had released a catalog of contemporary art titled *Art of This Century*, opened a gallery of the same name on West Fifty-Seventh Street, and made plans for a juried spring salon featuring a mix of European and American artists. Pollock submitted one of his recent paintings. (Krasner did not enter.) One of the salon jurors was Piet Mondrian, who called Pollock's work "exciting and unusual," earning him a studio visit from Guggenheim and inclusion in the salon. When it opened in April 1943, Pollock's painting was singled out for praise by the critics at *The Nation* and *The New Yorker*; the latter called his work "a real discovery." In July, Guggenheim offered Pollock a contract. She would give him his first solo show in November, and she would put him on a monthly stipend for a year. The money was an advance: He would receive $1,800 disbursed in twelve monthly installments of $150; at the end of the year, if his end of the sales of his paintings exceeded $1,800, he would receive further payment. If he didn't earn back that amount, he would make up the difference in paintings given to Guggenheim.

Francine Prose writes, "It was the first time that Pollock or anyone in his circle had heard of a modern artist being offered this sort of patronage." Thrilled, Pollock immediately quit his custodial job at the Museum of Non-Objective Art—though he subsequently realized that $150 a month "just about doesn't meet the bills." (When both Krasner and Pollock were working on the Project, they brought home around $190 a month total.) At one point, he asked Guggenheim if it would be possible to raise the amount to cover his and Krasner's living expenses. She refused. Though she wanted to support Pollock, she never liked Krasner and went out of her way to disparage her whenever possible. So when Pollock asked for more money, she had the perfect solution: "Tell Lee to go out and get a job."

Pollock wouldn't hear of it. Unusually for a male artist at the time, Pollock insisted that Krasner not look for work. He was committed to making a living for both of them from the sale of his paintings alone, a truly unheard-of feat. Krasner thought this absurd—it *was* absurd—but eventually she went along. However, with so much riding on Pollock's career, she gave herself another job: acting as a zealous and indefatigable promoter of his work and a reluctant manager of his mood swings, brought on by a drinking problem that was growing worse by the month.

In the fall of 1945, Krasner suggested they move out to Long Island for the winter, to a sleepy former fishing village in East Hampton called

Springs. Krasner thought they could get more work done away from the city—and, just as important, she was eager to get Pollock away from his drinking buddies. Pollock was hesitant at first, but then he did an about-face and embraced the idea. The couple married (Pollock insisted on a church ceremony), and soon after they found an empty farmhouse for sale in Springs. The price, $5,000, was far more than they could raise themselves. But the owners were offering a rent-to-buy option: With a $2,000 down payment, the purchasers could pay $40 a month until they had paid off the remaining $3,000 balance. But $2,000 was also more than they could raise. Krasner turned to Guggenheim, then sick in bed with mono, who recalled the ensuing negotiation in her autobiography:

> Lee was so dedicated to Pollock that when I was sick in bed, she came every morning to try to persuade me to lend them two thousand dollars to buy a home on Long Island. She thought that if Pollock got out of New York, he would stop drinking. Though I did not see how I could produce any extra funds, I finally agreed to do so as it was the only way to get rid of Lee.

Guggenheim came out to visit the newlyweds the following spring, in advance of Pollock's third show at her gallery. The house she helped pay for had no bathtub or hot water. To bathe, one had to fill a small basin with water drawn from a hand pump. And it was *cold*. Because wartime rationing was still in effect, Krasner and Pollock could get just one bucket of coal at a time (and firewood was expensive at twenty-one dollars a cord). When Guggenheim visited, "it was so cold there was ice in the toilet," Krasner recalled. "We gave her an oil stove for warmth and she carried it around with her. She came down in one of her negligees with the oil stove and said, 'This reminds me of the castles in England.'"

Despite the primitive living conditions, the Springs farmhouse became the site of major artistic breakthroughs for both partners. In the old barn that he converted into a studio, Pollock developed the drip-painting technique that would open the door to his remarkable next phase of work and before long make him America's most famous living artist. With Krasner's support, he stayed sober and productive—for a time—and through her efforts his work began attracting more and more notice. (It was Krasner who insisted that he allow a *Life* magazine photographer to shoot him at work in the barn, resulting in some of the most indelible images of postwar American art.) Meanwhile, working in an upstairs bedroom in the house, Krasner endured months of creative blockage before creating a brilliant series of what became known as her Little Image paintings, which were equally groundbreaking, though they were not properly recognized as such until decades later.

+ + +

The Project created a community of New York artists and gave that community several years in which they could live and work *as* artists, with all the confidence and risk-taking that that enabled. Peggy Guggenheim provided a crucial injection of money and vitality just at the moment Project funds were being cut off, making her new gallery into a nexus of the European and American avant-garde and a magnet for anyone who cared about those movements, plus a lot of people who didn't know they cared about them before that moment. Her moment was short-lived: In 1947, Guggenheim abandoned New York for Europe, which she always preferred, buying for herself the palazzo on Venice's Grand Canal that became her permanent residence and that still houses her art collection today. In her wake arrived a new generation of contemporary-art galleries, a whole new commercial art market, and, before long, a truly mindboggling boom in prices.

Remember that ambitious American artists in the 1930s and early '40s had pretty much no place to show their work and pretty much no one interested in buying it even if they did manage to show it. In the '50s, this began to change—but prices for paintings were still quite low: Peggy Guggenheim never sold a Jackson Pollock painting for more than $1,000 (around $15,000 in today's dollars), and the highest price Pollock ever reached in his life was $8,000, which only happened once. It was Pollock's death—on August 11, 1956, he flipped his Oldsmobile 88 convertible into the trees a mile from his house in Springs, killing himself and one passenger—that created a sudden and apparently irreversible acceleration in prices. And it was Krasner who set it off: Krasner, the Brooklyn daughter of Russian immigrants who painted lampshades to earn car fare to study art, who modeled nude to afford studio space, who convinced Peggy Guggenheim to give her the down payment that changed the course of art history—now, after Pollock's death, as executrix of his estate, she insisted that Pollock's new dealer quadruple the prices of his work and set strict limits on how many of his paintings could be sold and to whom. (One observer said that she refused to think "in terms of a current market, only a future market.") Prior to Pollock's death, the Museum of Modern Art had been considering buying his painting *Autumn Rhythm* for $8,000, but it couldn't raise the funds at the time; after Pollock's death, the museum returned to complete the sale. Krasner said the price was now $30,000—more than Pollock had received, while he was alive, from all his sales combined—and she refused to budge. MoMA balked, but the Metropolitan Museum of Art stepped in and bought the painting. The historian Mary Gabriel writes: "That single sale reset the entire market for modern American work."

From there, the market has only grown, and grown and grown. In subsequent decades, the path to art world prominence and critical recognition has also been, very often, the path to delirious wealth. And while more money in the art world always seems preferable to less money, it's hard not to feel nostalgic for the short-lived era of middle-class bohemia, particularly those years when the Federal Art Project created a new and vital community, when artists could draw a regular salary for making art, could afford comfortable but not lavish lifestyles, and could keep their heads focused on what was happening in the studio. "In fact, I do not like art today," Peggy Guggenheim wrote in her autobiography, when this sea change was just beginning. "I think it has gone to hell, as a result of the financial attitude."

TRUE FANS

The eighteenth-century English poet and satirist Alexander Pope scorned patronage. In 1723, he declared: "I take my self to be the only Scribler of my Time, of any degree of distinction, who never received any Places from the Establishment, any Pension from a Court, or any Presents from a Ministry." It's true that Pope did not receive any such patronage—but it was not because he eschewed these favors out of principle. Pope was Roman Catholic, which in the fiercely Protestant England of his era carried a humiliating array of penalties: Catholics were barred from attending public schools, holding civil office, or residing within ten miles of London, let alone enjoying state sponsorship of their poetry. So Pope had to find another way to fund his literary ambitions—and he did so in a way that feels startlingly contemporary.

Pope's father was a wholesale linen merchant who retired from commerce in 1688, the year Pope was born, with some £10,000 to his name, a fortune at the time. Unable to go to university because of his religion, Pope received private tutoring and attended Catholic schools for a spell, but as a writer he was mainly self-taught. He caught "the itch of poetry" at a young age, reading an illustrated edition of the *Iliad* with such wonder that, even in his last years, he remembered it with "a sort of rapture." His half sister, Magdalen, recalled that the young Pope "did nothing but write and read."

He taught himself Latin, Greek, French, and Italian and wrote his first extant poem, "Ode to Solitude," at age twelve.

That same year, Pope contracted a sudden, incapacitating illness that would plague him for the rest of his life. Though Pope guessed its cause was too much study, we now know that it was probably Pott's disease, a rare tubercular infection of the spine. The disease caused Pope's spine to curve sharply, giving him a hunchback, limiting his adult height to four and a half feet, and causing a never-ending succession of maladies throughout what he once called "this long Disease, my life." ("I do not think I ever shall enjoy any health four days together, for the remaining Sand I have to run," Pope wrote in his fortieth year.) The biographer Maynard Mack writes:

> Pope was afflicted with constant headaches, sometimes so severe that he could barely see the paper he wrote upon, frequent violent pain at bone and muscle joints . . . shortness of breath, increasing inability to ride horseback or even walk for exercise . . . recalcitrant wasting fevers, and such an exquisite sensitivity to cold as to require in winter almost a cocoon of waistcoats, in which "I live like an Insect, in hope of reviving with the Spring."

He counteracted his physical limitations with tremendous literary energy—and with a strategic approach to making friendships that might further his literary career. Though as a Catholic he could not hope for royal support, Pope could and did curry favor with his era's moneyed elite, starting at a young age. The historian Irvin Ehrenpreis writes, "As an adolescent, he began a career of seeking out men of talent, rank, or power, winning their friendship, and making them serve him. To do so, he learned to charm them with tact and wit, paying careful compliments and accommodating himself to the moods of the mighty."

Pope was also a brilliant entrepreneur, and these two attributes—his gift for cultivating useful friendships and his shrewd business sense—came together in one of the most successful publishing enterprises of his or any time. Indeed, Pope has been called "the first business man among English poets," and Mack writes that he did "more than any other eighteenth-century writer to improve the prospects of the writing class."

Pope made his publishing debut in 1709, a few weeks before his twenty-first birthday, when his verses were included in the sixth volume of a series called *Poetical Miscellanies* published by Jacob Tonson, himself a shrewd businessman described by one of his contemporaries as "Chief Merchant to the Muses." (Tonson was the poet John Dryden's publisher for twenty years, and he also bears the distinction of hosting, Mack writes, "what is probably the first expense-account publisher's dinner on record: a weekly feast at a local mutton-pie house.") Many writers disliked Tonson, but Pope, typically, set out to become his friend. At the same time, he avoided publishing with Tonson after his debut, recognizing that Tonson's terms were grossly unfair. At this stage in English publishing, the publisher and bookseller were still one and the same entity, and this individual typically paid writers a onetime fee to purchase their work, which the publisher-bookseller could then print and sell in perpetuity. This meant that a runaway hit was very lucrative for the publisher—and did not pay the writer anything beyond the initial fee. In a letter to a friend, Pope neatly summed up the situation in a couplet:

What Authors lose, their Booksellers have won,
So Pimps grow rich, while Gallants are undone.

If this system sounds too exploitative to last, well, pretty much the entirety of publishing was then an arena of embarrassment. Sophie Gee writes: "In the early eighteenth century, publishing and being published were often considered degraded and humiliating activities, on a continuum with prostitution, vagrancy and other forms of criminal marginality. But paradoxically publishing was also a path to cultural legitimacy, signaling writers' and booksellers' involvement in the new commercial systems of power and prestige."

Pope gained immense popularity and prestige in 1712, when his mock epic *The Rape of the Lock* was published (he was twenty-four). It was a year later that he contrived to revolutionize publishing. In October 1713, he announced his intention of embarking on a new verse translation of Homer's *Iliad* that would be distributed via subscription. Pope did not invent the subscription model—his predecessor Dryden had issued a subscription translation of Virgil in 1697—but he showed just how lucrative it could be. The scheme was as follows: Subscribers paid to receive one volume per year over six years, at the price of one guinea per volume. To buy in, subscribers had to pay two guineas up front, then one guinea for each successive volume except the last, which was free; this scheme frontloaded Pope's income, much like a publisher's advance today. For their investment, subscribers received handsome bound volumes printed "on the finest Paper . . . with Ornaments and initial Letters engraved on Copper."

To produce these volumes, Pope contracted with a rival of Tonson's named Barnaby Bernard Lintot, with whom he crafted a brilliant deal: Pope would receive a flat fee of two hundred guineas for each volume, just as in a typical arrangement with Tonson or another of his competitors. However, Pope would also receive an additional 750 copies for exclusive distribution to his subscribers—and these were to be the only editions published on special paper with engravings. Moreover, Lintot could not publish his editions until at least a month after Pope's subscriber editions appeared. "For the subscribers' edition," Mack writes, "Pope became essentially his own publisher, hiring Lintot by his other concessions to serve as agent."

Pope's scheme would only work if he could attract subscribers for most or all of the 750 volumes he would receive from Lintot. At first, it didn't look good: There are hints in Pope's letters that the subscription list was slow to take off. But then Pope's longtime efforts to make well-connected friends began to pay off, and by six months after his initial announcement Pope was able to rejoice that he was "in the good opinion of such a number of persons." Of course, fleshing out the subscriber list was only part of the challenge. Actually completing his promised translations was another thing entirely, and the labor of translating all sixteen thousand lines of Greek in Homer's *Iliad* proved so immense that Pope would have nightmares about it for years afterward.

But it worked: The subscription edition of the *Iliad* brought Pope an estimated £4,000 total, or around £200,000–£260,000 in today's currency, though these kinds of conversions are very imprecise. Pope quickly followed it with a subscription edition of Homer's *Odyssey* (this time enlisting the help of a co-translator to speed the enterprise along, releasing four volumes in 1720–21) and, after that, a subscription edition of Shakespeare's works. By the end, Pope was rich. He could, he wrote, "live and thrive / Indebted to no Prince or Peer alive."

+ + +

Pope's audience-funded publishing system was not too far removed from what you see happening on crowdfunding platforms today. Special bonus material, exclusive editions, the feeling of funding a work as it's being created—unknowingly, all these "new" schemes are channeling Pope's innovations with Barnaby Bernard Lintot, circa 1713. Today's creators enjoy much easier and more direct contact with their audiences—though this has its own pitfalls, too, at least in my experience. During the years I worked on this book, I joined many other writers trying to attract audience patronage via a much-ballyhooed email-newsletter start-up called Substack, which was, remarkably, enabling some writers to make six- or even seven-figure incomes through paid subscriptions. In the spring of 2022, I decided to invite the readers of my free newsletter—which at that point I had been sending out on a regular schedule for two years—to become voluntary patrons, chipping in a few bucks a month if they felt like they were getting something out of my dispatches and wanted to help keep them coming. But even making that pitch was complicated, mentally and emotionally, or so I mused aloud in one newsletter from April 2023.

That piece resonated with a number of my readers, particularly those who were trying to implement their own crowdfunding systems. But one reader was not impressed. A woman who went by the name Lynette wrote in reply: "To be honest, there's too damned many of you with your hand out when our bills have to be paid. Why is it that selling your book isn't enough for you?" She pointed out that Substack seems to expect readers to pay a separate subscription fee for each writer who interests them, which adds up very quickly. "Maybe you have that kind of money, but I don't," Lynette wrote. "I drive an 18yo old beater. You?" To Lynette, my supposedly complicated feelings about audience patronage weren't complicated at all: Writers like me were trying to milk money out of a readership that could hardly be expected to carry that burden—"and if you are at all honest, you realize this."

Was she wrong? Even as I was trying to find a way to fund my own writing projects through reader subscriptions, I had to admit that I felt a bit irritated by the many others who were making more or less the same pitch; my inbox was starting to feel like a giant echo chamber of writers wishing for patronage, but from whom? On the other hand—a lot of us were really quite gently asking readers to consider *voluntarily* supporting our writing, if they liked, which hardly seemed to warrant this level of scorn. I decided it was worth replying:

> Yeah, I hear what you're saying. For what it's worth, most authors make very little money off book sales, so we have to find other income streams. Substack is one that a lot of us are experimenting with. I certainly don't expect that everyone can afford to pay— that's one reason why all of my content is free for everyone. But some people can afford to pay and I don't think it's unreasonable to ask them to do so for writing they value.

Another writer piggybacked on my comment, adding some recent statistics about how little money the average professional writer makes, how the size of book advances has collapsed in recent years, and other very reasonable points about how authors are really suffering even as the biggest publishers are making record profits. "All in all," she wrote, "this means that if we as a society want to enjoy the fruits of other people's creative labour, we're going to have to find a way to collectively support them."

All fair points, except perhaps this writer went on for a little too long, and also perhaps she made a tactical error in favorably mentioning, near the end of her comment, the idea of universal basic income, because this seemed to really irritate Lynette. She wrote back:

> In other words you can't make it pay because YOU chose to write instead of labor and your answer is socialism? Because you can't pull your weight with a pen everyone else must support you? Aren't you special. I live on my SSI and food stamps entirely. I'm also re-tired after working standing on my feet 40+ hours a week helping to physically save lives and improve all manners of quality of life for the afflicted. If I buy a book, that's enough. It's not my fault you aren't Shakespeare.

Lynette went on from there, with escalating vitriol and in multiple replies to other writers who had by now piled on. I decided to disengage, but I followed the ongoing back-and-forth with fascination and anxiety. As much as I wanted to write Lynette off, I had to admit—she was making some good points. At least, she was making points that tickled my own insecurities: "Poverty isn't something new for most creative types, it's as old as time and the human condition, so why did you choose a field that put you there? What you are doing is panhandling. Just create your work and promote it as you ought. If you're any good people will buy it, but this begging crap has got to stop."

+ + +

Okay, maybe Lynette makes a valid point, though I am not entirely convinced. Fortunately, there is at least one audience that will always understand and empathize with artists' funding pleas, no matter how far-fetched, and that is their fellow artists. And some of the most suc-cessful instances of patronage in art and literary history have come not from powerful rulers, wealthy industrialists, enterprising heiresses, gov-ernment programs, or internet strangers but from other artists who have recognized a need and stepped in to meet it.

This has been especially true in historically marginalized communities, which have enjoyed fewer opportunities in pretty much every aspect of the artist's journey: access to arts education, places to show work or publish it, and exposure to audiences with the time, energy, and means to engage with it. But shoring up one's community also poses a dilemma for the individual artist, as is vividly illustrated in the case of Augusta Savage, who against long odds made her way from extremely humble beginnings to become one of twentieth-century America's most prominent sculptors, and certainly the most important Black woman sculptor of her time, but whose efforts to help her fellow artists threw roadblocks in the way of her own career.

"I was born in Florida of poor parents," Savage wrote in a brief auto-biographical sketch published in 1929, when she was thirty-seven and finally receiving widespread notice for her art, which she had been pursuing for pretty much as long as she could remember. In the sketch, Savage explained how she got started:

> I am the seventh child in a family of fourteen. Nine of us reached maturity. My father, who was burned to death in January this year, was a minister and very fond of good books. At the mud pie age, I began to make "things" instead of mud pies. I had very little schooling and most of my school hours were spent in playing hookey in order to go to the clay pit—we had a brick yard in our town—and make ducks out of clay.

Savage doesn't mention that her minister father so disapproved of her childhood sculpture-making—misunderstanding the Second Commandment, he thought that all man-made statues qualified as graven images—that he would beat her if he found any of her creations or caught her making them; Savage said that her father "almost whipped all the art out of me." Almost but not quite: Savage continued making sculptures throughout her youth and young adulthood (and an eighteen-inch statue of the Virgin Mary she made as a teenager finally won her father over). At age twenty-seven—after being twice married, widowed, and divorced—she received some crucial encouragement when her work won a twenty-five-dollar special prize at a county fair in West Palm Beach,

Florida. Fairgoers were so impressed that they urged Savage to get herself to New York for formal art training. Savage was eager to heed their advice, though it meant leaving her teenage daughter, Irene, in the care of her parents. She arrived in New York in 1921 with $4.60 in her pocket.

In the city, Savage attended the tuition-free Cooper Union, getting by on scholarship funds from the school and work as an apartment caretaker and a laundress. In 1923, she got her big break, followed by a stunning disappointment. Savage had learned of a summer art school sponsored by the French government, which would admit one hundred American women, selected by a committee of American artists and architects, to live and work together in Fontainebleau, thirty-five miles south of Paris. Savage applied and was in the process of gathering references and raising travel funds when her application was returned without explanation. In her studies at Cooper Union, Savage had seen how far ahead she was compared to most of her female peers, and she suspected that her race had something to do with the rejection. This proved to be the case: When the committee had learned that Savage was Black, it sought to avoid an "embarrassing" situation for the white women with whom she would have shared living and working quarters, and it rejected Savage instead of risking their discomfort.

Outraged, Savage sought to publicize the committee's racism, and succeeded—the story made the New York papers and drew widespread condemnation. She told the *New York World*:

> Democracy is a strange thing. My brother was good enough to be accepted in one of the regiments that saw service in France during [World War I], but it seems his sister is not good enough to be a guest of the country for which he fought. . . . How am I to compete with other American artists if I am not to be given the same opportunity?

In the years to come, Savage's energies were directed more and more toward creating these opportunities for her fellow Black artists. She made her own work, too—including busts of W. E. B. Du Bois and Marcus Garvey, and *Gamin*, a bust portrait based on her nephew that became one of her best-known pieces and that in 1929 earned her a Julius Rosenwald fellowship to travel to Paris, where she studied and exhibited her work. But after returning to Harlem in 1932, she invested much of her time and attention in community-building activities, opening the Savage Studio of Arts and Crafts in Harlem; becoming the first Black member of what is now the National Association of Women Artists; working with the Federal Art Project to establish and direct the Harlem Community Art Center, which offered workshops in the fine arts as well as weaving, pottery, quilting, and other disciplines; and organizing the Harlem Artists Guild, which advocated for Federal Art Project jobs for Black artists and also for Black history to be included in the public murals coming out of the program. In 1939, she also opened the Salon of Contemporary Negro Art, making her the first Black woman to open her own art gallery in America, though it closed after just three months.

In their landmark *History of African-American Artists*, the artist Romare Bearden and the journalist Harry Henderson wrote that for a generation of young Black artists in New York, Savage's "influence was critical. . . . She sought talent. She found jobs for young artists and helped them focus on their own experiences and values." For many, she was their first and fiercest patron. And yet, Bearden and Henderson point out, she "paid a heavy price for taking the lead in this fight."

> She was one of the first black American artists to challenge the art establishment head-on and, due to circumstances beyond her control, that struggle—rather than her art—came to be where she spent much of her life's energies. Throughout the rest of her life she was considered a troublemaker by those whose racial prejudice she exposed—a group that included influential artists, museum curators and directors, dealers, foundation personnel, critics, and government officials. No one knows how many times she was excluded from exhibits, galleries, and museums because of this confrontation.

Savage still made powerful work—including *The Harp*, a sixteen-foot-tall sculpture for the 1939 New York World's Fair, which was one of the most photographed sculptures at the fair—but without money to properly store it, and without the attention of museums and collectors, most of it has been lost or destroyed. (Numerous times, Savage made works in plaster and then couldn't raise the funds to have them cast in bronze, leaving only the fragile plaster original for posterity; this is what happened with *The Harp*, which, despite its popularity, was bulldozed after the fair.) Finally, she got tired of the struggle. In the early 1940s, she left New York City for the Hudson River valley, where she lived on an old chicken farm, worked as an assistant for a commercial mushroom grower, and stopped making artwork entirely. (A neighboring family discovered who she was and offered her free studio space, but she apparently never used it.) Bearden and Henderson write that "her resources, emotional and aesthetic, were depleted. More than a decade before she died in 1962, she abandoned all efforts to create and isolated herself."

Years before she reached this point, however, Savage recognized that her real legacy would lie not in her own work but in the succeeding generations of artists that she enabled through her activism. "I have created nothing really beautiful, really lasting," she said. "But if I can inspire one of these youngsters to develop the talent I know they possess, then my monument will be their work. No one could ask for more than that."

+ + +

Augusta Savage's fight to gain better opportunities for her community may have sidetracked her own art career, but—as she herself recognized—it was certainly no waste of energy. Other patronage legacies are more complicated. Probably the most prolific artist-to-artist patron of the twentieth century was the poet Ezra Pound, who throughout his life hustled to secure funding for writers he considered to have great promise but inadequate means. Ernest Hemingway called him "the most generous writer I have ever known." James Joyce, who benefited greatly from patronage arranged by Pound, called him "a miracle worker." T. S. Eliot wrote of Pound: "He would go to any lengths of generosity and kindness; from inviting constantly to dinner a struggling author whom he suspected of being under-fed, or giving away clothing . . . to trying to find jobs, collect subsidies, get work published and then get it criticised and praised."

Of course, Pound's efforts did backfire occasionally. My favorite example—for its mix of touching generosity and clumsy overreach—involved Eliot himself, the St. Louis–born poet who finished his landmark "Love Song of J. Alfred Prufrock" when he was twenty-three—though it wasn't published for another three years, and then only thanks to Pound's efforts. After completing his doctoral thesis at Oxford, Eliot embarked on an ambitious and draining mix of lecturing, freelance literary journalism, and, beginning in 1917, working as a clerk at Lloyds Bank in London, while also trying to write his own poetry. The strain proved immense. In late 1921, Eliot was granted a three-month leave from Lloyds to recuperate from nervous exhaustion; by the end, he had finished a draft of his long poem *The Waste Land*. This time, Pound served as collaborator, editing the poem down to its final form, and also the poet's financial savior, or at least that was his plan. The biographer Charles Norman writes: "To Pound, *The Waste Land* was 'a masterpiece; one of the most important 19 pages in English.' He could not understand why the author of those pages should have to work in a bank when he could be writing other masterpieces." So Pound set out to do something about it, with a plan that he dubbed Bel Esprit and announced via a March 1922 brochure, prefaced by a manifesto that began:

> There is no organized or coordinated civilization left, only individual scattered survivors.
>
> Aristocracy is gone, its function was to select.
>
> Only those of us who know what civilization is, only those of us who want better literature, not more literature, better art, not more art, can be expected to pay for it. No use waiting for masses to develop a finer taste, they aren't moving that way.

This was all a windup to the actual Bel Esprit proposal: Pound sought to establish a £300 annual fund by soliciting £10 a year from thirty subscribers, to be guaranteed for five years. In truth, this was a fairly humble sum; remember that in *A Room of One's Own*, published three years earlier, Virginia Woolf identified £500 as the annual amount that would "keep one alive in the sunshine." Indeed, Woolf was one of those informed of the Bel Esprit plan—by her friend Lady Ottoline Morrell, an important patron of several of the era's English writers—and she was skeptical. On August 1, 1922, she wrote to Lady Ottoline: "I have been thinking about the subscription. I find that the few people I have talked to would much prefer to give a lump sum down to Eliot himself, than to subscribe £10 yearly through the Pounds. One may so easily die, and still more easily go bankrupt; and where would poor Tom be then?"

A few days later, she had further thoughts on the scheme, and further questions, which she again shared with Lady Ottoline. Above all, she wondered "what Tom's own views are—has he agreed to accept the money, and for what amount will he give up his Bank?" In fact, Eliot hadn't even been informed of the scheme, which Pound had launched entirely on his own recognizance. When Eliot finally found out, he was mortified. It's true that Lloyds was a strain, but it also offered stability and financial security—and it guaranteed Eliot £500 annually, in perpetuity, rather than £300 for just five years. Indeed, Eliot's immediate reaction was fear for his job. He wrote to Pound on July 28: "If this Circular has not gone out, will you please delete Lloyds Bank to the mention of which I *strongly object*. If it is stated so positively that Lloyds Bank interfered with literature, Lloyds Bank would have a perfect right to infer that literature interfered with Lloyds Bank. *Please see my position*—I cannot jeopardize my position at the Bank before I know what is best."

Eliot's mortification increased many times over when, on November 16, 1922, the *Liverpool Post* published an article about the subscription scheme, writing that Eliot was to be the "first beneficiary under a unique scheme through which a co-operation of English, French, and American enthusiasts, known as 'Bel Esprit,' pledged themselves to give fifty dollars per year for life or as long as the author needs it." (Ten British pounds was then equal to around fifty US dollars.) The article went on to say— falsely—that Eliot had already been presented with a sum of £800 and had decided to keep his job at the bank anyway. Eliot protested and the paper later issued a retraction. By the end, Eliot confided in a letter to Woolf, the entire matter had become "an incessant strain." Finally, he was given what money had already been raised—around £100—in two installments, the matter was closed, and Eliot continued on at Lloyds. He remained at the bank for the next three years, until November 1925, when he accepted an editorial position at the publishing firm Faber and Gwyer (later Faber and Faber), where he would stay for the rest of his career.

If Eliot emerged from the affair embarrassed but also strengthened in his commitment to his day job, Pound did not fare quite as well. The Bel Esprit fizzle was part of his growing disillusionment over society's unwillingness to support its artists, an oversight that never ceased to vex and infuriate him. And the episode may have contributed to his growing sympathy for totalitarianism, which took a sinister turn during World War II, when Pound sided with the Axis powers and delivered hundreds of radio addresses for Mussolini's fascist government, which ultimately led to Pound being indicted for treason after the war and spending a dozen years in a psychiatric hospital in Washington, DC—an awful final chapter for a poet who had once done so much good for so many artists and convinced so many others to join him. As he wrote to the American lawyer and arts patron John Quinn in January 1915, in a statement that echoes Van Gogh's pleas with his brother Theo, and that neatly sums up the potential of genuine patronage, for the artist and the patron alike: "My whole drive is that if a patron buys from an artist who needs money (needs money to buy tools, time and food) the patron then makes himself equal to the artist, he is building art into the world. He creates."

SCHEMES

ART AND THEFT

The Belgian filmmaker Chantal Akerman wasn't born into any special artistic lineage. Growing up, she was, in the words of a friend, "a lower-middle-class nobody whose father owned a clothing store." (She was born in Brussels, in 1950, to Jewish Holocaust survivors from Poland.) And yet Akerman managed, with no money, to make her first film at age eighteen: a short film, only thirteen minutes long, filmed in one room and in one night with no retakes, but bursting with energy and ideas. Called *Saute Ma Ville*, or *Blow Up My Town*, it was figuratively and literally explosive—in the final moments, Akerman, who directed and stars, cranks up the gas on her kitchen stove and sets some papers on fire; the film ends with a black screen and the sound of an enormous explosion—and it was the beginning of a series of brilliant short films leading up to Akerman's audacious first feature, 1974's *Je Tu Il Elle*, and her follow-up the next year, the three-hour-and-twenty-minute *Jeanne Dielman, 23 Quai du Commerce, 1080 Bruxelles*. In *Sight and Sound* magazine's 2022 poll of the greatest films ever made, voters nominated *Jeanne Dielman* for the number one spot, edging out *Vertigo* and *Citizen Kane* and *Tokyo Story*. The greatest film ever made! By a twenty-four-year-old high school dropout (she quit film school, too, after three months) who originally wanted to be a writer until she discovered the work of Jean-Luc Godard and decided to be a filmmaker instead.

I said above that Akerman made her first film, the thirteen-minute *Saute Ma Ville*, on no money, but of course that's impossible. In a 1983 interview, Akerman explained how she really did it:

I wanted to make a feature film so I decided to sell stock in the film. I made a stock book and went to Antwerp and sold certificates on the Diamond Bourse, selling the pages for $3 each. By the end I had only $200 or $300, not enough to make a feature film. I made a short film with that. It wasn't enough to finish the film, so I worked in banks, in shops, sending telexes; Phillips Petroleum telex, American Express telex. Then, when I went to New York [in 1971], first I worked in a restaurant, La Poulade, in the Fifties. I took care of coats and hats, putting glasses of water and butter on the tables. . . . I worked at the New School, modeling for sculpture. I also worked in a photo lab blowing up pictures. Later I worked in a thrift shop, and then on Orchard Street. Then I worked at the 55th Street Playhouse, the porno pictures, as a cashier; and in three weeks I stole $4000, and I made [the short films] *Hotel Monterey* and *La Chambre* with that. That was the end of it for stealing, I stopped. Then I made *Je, Tu, Il, Elle*; for that I worked as a typist. Then that was finished because I got some grants from my government.

Above, Akerman neglects to mention another theft from around this time. In a 2015 documentary about her career, Akerman said that she stole boxes of old 35 mm film from a photo lab and used it to make *Je Tu Il Elle*: "I hid them under my bed and I was very scared that the police would come, but nobody cared about these boxes." In the same documentary, Akerman also elaborated on her porno theater theft: She would pocket the money from every other ticket sale; to make the ticket sales match the cash intake, she ripped each ticket in half, giving one half to the first customer and the other half to the next. "My pockets were filled with money," she tells the camera, eyes gleaming mischievously.

+ + +

Akerman was inspired to become a filmmaker after seeing Jean-Luc Godard's 1965 film *Pierrot le Fou* in the theater. "That was the first shock of my life," she later said of the movie, which she went to without knowing anything about it, simply because she liked the title. "I got crazy about movies immediately and I decided to make movies the same night. I was 15." Did she know that Godard financed his early filmmaking career through theft, too?

Unlike Akerman, Godard was born into a world of wealth and privilege: His father was a Swiss physician, and his mother was the daughter of one of the most prominent bankers in France. Born in Paris in 1930, Godard was raised mainly in Switzerland, where his father moved the family in 1934 so he could work at a private medical clinic on the shore of Lake Geneva. (He later started his own clinic near Lausanne.) Godard spent much of his childhood at a pair of family chalets on opposite sides of the lake. He later recalled, "I lived my childhood in an extremely rich family. . . . There was so much money that we didn't notice it." But for Godard to become a filmmaker, he needed to reject this world—or to force his family to reject him.

Initially, Godard sought to be an engineer, or at least that was the plan when he went to Paris in 1946 to study at the Lycée Buffon, a secondary school in the fifteenth arrondissement. Instead, the sixteen-year-old Godard fell hopelessly in love with movies, at the expense of his studies. In 1948, he failed his baccalaureate exam and had to retreat to a cramming school in Switzerland before retaking it; this time, he passed.

Godard considered going to the Sorbonne next, to study art, then changed his mind and applied to film school, but was rejected. So he embarked on his own course of study, obsessively attending a group of Left Bank film clubs, chief among them the Cinémathèque Française, an idiosyncratic temple of cinema cofounded by the film archivist Henri Langlois. In this era, Godard would see three or four films a day, or else sit through repeated screenings of the same film, sometimes entering the theater at 2:00 in the afternoon and not leaving until 10:00 at night. Previously, he had thought vaguely of becoming a writer, but cinema proved much more alluring to Godard and to the fellow young obsessives he met at the Cinémathèque, including the future filmmakers François Truffaut and Jacques Rivette. "When we saw some movies," Godard later recalled, "we were finally delivered from the terror of writing. We were no longer crushed by the specter of the great writers."

Godard's parents had planned to support his university studies, but they were not willing to fund him watching movies all day and cut him off. To stay afloat, Godard "borrowed" money from his mother's best friend with no intention of repaying it and then turned to outright theft. Godard's maternal grandfather, Julien Monod, the prominent banker, was also a key figure in the French literary world: He had been a close friend of the writer Paul Valéry and after Valéry's death became his literary executor. At the Monod family residence in Paris, Godard's grandfather kept his collection of first, private, and rare editions of Valéry's books, which Godard began to steal, selling them for cash at Paris book stalls. According to Richard Brody's book *Everything Is Cinema: The Working Life of Jean-Luc Godard*, he went even further than filching books and additionally "stole and sold a painting by Renoir that belonged to his grandfather." With the profits from his thefts, Godard not only funded his own lifestyle (a relatively meager one; according to a friend: "In Paris he had a big Bogart poster on the wall and nothing else") but produced his friend Jacques Rivette's short film *Le Quadrille*.

Around this time, Godard also began writing film criticism, first for the short-lived *La Gazette du Cinéma*, which he helped to found, and then for the hugely influential *Cahiers du Cinéma*, launched in 1951. Criticism did not make Godard and his fellow *Cahiers* critics any money, but it did prove a brilliant means of breaking into filmmaking. Brody explains: "By writing about the films they saw, they did two things: they elaborated and refined their ideas about the cinema, in anticipation of the day when they could make films; and they created for themselves a public identity that would get them the chance to make films." Indeed, Godard and his friends became notorious for their rejection of what they saw as classical

French cinema's excessive stuffiness and their embrace of popular directors like Alfred Hitchcock, Howard Hawks, and Orson Welles, whom serious cineastes had regarded as mere cogs in the American studio machine and hardly the major artists that the *Cahiers* crew now argued they were.

But Godard stole money from *Cahiers*, too, and got caught. According to the biographer Colin MacCabe, "*Cahiers* was a tiny magazine which lived from hand to mouth, and the incident was serious enough to make him *persona non grata* for a considerable time." The discovery of this theft apparently influenced Godard's decision to move from Paris back to Switzerland, where he stayed at his mother's house for a time (his parents' marriage had by then broken up) and, with her help, got a job at a Swiss television station, where he was again caught stealing, from the station's safe. This time, Godard was arrested and held in a Swiss jail for a few days, until his father managed to persuade the authorities to release him to the care of a psychiatric institution. After his stay there—the amount of time he spent in the institution is unclear, perhaps two or three months—Godard was thoroughly alienated from his family. He had little to do with them going forward and certainly could not expect their financial support.

Needing money, Godard turned to manual labor, getting a job at the construction site for the massive Grande Dixence Dam in Valais, Switzerland, which, when it was finished, would be the tallest dam in the world. If this sounds about as far away from filmmaking as one could get, Godard still managed to turn it into an opportunity. First he got himself transferred from manual labor to a position as a switchboard operator (apparently with the help of a cousin in a leadership position at the construction company—so even without family money, Godard was still benefiting from family connections). According to MacCabe, "because of the extreme weather conditions the construction site could operate fully only in the summer, but a twenty-four-hour telephone exchange operated all year round and Godard was taken on as one of three telephonists." Normally, the three telephonists would work back-to-back eight-hour shifts—but Godard suggested a new schedule, described by MacCabe: "Instead of working three eight-hour shifts, the telephonists should pool their labour and each spend ten days on twenty-four-hour duty and take the other twenty days off." The other telephonists were game, and thus Godard was able to draw a full wage while only working ten days out of the month, spending the other twenty days in Lausanne or Geneva. (A friend described how Godard managed to work nonstop for ten days: "He spent the nights there on a cot, he got up when the telephone rang.")

In his spare time, Godard dreamed up a new plan: He would use the money he had been saving from the Grande Dixence job to produce a documentary about the dam's construction and then sell this film to the construction company, to be used as promotional material. One of Godard's Swiss friends persuaded a pair of friends in Geneva to lend Godard a 35 mm film camera for the shoot, and one of these Geneva friends also served as cinematographer. Over the summer of 1954, Godard shot and edited a twenty-minute film that he titled *Opération Béton* (that is, *Operation Concrete*). Remarkably, his plan worked: When he showed the film to the construction agency, they were so impressed that they agreed to pay, Mac-Cabe writes, "a sufficiently large sum to bankroll himself for the next two years." He even got some publicity for the film. A journalist wrote in a Swiss film magazine: "For two years, he tightened his belt to be able to show what he could do. Like a medieval artisan, he created his masterpiece in order to obtain his mastery. Now, he wants to make a more ambitious film."

+ + +

Godard was ambitious, sure, but more than that he had nerve—as did many of his fellow New Wave filmmakers, including his friend François Truffaut, who as a teenage film lover founded his own cinema club in Paris and then, to keep it afloat, stole and sold a typewriter from his father's office, an incident he later dramatized in his first film, *The 400 Blows*, another of the era's masterpieces. (After the theft, Truffaut's father forced him to confess to the police, leading to Truffaut's three-month stay in a juvenile detention center.) But let's not pretend that theft is enough, that great films were made on porno theater or cinema journal cash register filching alone. Chantal Akerman was ultimately able to make *Jeanne Dielman* because she received a $120,000 grant from the Belgian government. Truffaut's filmmaking career was aided by a strategic marriage:

At the Venice Film Festival, he met, and soon after married, Madeleine Morgenstern, the daughter of Ignace Morgenstern, a Hungarian-born French film producer who owned Cocinor, one of the era's largest film distributors, and it was this new father-in-law who enabled Truffaut to make *The 400 Blows*. Claude Chabrol, another of the era's great filmmakers, had a similar connection: He was able to make his first film, *Le Beau Serge*, by drawing on an inheritance from his wife's family.

In fact, Chabrol played a key role in Godard eventually making *his* first film. Before *Le Beau Serge*, Chabrol had been working in the publicity department of Twentieth Century–Fox's Paris office. After *Le Beau Serge*'s modest success, Chabrol was able to quit working at Fox and continue making his own films, and he recommended that Godard be his replacement. Godard was interested because he thought he could use the job to meet producers for his own filmmaking efforts—and this is exactly what happened. Richard Brody writes:

> After one screening, in early 1958, of a French film called *La Passe du diable* (Devil's Pass), which was being offered to Fox for distribution, Godard confronted the producer and declared, "Your film is a disgrace." The relatively young producer, Georges de Beauregard (born in 1920), who made films on small budgets under eccentric and risky circumstances and barely scraped by . . . was curious about this audacious young man.

A year later, Beauregard was producing Godard's first film, *Breathless*, and he would go on to produce several of the brash young director's subsequent pictures, including *Pierrot le Fou*, which so inspired fifteen-year-old Chantal Akerman when it was released in 1965.

+ + +

Jean-Luc Godard was not the only French artist to fund his early creative endeavor by stealing books. Perhaps his most famous predecessor was the novelist and playwright Jean Genet, who, in the early 1940s, listed his profession as a "broker" of books, but who really shoplifted valuable secondhand editions from one bookseller and resold them to another—after he'd read the books himself, of course. To ply his trade, Genet employed a special leather satchel that he kept pressed under one arm. He wrote, "I perfected a trick briefcase and I became so handy in these thefts that I could push politeness to the point of pulling them off under the very nose of the bookseller."

But Genet didn't always evade detection, and during this time he spent multiple short stints in prison for stealing books as well as clothing from department stores and a bolt of fabric from a tailor. Prison was always good for Genet's writing; in fact, it was prison that made him a writer in the first place, because it gave him lots of time to read—the most essential training for any writer but especially for Genet, whose formal schooling ended at age twelve—and also because it gave him a kind of mission, at least if you trust what the narrator in Genet's autobiographical fifth novel, *The Thief's Journal*, says:

> The boredom of my prison days made me take refuge in my past life, even though it was vagrant, austere or destitute. Later on, when I was free, I wrote again, in order to earn money. The idea of being a professional writer leaves me cold. However, if I examine my work, I now perceive in it, patiently pursued, a will to rehabilitate persons, objects and feelings reputedly vile.

In a sense, Genet's whole life was about rehabilitating the "reputedly vile." He embraced homosexuality, vagrancy, theft, prostitution, prison; he made the subversive seem not just more adventurous but more honest than supposedly respectable lifestyles. The last sentence of the first chapter of *The Thief's Journal* gives a good taste of his approach: "With fanatical care, 'jealous care,'" Genet wrote, "I prepared for my adventure as one arranges a couch or a room for love; I was *hot* for crime."

Genet's very first acts of theft took place in September 1920, when, as a nine-year-old choirboy in the village church in Alligny-en-Morvan, in central France, he began to steal books, pencils, and sweets. He had been placed in the village by the state, after being abandoned by his mother in Paris at seven months old. (She was a twenty-two-year-old governess; Genet's father remains unknown.) His foster parents were modest artisans who sent Genet to the village school, a few meters from their front doorstep. Genet's success in school saved him from a life as a farmhand; instead, at age thirteen, he was apprenticed to a typographer at the École d'Alembert, near Paris. But after ten days he ran away, and over the coming weeks and months Genet continued to frustrate and evade all institutional attempts to contain him. Finally, two years after leaving the village, he was condemned to an agricultural penitentiary colony in Mettray, a "children's prison" where he lived for two and a half years. After that, he spent seven years in military service, in Syria, Morocco, and France; in between tours of duty, he vagabonded through Spain and eastern and northern Europe.

Genet's military career ended in 1936, when he abruptly deserted his regiment; for the next year, he drifted through Europe dodging the authorities, getting himself expelled from one country after another, finally making his way to Paris, where he was arrested for stealing a dozen handkerchiefs from a department store. Genet avoided prison in this case, but before long he was engaged in a seemingly endless cycle of theft, arrest, brief imprisonment (for weeks or months), and release, only to steal again and restart the cycle.

It was during one of these imprisonments, in late 1939, that Genet discovered that he was a writer. He had just turned twenty-nine. Before this point, he had never written anything other than letters, none of them showing any special literary promise. But during this particular imprisonment, something shifted. In an interview, Genet explained what happened:

> I was alone in the clink, in the cell. . . . I sent a Christmas card to a German woman friend who was in Czechoslovakia. I'd bought it in prison and the back of the card, the part meant for the message, was grainy. And this grain had really touched me. And instead of speaking about Christmas, I spoke about the grain of this postcard, and the snow it evoked. I started to write from that moment on. I believe that was the trigger.

In a different context, however, Genet said that he'd "always been writing, even before I ever tried to write anything. The career of a writer doesn't begin at the moment he begins to write. The career and the writing may coincide earlier or later." Perhaps that explains how he was able to find his voice on the page so quickly; the first book he wrote in prison, in 1941–42, titled *Our Lady of the Flowers*, was immediately recognized as a work of uncommon literary merit and began to circulate underground even before it was properly published. In the meantime, he wrote another novel, *Miracle of the Rose*, also while imprisoned. Indeed, when Genet finally broke out of his cycle of theft, arrest, and imprisonment—which only happened after he narrowly avoided being deported to a Nazi concentration camp at the end of 1943—it posed a problem for his burgeoning literary career. "I wrote in prison," Genet said. "Once free I was lost."

This isn't strictly true. Genet wrote his first two novels while in prison, but he wrote three more after serving his final prison sentence. However, as Edmund White points out in his 1993 biography of Genet, during the ensuing years Genet always felt the threat of imprisonment hovering over him—he had by this point been convicted of so many thefts that, under French law, he was now eligible for a lifetime sentence. When the French government finally issued an official pardon, and Genet could stop worrying about going back to prison, he really did stop writing. For the next six years, silence. When he finally resumed writing, in 1955, it was for the stage only—he never wrote fiction again.

But was it *prison* that enabled his writing, or was it the act of theft that he practiced so assiduously during all those years? In *The Thief's Journal*, his final novel, Genet described committing a burglary: "When I have broken the lock, as soon as I push the door it thrusts back *within me* a heap of darkness, or, to be more exact, a very thick vapor which my body *is* summoned to enter. I enter. For a half hour I shall be operating, if I am alone, in a world which is the reverse of the customary world." He could almost be describing the act of writing itself—and perhaps once he entered "the customary world" for good, Genet lost access to whatever it was that happened alone in that room, in that very thick vapor that was his natural element for so long.

SORT OF RICH, SORT OF QUICK

N ow listen to me. I'm 24 years of age and for the last eighteen months have been plaguing myself with something that is of complete indifference to me. An invention."

So begins a fragment of a story drafted in Robert Musil's diary in 1904 or 1905, when the Austrian modernist writer was in his mid-twenties and just beginning to find his way toward a literary career. The narrator, who bears a great resemblance to Musil himself, continues:

> At the age of 21 I was already a qualified engineer. I wanted to give it up and study philosophy. To do so one has to have complete financial independence. So all that needed to be done was to invent something and to buy freedom that way.

I love this matter-of-fact spirit, and when I read his lines I found it reassuring to know that I'm not the only one who has dreamed of a scheme like this: a quick, profitable diversion into another field, with the goal of attaining "complete financial independence," at least for a few years, in order to pursue one's true vocation free of the money pressure that smothers so many artistic and intellectual careers before they can really begin. In my case, I never actually came up with such a scheme; I was an English major who worked at a library and then in publishing, paths that are not exactly filled with easy moneymaking opportunities. But Musil did, and his story fragment is an intriguing glimpse into what it really means to try to buy your artistic freedom.

In the fragment—it is a little over six hundred words long; perhaps Musil envisioned it as a rough sketch for a short story—the young engineer does not say what he sought to invent, only that the idea came to him during a year-and-a-half-long period of factory work, following his engineering education. Once he had the idea for his invention, the narrator continues, he was determined to make it a reality:

> I spent three months working on calculations for it. . . . Time and again I threw the whole thing under the table. Hours of struggle within myself. . . . Good inventions have to be earned, one doesn't stumble upon them quite by chance.

In the end, however, the young engineer succeeds. After a year of struggle, he realizes his invention and sells the patent for "quite a nice sum of money." Huzzah! The complete financial independence that he craved is finally his to enjoy.

And yet, in Musil's fragment, the narrator is hardly in a celebratory mood. What leaves the greatest impression on him is not his success with the invention but that long year of uncertain striving, followed by another six months of work to secure the patent, which has perhaps, he now worries, sapped him of the energy needed for his true vocation as a writer:

> But what a year that was! Just imagine such a person in the first years of full maturity who, in order not to dissipate his efforts, cannot spare a single thought for what he considers his vocation. . . .
>
> Eighteen months ago I was talented and my [literary] drafts were well received. But what does it mean to have eighteen months cut out of one's development! Will there be anything left there to justify having made this sacrifice?

This sketch tracks closely with Musil's own biography. Born in Klagenfurt, southern Austria, in 1880, Musil grew up in Brno, where his father was the chair of mechanical engineering at the city's prestigious Technical University. When it came time for his university studies, Musil enrolled in his father's department and, at age twenty-one, qualified as an engineer. Musil's father then arranged for him to begin work as an unpaid assistant to a distinguished colleague in Stuttgart. But young Musil was rapidly losing interest in the family profession. While he was an engineering student, he had developed a fierce love of literature and philosophy, and he began to suspect that his proper path lay in that direction. During his time working in Stuttgart, he began writing a novel, *The Confusions of Young Törless*, based on his youthful experiences at military boarding school. And like the narrator of his story fragment, which he would draft a few years later, Musil began to dream of an invention—a wonderfully profitable one that would free him from the unfortunate necessity of earning a living.

Remarkably, like his narrator, Musil succeeded: He invented an optical instrument that he called a *Variationskreisel*, used to help in investigating perceptions of color, and he also succeeded in selling the patent. (Musil's instrument was manufactured commercially into the 1920s.) Unlike in his story fragment, however, the patent sale did not make Musil financially independent—that part, alas, is fiction. In reality, Musil finally had to appeal to his parents to support a change of direction. He proposed leaving Stuttgart and engineering to study philosophy in Berlin (his ultimate trajectory was toward writing fiction, but philosophy was a stepping stone in that direction and would inform all his writing), and his parents agreed to pay him an allowance while he worked toward a doctorate.

It was from Berlin that Musil wrote his fragment about the young engineer; obviously, the experience of trying to buy his freedom with an invention—and the worry that he had lost crucial months of artistic development in the process—was still fresh, almost excruciatingly so. In Musil's case, the worry seems unfounded; shortly after writing this sketch, he succeeded in publishing *The Confusions of Young Törless*, to favorable reviews. But who's to say that things might not have gone otherwise? Musil's play for artistic freedom was a gamble, and he knew he was lucky to emerge whole, more or less.

+ + +

Musil is hardly the only young person to dream of funding a life in the arts through a short-term diversion into a more profitable project. And, alas, he is hardly the only one to discover how difficult this twin-track existence really is.

In the late 1940s, the Harlem-based painter Romare Bearden found himself with a similar craving for financial and artistic independence. Well, what he was *really* craving was Paris: After serving three years in the army during World War II, Bearden enjoyed a postwar stint studying in Paris on the GI Bill and discovered that the city was "like a thing of dreams." In Harlem, he had been trying to figure out how to develop as a painter while laboring as a caseworker for the New York Department of Welfare. (He painted in the evenings after work. Though he had succeeded in exhibiting in galleries in New York and Washington, DC, Bearden's income from gallery sales was not enough to live on.) In Paris, by contrast, he was living an artist's fantasy existence. Thanks to his GI Bill benefits—seventy-five dollars a month, or about twice a French worker's wage at the time—Bearden was able to rent a furnished room on the Left Bank with, the biographer Myron Schwartzman writes, "a skylit studio, ample heat, laundry, and three plentiful meals daily, all for forty dollars a month."

Ironically, Bearden later admitted that he painted "nothing" during this time; he was too busy roaming the city and hanging out with other artists. But this was important in its own right. The scale of the city, the architecture, the cafés, and the pace of café life—it all came to Bearden as a tremendous jolt of freedom. He wrote to his cousin, the painter and teacher Charles Alston: "You can sit down at a cafe, no one bothers you, it's hard to find a waiter even to pay your bill—no one would say 'You lazy bastard, why don't you paint a picture, or write a poem.'" For the first time, Bearden stopped feeling that he needed to prove himself as an artist, and this gave him the mental space to start actually becoming an artist. It was almost too good—when Bearden's five months of study were up and he was forced to go back home, reluctantly, to Harlem, he immediately started plotting his return.

Robert Musil drew on his engineering training for the invention that he hoped would fund his writing career; Bearden turned his attention to an old upright piano someone had left in the corner of his studio. Growing up in Harlem, Bearden had benefited from his mother's vigorous involvement in local Democratic politics, which had brought into the family's orbit some of the major figures of the Harlem Renaissance, including many of the era's great musicians: Duke Ellington was a family friend, and Fats Waller dropped by the Bearden apartment regularly. As an adult, Bearden counted among his friends the composer and arranger Dave Ellis, the classical music composers Joshua Lee and Frank Fields, and the pop composer Fred Norman. He knew that successful songwriters could make a lot of money on a single tune, and he began to ask his friends to teach him how to do it. *This* would be his return ticket to Paris, he thought—a hit song! How hard could it be?

In fact, Bearden did have a knack for songwriting, or enough of one that he managed, over the next few years, with the help of Norman and a publicist named Larry Douglas, to publish about twenty tunes. His biggest success was "Seabreeze," which became a minor hit in the mid-1950s, recorded by Billy Eckstine and Tito Puente, among others, and used by Seagram's to promote a gin-based mixed drink of the same name. But neither this nor any of his other songs earned enough for Bearden to fund a return to Paris. And the strain of trying to make it big in songwriting, while resuming his full-time position at the New York Department of Welfare *and* still trying to make progress as a painter, weighed on him—especially since painting, for Bearden, was never an easy or straightforward thing. "You know, when you're serious about something, you don't really like doing it," Bearden said. "Painting is so difficult; the canvas was always saying no to me."*

---

* Musil would have been able to relate: "Spend eight days of torture on this and have nothing to show for it, it is still nothing—it's almost something and yet it's nothing," he wrote in his diary on August 29, 1910, while working on his second book. "Deepest depression."

At this time, Bearden was friends with the married philosophers Hannah Arendt and Heinrich Blücher, who lived in Morningside Heights near Columbia University. As a student in Berlin in the 1920s, Blücher had had some success of his own as a musician, writing songs for musicals to help fund his studies. But now he told Bearden that his own experience had been vastly different—songwriting was just a paycheck for him. "What you're doing is something else altogether, because you're not painting," Blücher said. "If you keep on, you're going to ruin yourself as a painter, because you're just not attuned to this."

Before Bearden could take Blücher's advice, he collapsed in the street and woke up in the hospital—he'd had a nervous breakdown. When he recovered, after a month in the hospital, he was done with songwriting and done with trying to return to Paris, too. He wrote to his friend and fellow artist Carl Holty, "Now I'm going to do nothing but paint—no more wildcat schemes to get rich quick with a hit song."

+ + +

As it happens, Musil's story fragment also ends with a kind of breakdown. The engineer, having succeeded with his invention, assures himself that the "deep discouragement" he is left with will soon lift. His literary capabilities will return, of course! After a fortnight, he will begin "to pick up the threads again." But then, in a cruel twist of fate, the narrator is diagnosed with "a nervous condition of the heart as a result of overexertion." His literary future is once again in doubt; perhaps he missed his chance?

In reality, Musil did not develop a heart condition like the one he describes, though he certainly suffered from a lifelong nervous temperament. (As the critic John Simon once wrote, everything Musil touched "was or became difficult. Simplicity was not for him: in style, thought, or life.") Nervous afflictions aside, Musil and Bearden are not exactly cautionary tales. Musil's various vocational dead ends—not only as an engineer and an inventor but, later, as a librarian and a civil servant—never stopped him from writing, or not for long. As for Bearden, after recovering from his collapse and pledging "to do nothing but paint," he eventually did break through as a painter, though it took quite a few more years of searching and striving.

The Paris sojourn was a turning point. His early paintings were based on his childhood memories of the rural South,* done in tempera on brown paper, or they were based on literary and biblical themes, as in Bearden's 1945 exhibition *The Passion of Christ* at the Samuel Kootz Gallery, in New York. After Paris, he lost interest in this early subject matter and found himself drawn toward abstraction. When he returned to Harlem, he wrote, "I began experimenting in a radically different way. I started to play with pigments, as such, in marks and patches, distorting natural colors and representational objects." Later, a meeting with a scholar of Chinese art and calligraphy led him to study Chinese landscape painting and to begin incorporating rice paper into his work, gluing it to the canvas and tearing away sections, adding paint and more paper in stages. But Bearden's real and most lasting breakthrough occurred via Spiral, the Black artists collective that formed in Bearden's Canal Street loft in 1963. (Bearden had moved from Harlem to Canal Street in 1956, with his new bride, Nanette, whom he met not long after his nervous breakdown and who played a major role in his subsequent reenergization as a painter.) At one of the group's meetings, the idea of a collaborative project came up. Pondering how this might work, Bearden thought of collage and began cutting out photos from his wife's magazine collection. At the next Spiral meeting, no one else was interested in this direction—but Bearden kept tinkering with small collages, until another Spiral artist suggested he take them to a photo lab to be blown up. These enlarged photomontages, which he called "projections," became a major breakthrough for Bearden and the basis of all his subsequent work. They allowed him to create arresting, dreamlike scenes of Black life that transcended any particular time and place, or any particular social message, and that proved an endlessly rich source of experimentation and development.

---

* Bearden was born in Charlotte, North Carolina, in 1911. When he was a child, his family moved to Harlem—but Bearden also spent long stretches of time with relatives in North Carolina and Maryland.

Would he have gotten there if the songwriting had worked out and he'd struck it rich with a popular tune? Perhaps. But it's hard to resist the conclusion that it was Bearden's years of gradual muddling forward that allowed him to arrive at his mature style. Working days at the welfare department,* painting nights and weekends in his Harlem studio—did it suit him, in a way? (Remember that he painted nothing while he was in Paris, living his dream artist lifestyle.) Bearden seemed to recognize this himself. "I think the artist has to be something like a whale," he once said, "swimming with his mouth wide open, absorbing everything until he has what he really needs. When he finds that, he can start to make limitations. And then he really begins to grow."

+ + +

Romare Bearden decided that his "wildcat scheme" to get rich with a hit song was a diversion from his true development as a painter—and Robert Musil fretted that his months spent trying to realize a profitable invention might have deprived him of a crucial period in his artistic development. But these kinds of schemes can be generative, too, can't they? For the German conceptual artist Martin Kippenberger, gambling—figuratively and literally—was a way of life, part of the fabric of his daily existence. Instead of trying to buy a stretch of artistic freedom through one big payday, he was continually extending himself credit—or convincing others to extend it to him.

Kippenberger was, in the words of his *New York Times* obituary, "a dandyish, articulate, prodigiously prolific artist who loved controversy and confrontation." Born in 1953, his obituary appeared far too early, in 1997; Kippenberger was forty-four, felled by alcohol-related liver disease. In his short life, he was astonishingly productive. His motto was "Think

---

* In the end, Bearden was a caseworker for the New York Department of Welfare for three decades, until 1967, when he was finally able to quit and live off the sales of his paintings. (He was fifty-six.) He didn't regard the job as a terrible burden. Asked about it in a 1968 interview, the year after he finally retired to live off his painting sales, Bearden said merely: "It was easy and I did have time to paint." In a different interview, he said that he only had two or three hours of peak creative energy a day anyway, and he could get that in the evenings. "If you're working intensely—composing a piece of music, or writing a novel, painting, or whatever art you're in—about three hours is enough for anyone."

today, done tomorrow"—as soon as he had an idea for a new project, he executed it as fast as possible, often the very next day.

Another of Kippenberger's favorite sayings was "*Nicht sparen—Taxi fahren*," or: "Don't save money—take a taxi." This is according to the artist's youngest sister, Susanne Kippenberger, who, after his death, wrote a fascinating biography, *Kippenberger: The Artist and His Families*, published in English in 2011. In unpacking what drove her brother's art and life, Susanne can't help but return to the theme of money—and Kippenberger's extremely loose, almost porous relationship to it. Even as a young child, she writes, "his monthly allowance was spent by the first of the month, usually on candy." As an adult, he was no different. She writes:

> Warnings were always turning up: from the tax office, from the printer's. Money was always tight; his bank account was constantly overdrawn. He looked for jobs and had a special talent for "finding jobs where he didn't have to work himself to death," as [the artist] Jochen Krüger recalls. He painted three hundred windows for a health insurance company, licked envelopes, set up chairs, and signed up when the labor office needed "2 Men, strong" to load trucks for seven marks an hour. . . . Sometimes he said yes to two jobs at the same time, so he could call in sick to one and make twice as much money.

When Kippenberger's mother died in 1976, the artist was poised to receive an inheritance of "several hundred thousand marks." Knowing his profligate ways, Kippenberger's uncle was determined that he should receive the inheritance in installments rather than as a lump sum, but, Susanne writes, "in the end Martin got it all at once, and spent it all at once too." She continues:

> The inheritance was a great stroke of luck for him: it gave him the means to start squandering himself in Berlin. Finally he could do what he wanted, unchecked and uninhibited and with no regard

to the cost. He didn't have to fritter away his time on furniture-moving jobs or beg people to buy his art supplies for him; he could hire expensive bands at S.O.36 [the Berlin nightclub he began managing in 1979], furnish Kippenberger's Office [his studio] the way he wanted, go out to eat every day (and drink, too), make his own records and produce other people's, make books, hire sign painters, shoot movies and photographs at will, risk flops, and plaster bar walls with his stickers and posters. He could stretch out and make himself known.

How did he get by once the inheritance was gone? He did sell artwork but often didn't make enough even to recoup the cost of making it. (Now his work sells at auction for eight figures.) He filled the gaps by borrowing money from friends and colleagues (and not repaying it), by bartering—according to Susanne, he once traded a series of paintings "for lifetime free food and drink for himself and a guest at the Paris Bar in Berlin"—and, when he was really in trouble, by gambling. His specialty was mau-mau, a card game similar to Uno. Susanne writes:

> He played mau-mau to excess, with anyone and everyone, some-times for days and nights on end. In Tokyo he taught a distin-guished Japanese lady how to play; on an airplane flight to San Francisco he passed the time playing mau-mau with the artist Rosemarie Trockel and won seventeen drawings from her. Martin always wanted to win and usually did (and if he didn't, look out: you had to keep playing with him until he came out ahead, no matter how long it took). No one was ever as much in practice as Martin, and no one cheated as much as he did, either.

As much as the lack of money caused problems—chiefly, by hamper-ing his ability to fund new work—Kippenberger thought that having money was even worse for an artist. "It's a kind of engine, this never hav-ing enough," he said. "It's probably from nature somewhere, and we have to work to live, you know? And when you suddenly do have money . . .

me, I'd get lazy, and when I'm lazy, and don't work, right away I get drunk." Given that his drinking would eventually kill him, Kippenberger's finances were therefore literally an existential concern; he needed just enough to keep working and no more. Work redeemed his excesses and kept him continually moving forward. Susanne reports that he never had a credit card and "always paid from a thick wad of cash he had in his jacket pocket." When someone asked him why, he replied: "I'm on the run."

THE BRIDGE

R obert Musil's and Romare Bearden's attempts to "buy freedom" through a diversion into a more profitable enterprise do beg the question: Why not try to make a profit from your actual artistic discipline, or at least an offshoot of it? Wouldn't that be easier and more practical, and mightn't it make good sense to try to meld your artistic and commercial aims?

In fact, much earlier in his career, Bearden had tested this exact route. His introduction to the art world had been through cartooning, which he embraced near the end of his high school career and throughout his college years. He briefly attended the all-male Lincoln University, outside Philadelphia, before transferring to Boston University and, finally, New York University, living at home in the family apartment in Harlem and taking the subway downtown to attend classes in Washington Square. At NYU, Bearden published political cartoons steadily in the university humor magazine, the *Medley*, and in outside publications, too. By the time he graduated, Bearden recalled later, he "had already become something of a semiprofessional cartoonist with a weekly feature in the Baltimore *Afro-American*, a Negro newspaper of nationwide reputation and circulation."

During this time, he met Elmer Simms Campbell, one of the first Black cartoonists to get published regularly in major national magazines.

Campbell helped Bearden place his work in a few of these, including *Life* and *Collier's*, but he also encouraged Bearden to get more formal training by enrolling at the Art Students League, a fine arts school on West Fifty-Seventh Street that was a formative training ground for many of the era's artists. Bearden took his friend's advice and, in 1936, began studying life drawing and painting with the German émigré artist George Grosz, who dramatically expanded Bearden's horizons, leading him to the work of Ingres, Hans Holbein, Albrecht Dürer, and Pieter Bruegel the Elder. It was during this period, Bearden later wrote, "that I began to regard myself as a painter rather than a cartoonist." And as he wrapped up his studies, he thought, well, why not use cartooning to pay the bills and pursue painting at the same time?

He tried to do exactly that—and found that it did not work for him at all. He could pour his creative energy into cartooning or painting, not both at the same time; trying to do so hopelessly diluted both efforts. "There is unfortunately no bridge between the fine arts and the arts of commerce," Bearden concluded in his journal on September 7, 1947. "The artist must decide which of the two endeavors is most compatible to his talents and personality."

+ + +

Other artists have had better luck finding this bridge and crossing it. British writers, in particular, seem to have a talent for combining artistic and commercial aims. The Wimbledon-born writer Robert Graves is a good example. In the early 1930s, Graves got himself into trouble with a real estate deal in Majorca, Spain, where he had relocated in 1929; the Mediterranean island was to be a refuge for him after the horrors of World War I, where he was badly wounded, and the breakup of his first marriage. It was Gertrude Stein who suggested that he consider Majorca, and after renting a house that proved unsuitable, Graves had a new one built to his specifications: a study for himself, another for his partner and fellow writer Laura Riding, and a spare study for visiting friends, plus a light-filled room for the printing press that Graves and Riding operated together. But almost as soon as the house was completed, he found himself in danger of losing it. "I'd been let down in a land deal," he explained in a 1965 interview. "I had to find four thousand pounds, and I'd mortgaged my house."

Graves had by this time already had one major publishing success. The autobiography *Good-Bye to All That*, which described his near-death experience in the war and the brutality of trench warfare, was a bestseller and funded his Majorcan escape to begin with. So the solution to his land-deal woes was, clearly, to write *another* bestseller, as fast as possible, to clear his debts and save his new house. Graves set to work on a historical novel set in the Roman Empire, taking readers behind the scenes of the elaborate plots and brutal machinations that led from one emperor to another, and from Rome's glory to its decline. It was Graves's first attempt at melding historical research with the irresistible forward momentum of a page-turner, and he proved to have an astonishing gift for it, not to mention a remarkably accurate sense of its sales potential. *I, Claudius*, published in 1934, did exactly what Graves hoped. "I wrote it and I made eight thousand pounds in six months, and that saved my house," he recalled. He quickly followed it with a sequel, *Claudius the God*, published the same year, and the two books' massive popularity not only allowed Graves to clear his debts but to hire a typist as well.

I, Claudius is now Graves's best-known book, adapted into a beloved BBC miniseries in 1976 and hugely influential on subsequent authors of historical fiction. Even so, Graves was dismissive of it. "It was purely a practical job," he said, written to save his house—and in the years to come, he would write several more historical novels as additional income sources. In fact, Graves didn't really think of himself as a novelist at all—he saw himself primarily as a poet, and he saw prose writing merely as a way to pay the bills. "Prose books," he said, "are the show dogs I breed to sell and support my cat."

+ + +

Just a few years after Robert Graves saved his house with the *I, Claudius* books, his fellow Englishman Graham Greene was trying to figure out how to secure his family's future through a bestseller of his own. It was 1939; World War II was fast approaching, and Greene was growing fearful. Once Britain entered the war, he felt it would be his duty to serve his country in the army—but he was, at this time, struggling through a new novel that he considered "unsaleable" and, worse, that he could not seem to finish. "There was no money in the book as far as I could see," Greene wrote in the second volume of his autobiography. "Certainly my wife and two children would not be able to live on one unsaleable book, while I satisfied my conscience in the army." What was he to do?

His solution, similar to Graves's but even more extreme, was to simultaneously write another novel, this one purely for money, and to do it as fast as possible. To be fair, he knew his capabilities pretty well by this point. Greene was thirty-five and had been publishing books for a decade, though he had dreamed of doing so for much longer. As a schoolboy, his fantasy was not to be an athlete or a race car driver but, touchingly, "an established writer who was making enough money to support himself," Greene recalled in his autobiography. At Oxford, he made his first attempt at a novel, and finished it, but was unable to find a publisher. After graduation, he worked briefly as a tutor, then moved to the *Nottingham Journal* as an unpaid apprentice subeditor (living off an allowance from his father), meanwhile writing five hundred words a day on a second novel. The apprenticeship paid off: From there, Greene was able to land a job at *The Times* in London, a magical place for him, where he thought he would stay for the rest of his life. We've seen that Franz Kafka believed journalism would detract from a writer's more imaginative work, but Greene found the opposite was the case. "I can think of no better career for a young novelist than to be for some years a sub-editor on a rather conservative newspaper," Greene wrote.

The hours, from four till around midnight, give him plenty of time to do his own work in the morning when he is still fresh from sleep—let the office employ him during his hours of fatigue. He has the company of intelligent and agreeable men of greater experience than his own: he is not enclosed by himself in a small room tormented by the problems of expression; and, except for rare periods of rush, even his working hours leave him time for books and conversation (most of us brought a book to read between one piece of copy and another).

At *The Times*, Greene finished his second novel but again failed to interest a publisher. He started a third book—a detective novel—and abandoned it, then started another one, now resolving to give up on novel writing entirely if this effort proved unsuccessful. But this time, he pulled it off: *The Man Within* came out in 1929 and sold eight thousand copies, more than enough to earn out the £50 advance Greene had received from his publisher—enough, in fact, that his publisher offered him £600 a year for the next three years, in exchange for three new novels. Greene, who had been making £5 a week at *The Times*, eagerly agreed, resigning his subeditor position in order to write full-time.

But one success did not guarantee another, and his next two books— *The Name of Action* and *Rumour at Nightfall*, published in 1931 and 1932—were both commercial flops, and artistic ones, too; in later years, Greene would excise them from his official bibliography. ("Both books are of a badness beyond the power of criticism properly to evoke" was his evaluation late in life.) He was more than a little disappointed. "If *The Man Within* had shown promise," he wrote, "it was the brief promise of a dud rocket on Guy Fawkes night." He found himself in a sickeningly familiar position: Everything rode on his next novel; if it failed, his career was over.

Apparently, Greene responded well to this kind of pressure, because his next book, *Stamboul Train*—published in the United States as *Orient Express*—was his best book so far and his biggest success, too; it sold briskly and, in 1934, was adapted into an American film. If Greene still didn't feel that he had fully made it—and perhaps never would—at least he had bought himself a fresh set of attempts; his publishers would be delighted to have more books like *Stamboul Train*. And surely *now* he had found the secret to producing well-written, propulsive thrillers that would appeal to a wide readership? Well, no. Believe it or not, Greene now repeated the same pattern for a third time, following *Stamboul Train* with another series of duds.

The problem was that Greene was not satisfied writing mere thrillers, but he hadn't yet figured out how to write the kind of book that did satisfy his larger ambitions. It was only with *Brighton Rock*, in 1938, that he cracked the code, producing a work that was at once a page-turner and a subtle, complex character study soaked with the themes of guilt and paranoia that reflected his persistent conflicts as a Catholic convert (and later a "Catholic agnostic"). It was the tenth novel Greene had written and the eighth he had published, but as far as Greene was concerned it was his first *real* novel, an entirely different beast from the thrillers he had produced until that point—and that he felt he would need to keep producing to fund his writing life. Starting around this time, he would divide his output into "entertainments" and "novels"—the first were page-turners that he produced quickly for money, while the second were intended as serious works of literature.

Which brings us back to Greene in 1939, at the cusp of World War II. Clearly his scheme of producing another moneymaking thriller at the same time as he worked on a new novel proper wasn't entirely far-fetched—but now, with war on the horizon, he had to do so *fast*. He resolved to work on the "entertainment" in the morning, then in the afternoon switch over to what he felt certain would be his masterpiece, even if he had little hope for its sales potential: *The Power and the Glory*, an allegorical novel about a nameless Mexican "whisky priest" fleeing the soldiers who are determined to stamp out religion in their country. But writing two books at once was a herculean task even for the disciplined Greene, and especially with all the pressures of looming wartime. Needing some extra stimulus, he turned to Benzedrine, the brand name of an amphetamine then available without a prescription. He wrote:

> I fell back for the first and last time in my life on Benzedrine. For six weeks I started each day with a tablet, and renewed the dose at midday. Each day I sat down to work with no idea of what turn the plot might take and each morning I wrote, with the automatism

of a planchette, two thousand words instead of my usual stint of five hundred words. In the afternoons *The Power and the Glory* proceeded towards its end at the same leaden pace, unaffected by the sprightly young thing who was so quickly overtaking it.

That "sprightly young thing" was *The Confidential Agent*, and it was completed a mere six weeks after he began writing it. Revisiting the book years later, Greene said, "It is not really one of mine. It was as though I were ghosting for another man." This act of speed ghostwriting took its toll. Greene's new Benzedrine habit, he wrote, "left my nerves in shreds and my wife suffered the result." It took him six weeks to wean himself off the drug, taking smaller and smaller doses each day, and when he looked back on the factors that led to the breakup of his marriage—which also included the couple's separation during the war, and Greene's infidelities around the same time—he wondered if *The Confidential Agent*, and the Benzedrine it took to write it, weren't among the root causes.

+ + +

Graham Greene may have stretched himself too thin trying to write entertainments and novels simultaneously. But in the end he succeeded: Not only did he manage to finish *The Power and the Glory*, and not only did it live up to his artistic aspirations, but in the subsequent years he completed several more novels that matched or perhaps even surpassed this standard, while also continuing to write his entertainments for money.

Greene was both unusually talented and quite lucky. In truth, it's not so easy to make one version of your art just for money and then pivot to the other version, the one you make without worrying about money and maybe even in defiance of it. Trying to do both things at once may prevent you from doing either of them well. And if you succeed at one, the world may not let you pivot to the other.

Perhaps no writer knew this as well, and felt it as bitterly, as Louisa May Alcott, who from a young age dreamed of becoming a successful novelist, but whose enormous and unexpected breakthrough with a children's book she never wanted to write trapped her in that genre and prevented her from ever realizing her larger ambitions. She gave pleasure to generations of young readers around the world—no small thing—but felt creatively stymied and never fully reconciled herself to the career that erupted out of *Little Women* and took over her life.

Alcott had always dreamed of making a lot of money through a creative pursuit. In her "Recollections of My Childhood," written near the end of her life and published posthumously, she recalled being fifteen years old and feeling so overcome by ambition that she literally shook her fist at the sky, vowing: "I *will* do something by-and-by. Don't care what, teach, sew, act, write, anything to help the family; and I'll be rich and famous and happy before I die, see if I won't!" These were outsize hopes for a girl born in 1832, when women were still expected to limit their ambitions to the domestic sphere. But Alcott was an unusually willful spirit almost from birth, and she was born into an unusually progressive family: Her mother, Abba, was an abolitionist and pioneering social worker who everywhere saw "woman under the yoke"; her father, Bronson, was a philosopher, an influential educational theorist, and a member of the transcendentalist circle. But her father's progressive ideals meshed poorly with worldly success, and for thirty years he made virtually no income, relying instead on his wife and daughters to keep the family afloat, often just barely. (His friend Ralph Waldo Emerson helped them out numerous times.) Louisa was the second of four daughters, and as her mother slowed down with age and illness, and her older sister married and began her own family—and Bronson Alcott continued to contribute nothing but the vegetables from his garden—it fell upon Louisa to act as primary breadwinner for the family, living with and financially supporting her parents for most of her adult life.

Alcott's early contributions to the family's coffers came from working as a teacher, a seamstress, a governess, a domestic helper, and a laundress, positions that she disliked or outright loathed; confined to a basement kitchen at one point, she felt like "a caged sea-gull" and wrote that she was beginning "to know something of the pathetic side of life with its hard facts, irksome duties, many temptations and daily sacrifice of self." Writing was a crucial outlet for her imagination, and Alcott finished her first novel,

The Inheritance, before she was twenty. (The biographer Susan Cheever writes: "A short romantic Cinderella story written in girlish, sentimental prose, it is weirdly enlivened by the desperate feelings of its author.") That book was not published in her lifetime, but another, *Flower Fables*—a collection of tales first written for Emerson's daughter—was published in 1854, when Alcott was twenty-two. Thereafter, writing became a viable source of income. Alcott discovered that she could supplement teaching and tutoring with selling melodramatic short stories with titles like "The Maniac Bride" and "The Mysterious Key and What It Opened," published under a pseudonym (and not discovered to be Alcott's work until almost a hundred years later). Though she much preferred this to her other jobs and was gifted at cranking out overheated Gothic melodramas, this kind of writing was still not artistically satisfying; in the meantime, she labored on *Moods*, her attempt at a serious novel for adult readers, completed in 1860, though not published for another four years.

A turning point came during the Civil War, when shortly after her thirtieth birthday Alcott served for six weeks as a volunteer nurse for the Union army, working in a hospital in Washington, DC. The letters she sent home were shared by someone—probably her father—with the editors of an antislavery journal, who asked if Alcott would consider revising them for publication. She agreed, and her *Hospital Sketches* were serialized in four parts starting in May 1863, and proved immediately popular with readers. With her Gothic melodramas, Alcott had already figured out how to make money with her pen; now she had, she wrote, "discovered the secret of winning the ear & touching the heart of the public." And it was the success of *Hospital Sketches* that finally enabled her to publish *Moods*, after significant revisions.

But before she could figure out how to apply these skills to a new novel for adults, her editor and publisher Thomas Niles suggested that Alcott write a "girl's book," an idea that did not appeal to her at all: "Never liked girls or knew many except my sisters," she wrote in her journal. She avoided starting it for almost an entire year before her publisher's entreaties, and her father's, wore her down. The pressure from her father was doubly self-serving: Not only did he agree with Niles on the lucrative potential of children's literature, but he was maneuvering to get his own book *Tablets* published, which Niles had suggested would be possible if his daughter agreed to pen the "girl's book." Alcott finally set to work in the spring of 1868, though her initial ambition was to prove she could *not* write books for girls, and thus put the matter to rest for good. At first, Niles agreed: He found the early chapters dull. But the reaction of his young niece—the pages moved her to laughter and tears—convinced him that they were onto something.

Alcott wrote the remainder of the manuscript with incredible speed, completing four hundred manuscript pages in two and a half months. When the book came out in late 1868, the first edition sold out so quickly that Niles asked Alcott to immediately begin work on a second volume, which she delivered three months after the publication of the first part. *Little Women* went on to sell hundreds of thousands of copies, making Alcott rich and reluctantly famous, sought out by legions of fans who made the pilgrimage to meet their favorite author at her home in Concord.*

So why not then focus on the serious literary books she really wished to write? After a lifetime of financial insecurity, Alcott simply was not capable of turning away from the moneymaking potential of the children's stories she once called "moral pap for the young." And with financial success came more financial commitments. The novelist and academic Alison Lurie writes:

> The financial needs of her family were so great that Louisa felt unable to stop producing stories for children that were sure to sell. Her mother was too ill to work, and her father had heavy debts. In 1870 her sister Anna's husband died, leaving two young sons, and in 1879, her sister May died in Europe, leaving a baby daughter, who was sent back to her aunt in Massachusetts. Louisa

---

* As the historian Ann Douglas has written, Alcott was an "intensely private person" who found that encounters with fans were "usually painful to her, and sometimes to her visitors"—in one case resulting in a little girl weeping inconsolably because she could not believe that "this sharp-featured, grim, middle-aged woman was the author of *Little Women*."

took financial responsibility for all three children, and it never seems to have occurred to her that she might have declined to pay her father's debts or support her niece and nephews. As Bronson Alcott told everyone proudly, and in some critics' view rather smugly, she had become "The Child of Duty."

The Child of Duty did attempt additional novels for adult audiences— her 1872 novel *Work*, for instance, is based on the string of menial jobs she endured in her youth—but she never became the mature novelist she wished to be, focusing most of her energy on two additional *Little Women* sequels and other works for children. Especially as her health failed in her later years, it no longer seemed worth the effort to fight against her fate. "Though I do not enjoy writing 'moral tales' for the young," Alcott told a reader in 1878, "I do it because it pays well."

Alcott's story raises an interesting question: If you have a rare talent for a particular type of creative work, and audiences are hungry for what you're producing, and you are getting paid handsomely for it, isn't it a touch masochistic to insist that said work is not your *true* passion and to fixate on what you might have done otherwise had it not been for the piles of money laid at your feet? *Little Women* has endured for more than a century and a half; meanwhile, Alcott's attempts at writing serious novels for adults are really only read by scholars who want to know more about the woman behind Meg, Jo, Beth, and Amy. If it hadn't been for *Little Women*, would Alcott have eventually become a mature literary artist like Henry James, her hero? Perhaps. But to achieve that, she may have needed to start with much different goals in mind. Remember that Alcott's teenage dream was to do something creative, to help her family—no small thing, given how financially irresponsible her father was—and to be "rich and famous and happy" before she died. She achieved all those goals except the very last. And as for *that* goal, well, Alcott would hardly be the first, or the last, to discover that writing and happiness rarely go hand in hand.

DOUBLE OR NOTHING

———————————————————

The painter Romare Bearden thought that the artist has to be "something like a whale, swimming with his mouth wide open, absorbing everything"—but he also thought that what the artist *really* needed was limitations. And it was absorbing everything that eventually allowed him to make those limitations.

The American avant-garde composer John Cage would have appreciated this sentiment. So much of his career was about creating a space for things to happen, using limitations as a tool. And so much of his early path as a composer was shaped by his own limitations, chief among them a lack of money—"I never made enough money (from my music) to live on until I was fifty," he wrote in a 1973 letter—but also a lack of natural talent in areas generally considered indispensable for a composer. When a twentysomething Cage sought out and studied with the legendary Austrian composer Arnold Schoenberg, who had fled Nazi Germany for Cage's native Los Angeles (buying a house in Brentwood Park directly across the street from Shirley Temple's house), he eventually had the following exchange with his hero and mentor:

After I had been studying with him for two years, Schoenberg said, "In order to write music, you must have a feeling for harmony." I explained to him that I had no feeling for harmony. He then said that I would always encounter an obstacle, that it would be as though I came to a wall through which I could not pass. I said, "In that case I will devote my life to beating my head against that wall."

But if Cage was always beating his head against that wall, he did so with a smile on his face. Obstacles brought out the best in him; he didn't attempt to surmount them so much as he rushed over to greet them with warm interest. It was this spirit that had allowed him to study with Schoenberg in the first place. Cage recalled their first meeting, circa 1935: "He said, 'You probably can't afford my price,' and I said, 'You don't need to mention it because I don't have any money.' So he said, 'Will you devote your life to music?' and I said I would."*

Cage might have never even heard of Schoenberg if it hadn't been for an earlier moneymaking scheme. First, some background: Cage took piano lessons starting as a child, but by the time he started at Pomona College—at age sixteen, after graduating as valedictorian of his Los Angeles high school—he had decided to become a writer. After two years, convinced that college was of no use to a writer, he dropped out and persuaded his parents to send him to Europe instead. Staying in Paris, he developed an obsession with Gothic architecture, worked for a time for a Hungarian-born architect named Ernő Goldfinger, and discovered modern painting and music. After a year and a half in Europe and northern Africa, Cage returned to Los Angeles. It was the Depression years; he was still trying to find his path in life, and he also had to find a way to support himself. To satisfy all these needs at once, Cage settled on an inspired combination of gardening and lecturing. As he explained it:

> I found an auto court in Santa Monica where, in exchange for doing the gardening, I got an apartment to live in and a large room back of the court over the garages, which I used as a lecture hall. I was nineteen years old and enthusiastic about modern music and

---

* Schoenberg then agreed to give Cage lessons for free. He knew what it was like to be broke. Cage once said: "Like most composers, Schoenberg had more or less constant money problems. The thought arises whether these are not the true subject of music."

painting. I went from house to house in Santa Monica explaining this to the housewives. I offered ten lectures for $2.50. I said, "I will learn each week something about the subject that I will then lecture on."

Cage drew an audience of thirty to forty housewives each week, using the lectures to continue his ambitious self-education in music and art. He said, "In this way I taught myself, so to speak, what was going on in those two fields." And it was in prepping for one of his lectures that Cage learned of Schoenberg and resolved to seek him out. In Paris, Cage had overheard Ernő Goldfinger telling someone that to become an architect, you had to devote yourself to it to the exclusion of all else. Upon hearing this, Cage quit—he wasn't ready to rule out all the other possibilities. But when Schoenberg asked him the same question, he said yes.

Going forward, Cage's entrepreneurialism—and his thriftiness—continued to create unexpected opportunities. Around 1940, while Cage was working on the faculty of the Cornish School of Music, in Seattle, a dancer asked him to compose a piece of music for an energetic solo dance she would be performing a few days later. The performance space only had a small grand piano for Cage to work with, but the dance called for something more primitive and percussive than he could coax out of the instrument. "I decided that what was wrong was the piano, not my efforts," Cage said. So Cage—whose father's career as a stay-at-home inventor had a profound influence on his music life*—resolved to alter the instrument, placing various objects between the strings to see what other sounds he could make. He tried newspapers, magazines, ashtrays, books, and a pie plate before settling on a small bolt, a screw with nuts, and some weather stripping. This experiment became the "prepared piano," Cage's earliest musical invention, which allowed him to create an ensemble's worth of sounds in a single instrument. The prepared piano became Cage's principal musical resource for the next decade, especially after he moved from Seattle to Chicago and then New -

---

* "I had the example every day of a person in the house inventing," Cage recalled. "And I knew that that was the only thing I would be able to do in the field of music."

York and discovered how difficult it was to assemble a proper ensemble in the city. "You can't get a group of people to work together in New York for any length of time, because they're all too busy making money," Cage said. "So that when I had to give a concert of percussion music at the Museum of Modern Art, I found that I couldn't get a full rehearsal—ever. Even for just a short time. So I threw my energy and everything into the prepared piano."

Cage's inventiveness also led him to one of the most unlikely money-making schemes in music or art history. It began, like so many artist schemes, with hunger. In the mid-1930s, Cage lived for a time in Carmel, California, where, short of cash as always, he went foraging for wild strawberries to supplement his meager diet. Instead of strawberries, he found mushrooms—and after doing some research at the local public library to determine if they were edible, he made the foraged mushrooms a staple of his diet. Later, this clever adaptation became a passion of Cage's: He would become a dedicated amateur mycologist, eventually building an extensive collection of books on the subject and joining several mycological societies. He came to see it as a useful corollary to his musical work, writing: "I have come to the conclusion that much can be learned about music by devoting oneself to the mushroom."

In the late 1950s, while on a six-month tour of Europe, Cage managed to turn this hobby to profit. A letter he wrote from Italy in late 1958 gives a hint of what was to come: "Will lecture here in Italian + concertize but most surprising is that I will probably be on a quiz show (mushrooms!) + come home rich! Of course that is a vague possibility but it looks p o s s i b l e." In fact, this is exactly what came to pass. Cage was accepted as a contestant on *Lascia o Raddoppia* (roughly: *Double or Nothing*), a hugely popular television game show, which invited contestants to answer questions on a subject of their choice; as long as they answered correctly, they would return week after week to answer more and more difficult questions for increasing amounts of cash. Cage appeared in five episodes in January–February 1959, answering questions on—of course—his beloved mushrooms. He also negotiated to put on a brief music performance for each episode he appeared in, and he quickly became a minor celebrity as a result of these appearances. The biographer David Revill writes that Cage

was besieged by autograph hunters and photographers and interviewed every day. . . . A little Italian girl gave him a good luck card,
"Buonviaggio et buoni funghi." The press depicted him as a classic
American, tall, square-jawed, "pleasantly reminiscent of Franken-
stein." Cage was a curiosity not only as an American, and one who
knew everything there was to know about mushrooms, but one
who performed such curious music on such strange instruments.

Week after week, Cage correctly answered the host's questions. In the
fifth and final week, he was asked to name every type of white-spored
mushroom. In a soundproof booth in front of a live audience, Cage calmly
listed them one by one, naming the final type just before his time ran out.
The forty-six-year-old composer walked away with five million lire, or
about $8,000 dollars—almost $90,000 at present-day values; it was, Cage
said, "the first consequential amount of money I'd ever earned"*—which
he used to purchase a Steinway piano for himself and a Volkswagen station wagon for his partner Merce Cunningham's dance company to use
when it toured.†

Going forward, Cage's love of mushrooms would provide additional
rivulets of income. The next spring, he would teach a course in New
York on mushroom identification. And he even dealt (non-psychedelic)
mushrooms for a time, selling them through a middleman to a pair of
food-service organizations that supplied high-end New York restaurants.
According to Revill, in one month in 1959 Cage made more than $200

---

* Remarkably, Cage wasn't the only mid-century New York artist to appear on a television game show. Two years
earlier, in 1957, the painter Larry Rivers had appeared on CBS's *The $64,000 Challenge*, a national sensation for its
record-high prize (more than a half million in today's dollars). The format was similar to *Lascia o Raddoppia*: The
show took two ordinary people with an extraordinary knowledge of a particular topic and had them face off against
each other, answering questions of increasing difficulty for increasing amounts of cash, one question per episode
over the course of a few weeks. (There were several pairs of contestants per episode.) The show's producers enlisted
Rivers to compete on the topic of "Painting 1850–1950," which could hardly have been a better fit: Rivers had
been immersing himself in that era's history for years. In a soundproof box in front of forty million viewers, Rivers
faced off against his competitor: a working jockey who was also an art history buff. In the end, both contestants
made it through the full series of questions and split the $64,000 prize.

† Cage and Cunningham were creative as well as life partners and frequently toured together. "That began from
'43 on," Cage said in an interview. "We gave more and more concerts and finally tours across the country, giving
programs. Mostly we didn't make money that way but we would make ends meet."

in this manner (more than $2,000 at present-day values), enough that he decided to invest $50 in a secondhand mushroom dryer.

+ + +

John Cage's career had several major turning points. There was his decision, at seventeen, to drop out of college and go to Europe, where he first learned of modern art and music; his discovery of the work of Arnold Schoenberg and his successful effort to study at the master's feet in Los Angeles; his invention of the prepared piano, which opened up a world of musical possibilities and brought him widening opportunities, though not much income. ("I discovered that no matter how well-known you are, it doesn't mean anything in terms of employment or willingness to further your work or do anything," Cage said of this period.) Later, in the 1950s, there was his embrace of Zen Buddhism, and the incorporation of "chance processes" into his work, starting with *Music of Changes*—a four-volume solo piece for piano composed using the *I Ching*—in 1951 and continuing the following year with "4'33"," still his most famous piece, for which a pianist sits silently at the piano for four minutes and thirty-three seconds, while the audience listens to whatever sounds naturally occur in the performance space. With this turn to "nonintentional music," Cage thought that he had found a way to transcend his own personality and taste, which he increasingly considered a rather flimsy basis for art. "Chance is a leap," he said, "out of reach of one's grasp of oneself."

Was this artistic leap enabled by an earlier leap of faith regarding his finances? Cage had always tried to avoid getting a traditional day job. Before *Music of Changes*, he said, "I only took other employment if it was absolutely necessary, to eat; but I could go a long time without working, I mean without getting a job." But he would look for work when necessary—until a certain point at the beginning of 1951, when he spent two or three days looking for a job and didn't come up with anything, and decided: no more. He resolved, he said, "to limit my work to my composition, not to look for another kind of work"—and "if necessary, to die as a result." If this sounds overdramatic, he wasn't kidding: Working to finish the incredibly labor-intensive composition process for *Music of Changes* and at the same time experiencing an all-time low in his personal finances, Cage at one point gave instructions to his collaborator David Tudor on how he could finish the piece in the event of his death.

This may be the ultimate artist scheme: to insist that one's art will keep one afloat financially even as it shows no indication of doing so—to take the leap "out of reach of one's grasp of oneself" that Cage was always seeking. In his case, it mostly worked out. There was the unexpected infusion of mushroom money at the end of the 1950s, and later he became increasingly in demand as a lecturer, which covered his expenses and, as his fame grew, eventually allowed him to support his parents in their old age. (For Cage, lecturing was a natural extension of his art, which always had a bit of a crusading quality. Even so, he wrote in a 1966 letter, "I long for the opportunity to sit, relatively still, writing and composing.")

In other cases, let's admit, the leap-of-faith scheme does not work out as well. In 2019, a public radio program called *The Organist* broadcast an almost hour-long episode on the financial life of the poet Bernadette Mayer a few years before her death in 2022 at age seventy-seven. Mayer was one of the most important poets of her generation, the only woman included in the landmark 1970 *Anthology of New York Poets* ("The only woman. I thought that was weirdly stupid," she said), who published more than thirty books of poetry and prose and whose poetry workshops were a formative influence on legions of young writers. To kick off the episode, the host, a younger poet and artist named Rachel James, asked an important question about this important poet: "Why is Bernadette Mayer so broke?" She continued: "Maybe I was naïve to think if you're pretty famous and you've been influential in the literary scene and in the art world for over five decades, and you're living, you'd be set. And *set* is relative, but living in the United States you'd make more than seventeen thousand a year, which is what Bernadette made last year."

Actually, it's not much of a mystery why Bernadette Mayer was broke. As she told James, "As a poet I always tried to earn a living as a poet. I know it's stupid, I know it can't be done. But I figured—let's do it." (She said something similar to a visiting *New Yorker* writer in 2016. "I'm an idiot: I keep writing poems, trying to make money.") That wasn't the *only* thing she did for money—over the years, she taught school in Harlem, worked as a proofreader for Random House, edited magazines and books, and served as director of the St. Mark's Poetry Project from 1980 to 1984, to mention just a few of her various jobs—but to an uncommon degree Mayer tried to make poetry pay, and endured the consequences of it mostly not paying very much, and was perhaps inspired by this fundamental paradox. "I have never lost interest in writing poetry," she told *The Organist*, "maybe because it's so impecunious."

If John Cage approached obstacles with sunny fortitude, Mayer's response was more like a cackle. She had a long history of stubborn refusal. Growing up in Ridgewood, on the line between Brooklyn and Queens, Mayer's strictly Roman Catholic parents forbade her and her sister from socializing with any non-Catholics. An interviewer once asked Mayer what it was like to be raised in such a household. "I was in this weird position that I was just learning about the world," she replied. "I thought, *Well, if this is the way the world is . . . fuck it!* I couldn't believe that people could behave this way." After an oppressive childhood came a tragic adolescence: Mayer's father died from a cerebral hemorrhage when she was twelve, her mother from breast cancer two years later; and then the uncle who became Mayer and her sister's legal guardian died as well. "Everybody died by the time I was sixteen," Mayer wrote. "My relatives were afraid that if they adopted me, they would die too."

After a brief, miserable stint at a Roman Catholic college, Mayer switched to the New School for Social Research in Manhattan, where she took a poetry class with Bill Berkson and found her path as a poet of the everyday, in all its beauty, absurdity, and bafflement. (Asked how she survived after losing both her parents, she said, "I don't know, I was just fascinated by the world, so I guess that's how I survived.") She seemed to be able to live in the present to an uncommon degree, in 1978 composing *Midwinter Day*, a book-length poem written on a single day, about that day, which her fellow poet Alice Notley called "an epic poem about a daily routine." Above all, she stuck to her honest reaction to things and refused to make sense where she saw none. A line from one of her poems: "i write unbalanced poetry, i cannot balance my checkbook, nor do i have one."

That last part is true, or was true for a long time. Speaking to *The Organist*, Mayer's eldest daughter, Marie, said: "Bernadette didn't have a bank account. She kept her money, actually, in a book of Shakespeare's sonnets." Reminded of this, Mayer laughed and explained her reasoning: "So my kids always knew where to find the money. It was in the sonnets. Sometimes a lot, sometimes a little. What better book to put it in?"

According to the poet Anselm Berrigan—the son of the married poets Alice Notley and Ted Berrigan, close friends of Mayer's—this was normal in the East Village of the 1970s, or at least among the poets he observed. "I mean, we didn't have a telephone," he told *The Organist*. "My parents didn't have a bank account. When my father died, my mother only had about forty dollars. They would raise money on a regular basis." "Raising money" meant they were well and truly broke and needed to do something about it—and one of Ted Berrigan's favorite methods was selling letters from the famous writers he corresponded with. "My father would write to people, and then he'd get their letters back, and then he'd sell them," Anselm Berrigan explains. "He also forged signatures. He learned certain people's signatures and would then go and sell these things."

Berrigan also taught Mayer to forge *his* signature, so if she ever needed to sell his books for money she could get a little more for them. A good trick—but Mayer always wished for more radical and durable solutions to the money problem. In a 1978 letter to her sister, the artist Rosemary Mayer, written on Veterans Day, Bernadette wondered why there wasn't "a poets and artists day which is a so-called federal holiday on which the post office would be open 24 hours instead of closed and the banks would give us money free & the market free food and so on?" And she was an advocate of something like universal basic income, with her own exceedingly simple calculation for how it could work: Take all the income that everyone in the United States makes in a year and divide it by the number of people in the country, including babies, and there you have it, done. "Give everybody everything," she wrote in a 2016 poem, and meant it.

+ + +

Working on this book, I wanted to give you, dear reader, everything, too—everything that I turned up in my endless reading and thinking about artists' financial lives; every anecdote about squandered inheritances, unbearable day jobs, capricious patrons, and unlikely fundraising schemes; every brilliant and foolhardy way that artists circumnavigated this eternal, insoluble dilemma—making art *and* making a living, how?—and yet, as we arrive at the end, all I can think about are the many stories that I did not manage to squeeze into the book as it now stands. What about the German choreographer Pina Bausch, who, at age eighteen, received a scholarship to study dance for one year at the Juilliard School, in New York, and who was so inspired that she resolved "to stay two years on the money that was only intended for one," a feat that she accomplished through extreme frugality, for a time living "almost exclusively on ice cream"? Or the German-born English novelist Sybille Bedford, whom *The New York Times* once described as "a world-class writer and a world-class freeloader," and who indeed seemed to possess a special gift for attracting her friends' financial assistance, which proved a crucial counterbalance to her self-described "great natural sloth" as a writer? Or the seventeenth-century playwright Aphra Behn, the first Englishwoman to earn a living solely by her pen, who, before she found her way to the London stage, found employment as a spy for King Charles II, landing herself in debtor's prison when the king's intermediaries failed to pay her as expected? Or the English Romantic poet Samuel Taylor Coleridge, who was promised a generous lifetime stipend by two heirs to the Wedgwood pottery fortune, but whose worsening opium habit prompted his disillusioned patrons to scale back and finally cut off his allowance altogether? Or the American short-story writer and novelist John O'Hara, who once began a letter to *New Yorker* editor Harold Ross by writing, "I want more money I want more money I want more money I want more money I want more money I want more money I want more money I want more money I want more money I want more money I want more money"? Or the writer Dorothy Parker, who described the money she made in Hollywood as "like small ice in your hand. It all vanishes. That's all"? Or, for that matter, the many other fiction writers who turned to Hollywood for an easier payday—

including Nelson Algren, William Faulkner, F. Scott Fitzgerald, Aldous Huxley, and Nathanael West—and then, more often than not, found that it was hardly as easy as they had imagined? Or the Indian filmmaker Satyajit Ray, who said of shooting a film in primitive conditions in Calcutta (without air-conditioning, with rolling blackouts citywide, with ineffective soundproofing, and with pigeons roosting in the roof of the studio, which had to be periodically driven away with stones): "After all, we do have the bare essentials—and the rest is here, in my head. I don't think you need any more than that really"? Or the poet Kenneth Rexroth, who once griped, "I've had it with these cheap sons of bitches who claim they love poetry but never buy a book"? Or the Venetian painter Titian, who routinely set uninspiring commissions aside, neglecting them for months, years, or even decades, and whose delays prompted the powerful Duke of Ferrara to assign one of his ambassadors to shadow Titian for more than a year, delivering up-to-the-minute reports on the artist's activities, health, moods, and the likelihood of the duke's painting being completed (which finally occurred twenty months after Titian had promised to begin it "that very morning")? Or the several dozen other artists I researched and planned to squeeze into this book, somehow, even as it became more and more apparent that doing so would not only be unwieldy and impractical but almost literally impossible?

At various points, the pressure I felt to create a container for all these stories, and make some kind of sense of them, truly overwhelmed me, especially as draft after draft of this book really did not cohere and my own personal finances—ironically or appropriately, I could never decide—threatened to implode from the ever-lengthening delay. (I originally budgeted eighteen months for this project; I'm writing this sentence near the midpoint of month fifty-three.) And it was during one of those moments of low confidence that Lynette, the effusively cynical Substack commenter we met in "True Fans," left her series of disdainful replies about how writers and artists need to stop asking for a handout from hardworking folks like herself, which I didn't know how to answer at the time. Well, maybe this book is my answer—not because it shows how generous and wise artists have always been but because it shows what a funny, fretful business it is, trying to fund a life as an artist, and I hope celebrates the figures who hung in there anyway and remained committed to their idiosyncratic personal visions. I think the reason Lynette got under my skin is that she felt like the avatar of a kind of stingy, withholding, resentful energy that seems to be trending in our society, when what I love about the artists in this book is their embrace of the opposite values: of possibility, of giving yourself permission, of staying true to your instincts and indulging them even when they lead someplace totally impractical—especially then—and asking necessity to wait while you figure things out, even if you never quite figure things out.

In a funny way, that's the attitude that finally allowed me to finish this book. So it took me a long time to get here, and it's still far from perfect. So what? Not being able to do something, and trying to do it anyway—this creates a certain kind of energy that's good for the work and perhaps good for the world, too. It's the energy of Arthur Schopenhauer squirming in frustration at the merchant's office in Hamburg; of Vincent van Gogh hitting Theo up for money just one more time; of John Cage and Bernadette Mayer resolving to make their art pay no matter what, even though it had very little chance of paying and, in fact, did not do so for long stretches; of Kathy Acker thinking aloud that "what we know of as 'life' is so thin and juiceless and boring, frankly—we're ground into nothing before we even start out!" Yes! The artist's first job is not to get ground into nothing before they even start out. And the artist's second job? To keep going, to not let money get in the way, or not for long, and when in doubt to remember what Charles Baudelaire wrote to his mother on December 20, 1855—asking for money again, of course—in what could really be every artist's message to their funders, their families, their friends, their community, the universe:

I won't say: "I beg you." I'll just say: "Have a little boldness and trust."

ACKNOWLEDGMENTS

This is a book about funding creative work, so it's only fair to start by thanking my wife, Rebecca, whose steady full-time income allowed me to have a very unsteady and frequently inadequate income while I carried this book through its much-lengthier-than-expected gestation process. I couldn't have completed it without her support; her discerning feedback on numerous iterations of the manuscript; her own long history of trying to make art and make a living, which exerted a subtle influence on every page; and the restorative joy of our daily life together.

I'm grateful to my editor, Jamie Raab, for her unflagging belief in this project, her unerring good judgment, and for telling me, at a crucial moment, perhaps the greatest thing an editor can say to a writer: "You're closer to being done than you think you are." (She was right.) Her colleagues at Celadon Books have been uniformly superb collaborators. I'm especially indebted to the book jacket designer, Evan Gaffney; the creative director, Anne Twomey; the text designer, Michelle McMillian; the production editor, Molly Bloom; the copy editor, Sara Robb; Anna Belle Hindenlang and Jaime Noven in publicity and marketing, respectively; and Margaux Kanamori for graciously and efficiently shepherding the book through its various phases. Thanks as well to Michael Cantwell for his careful attention to legal matters.

This book and my previous books may never have happened without my agent, Meg Thompson, who plucked me out of the blogosphere in 2009 and has skillfully and cheerfully guided me through the publishing world ever since. I'm also grateful to her colleague Tess Brown for her speedy assistance in all matters and to Sandy Hodgman for brilliantly arranging the foreign editions of my work.

Another person without whom this book might not exist: my therapist, who week after week evinces an amazing ability to convert insecurity into confidence, exasperation into resolve, confusion into insight. I'm grateful for her wisdom, intelligence, and humor.

Thanks to the Los Angeles Public Library, Walt's Bar, and Uno the dog.

When I was feeling really stuck on this project, I took an online workshop with the writer Sheila Heti during which she offered to help participants form local in-person writing groups. Through that, I found myself among a group of terrific Los Angeles writers whose feedback and enthusiasm proved incredibly helpful to moving this project along. My sincere thanks to Sheila and to Joshua Conkel, Maddie Connors, Cora Currier, Liz DeWolf, Anna Furman, Sammy Loren, Radhika Menon, William Nedved, Agatha Palma, Neha Potalia, Lindsay Reeve, and Annakeara Stinson.

Have I mentioned that this book took far longer than I anticipated? Deepest gratitude to my friends and family for putting up with my frequent spells of moodiness and distraction during its overlong production, and for their loving support of everything I do. My writing brain is a product of my mom's warmth and creativity, my dad's intelligence and tenacity, my stepmom's great taste—how lucky was I to be introduced, as a teenager, to Walker Percy, John Kennedy Toole, and *The New Yorker*?— and my brother's empathy and bonhomie. Thanks as well to Antoinette Albano and Pennell Whitney, my generous patrons in Portland, Oregon, and the Poconos; Albert Chu, Robert Kett, and Acorn for all the late-afternoon beers at picnic tables; and Anna Brones, Matt Evans, and Sabrina Y. Smith for the cathartic kvetching sessions.

Finally, I want to offer heartfelt thanks to the readers of my *Subtle Maneuvers* newsletter, many of whom have written over the years with research leads, notes of encouragement, and offers of assistance (special thanks to Laura Tucker for her volunteer editorial consulting at a moment when I really needed it), and who have made me feel part of a true community of creative strivers wriggling along on our weird, impossible projects. What a privilege—thank you.

NOTES

This book is based on material I found in biographies and interviews, in my subjects' published diaries, journals, and letters, in their autobiographies and memoirs, in documentaries about their work, and in their friends' and colleagues' published recollections. I'm grateful to the many scholars, editors, translators, journalists, and publishers who have made this material available to the public. To credit their work, I have done as follows: After the first appearance of a subject's name, I have supplied the main source or sources I used to write about them, with a short explanatory note when needed. Then I have cited the source of every quotation in the text. For readers who want to know more about a particular figure, I hope this will also provide useful suggestions for further reading.

INTRODUCTION

1   **Arthur Schopenhauer:** R. J. Hollingdale, introduction to Arthur Schopenhauer, *Essays and Aphorisms*, trans. and ed. R. J. Hollingdale (1970; repr. Penguin, 2004), Kindle, 9–35.

2   **"the attitude towards":** Hollingdale, 28.

3   **"like a pauper":** Quoted in John Richardson, *A Life of Picasso: The Cubist Rebel, 1907–1916* (Alfred A. Knopf, 2007), 43.

3   **the same routine:** Hollingdale, 24–25.

5   **An excellent, if depressing, book:** William Deresiewicz, *The Death of the Artist: How Creators Are Struggling to Survive in the Age of Billionaires and Big Tech* (Henry Holt, 2020).

6   **"financial stress is":** Anne Trubek, "Debt, Anxiety, and James Patterson," *Notes from a Small Press*, June 14, 2022, https://notesfromasmallpress.substack.com/p/debt-anxiety-and-james -patterson.

INHERITANCE

11   **Fernando Pessoa:** Richard Zenith, *Pessoa: A Biography* (Liveright, 2021). The story of Pessoa's inheritance, Ibis, and its aftermath is all from Zenith's biography.

12   **"a huffy, slightly insulting letter":** Zenith, 245.

12   **a "commercial code":** Zenith, 247.

12   **"with his face":** Zenith, 279.

12   **"In September":** Zenith, 281.

14   **"In less than":** Zenith, 286.

14   **"some part of him":** Zenith, 305.

14   **"How can I think":** Fernando Pessoa, "Sonnet V," *35 Sonnets* (Project Gutenberg, 2006), https://www.gutenberg.org/ebooks/19978.

14   **Virginia Woolf:** Hermione Lee, *Virginia Woolf* (Vintage, 1999); Phyllis Rose, *Woman of Letters: A Life of Virginia Woolf* (Oxford University Press, 1978); Leonard Woolf, *Beginning Again: An Autobiography of the Years 1911–1918* (Hogarth Press, 1964); Leonard Woolf, *Downhill All the Way: An Autobiography of the Years 1919–1939* (Hogarth Press, 1967); Virginia Woolf, "A Sketch of the Past," *Moments of Being*, 2nd ed., ed. Jeanne Schulkind (Mariner Classics, 1985), 64–159.

15   **"born not of rich parents":** Virginia Woolf, "A Sketch of the Past," 65.

15   **"Over the whole week":** Virginia Woolf, "A Sketch of the Past," 144.

16   **"Like my father":** Virginia Woolf to Ethel Smyth, January 12, 1941, in *The Letters of Virginia Woolf, Volume Six: 1936–1941*, ed. Nigel Nicolson and Joanne Trautmann (Harcourt Brace, 1980), 459.

16   **"a penniless Jew":** Virginia Woolf to Violet Dickinson, June 4, 1912, in *The Letters of Virginia Woolf, Volume One: 1888–1912*, ed. Nigel Nicolson and Joanne Trautmann (Harcourt Brace, 1975), 500.

17   **"Both would work":** Lee, 321.

17   **Leonard tallied the earnings:** Leonard Woolf, *Beginning Again* and *Downhill All the Way*. All the financial figures in this section come from these third and fourth volumes of Leonard's five-volume autobiography.

17   **"Virginia was 40":** Leonard Woolf, *Downhill All the Way*, 17.

18   **Alison Light points out:** Alison Light, *Mrs. Woolf and the Servants: An Intimate History of Domestic Life in Bloomsbury* (Bloomsbury Press, 2008), Kindle, loc. 2774 of 5765.

18   **"After 1928 we":** Leonard Woolf, *Downhill All the Way*, 145.

19   **"But, rather quickly":** Lee, 359.

19   **"a woman must":** Virginia Woolf, *A Room of One's Own* (1929; repr. Penguin, 2004), Kindle, 1.

20   **"Neither of us":** Leonard Woolf, *Downhill All the Way*, 156–57.

21   **Charles Baudelaire:** Rosemary Lloyd, *Baudelaire's World* (Cornell University Press, 2002); Rosemary Lloyd, *Charles Baudelaire* (Reaktion Books, 2008); Rosemary Lloyd, ed. and trans., *The Selected Letters of Charles Baudelaire* (University of Chicago Press, 1986); Joanna Richardson, *Baudelaire* (St. Martin's Press, 1994); Lewis Piaget Shanks, *Baudelaire: Flesh and Spirit* (Little, Brown, 1930).

22   **"You've told me":** Baudelaire to Caroline Aupick, summer 1844, *Selected Letters*, 24.

23   **"I'm writing to you":** Baudelaire to Caroline Aupick, March 26, 1853, *Selected Letters*, 54.

23   **"the horrible life":** Baudelaire to Caroline Aupick, February 19, 1858, *Selected Letters*, 107.

23   **"that shocking error":** Baudelaire to Caroline Aupick, October 11, 1860, *Selected Letters*, 159.

23   **"I need to be saved":** Baudelaire to Caroline Aupick, May 6, 1861, *Selected Letters*, 169.

24   **"When I'm unfortunate":** Baudelaire to Caroline Aupick, December 25, 1861, *Selected Letters*, 177–78.

24   **"Habit alone can":** Baudelaire to Caroline Aupick, June 3, 1863, *Selected Letters*, 194.

24   **"The great aim":** Baudelaire to Caroline Aupick, November 25, 1863, *Selected Letters*, 198.

24   **"I've acquired the":** Baudelaire to Caroline Aupick, December 31, 1863, *Selected Letters*, 200.

24 **"Truly, I consider"**: Baudelaire to Caroline Aupick, December 31, 1863, *Selected Letters*, 201.

25 **"saw his poems"**: Richardson, xiii.

25 **"I have in my head"**: Baudelaire to Caroline Aupick, February 19, 1858, *Selected Letters*, 108.

25 **"eking out a"**: Virginia Woolf, "George Moore," *Vogue*, June 1925, in *The Death of the Moth and Other Essays*, 2nd ed. (Hogarth Press, 1942), 103.

25 **"Because the form"**: Baudelaire to Armand Fraisse, February 18, 1860, *Selected Letters*, 148.

25 **"he came and went"**: Richard Zenith, introduction to Fernando Pessoa, *The Book of Disquiet*, ed. and trans. Richard Zenith (Penguin, 2001), Kindle, loc. 133 of 8273.

26 **"Opportunity is like"**: Pessoa, *The Book of Disquiet*, 272.

ALLOWANCE

27 **Paul Cézanne**: Alex Danchev, *Cézanne: A Life* (Pantheon, 2012), Kindle; Ambroise Vollard, *Cézanne*, trans. Harold L. Van Doren (1937; repr. Dover, 1984).

27 **"had not made"**: Vollard, 57.

28 **"installed himself in"**: Danchev, 44.

28 **"moneylending bordering on"**: Danchev, 44.

28 **"Monsieur Cézanne asked"**: Vollard, 14.

29 **"Alas, I took"**: Quoted in Danchev, 57.

29 **"Paul will be"**: Quoted in Danchev, 50.

30 **"A room at"**: Quoted in Vollard, 19.

30 **"it was Cézanne's"**: Vollard, 25.

30 **"The banker Cézanne"**: Quoted in Vollard, 23.

31 **"It would be"**: Danchev, 52.

32 **"*Nota-Bene*: Papa"**: Quoted in Danchev, 155.

33 **"That armchair in"**: Quoted in Danchev, 321.

33 **Louise Nevelson**: Laurie Lisle, *Louise Nevelson: A Passionate Life* (Summit, 1990); Louise Nevelson, prologue to Arnold B. Glimcher, *Louise Nevelson* (Secher & Warburg, 1972), 19–24; Louise Nevelson with Diana MacKown, *Dawns + Dusks* (Charles Scribner's Sons, 1976); Laurie Wilson, *Louise Nevelson: Light and Shadow* (Thames & Hudson, 2016).

33 **"earliest, earliest childhood"**: Nevelson, *Dawns + Dusks*, 1.

34 **"Who in this absurd"**: Quoted in Wilson, 391.

34 **"I explained very carefully"**: Nevelson, *Dawns + Dusks*, 31.

34 **"My husband's family"**: Nevelson, prologue to Glimcher, 20.

34 **"I wasn't equipped"**: Quoted in Lisle, 57.

35 **"dreaded" being home**: Quoted in Lisle, 57.

35 **"I don't think"**: Quoted in Lisle, 57.

35 **"I knew where"**: Nevelson, prologue to Glimcher, 20.

35 **"It is always"**: Nevelson, *Dawns + Dusks*, 95.

35 **"For thirty years"**: Nevelson, *Dawns + Dusks*, 94.

36 **"an enormous, four-story"**: Nevelson, *Dawns + Dusks*, 96.

36 **"so there was"**: Nevelson, *Dawns + Dusks*, 96.

37 **"had an account"**: Wilson, 132.

37 **"I trained myself"**: Nevelson, *Dawns + Dusks*, 73.

37 **A story related by Nevelson**: Nevelson, prologue to Glimcher, 20.

38 **Christopher Isherwood**: Katherine Bucknell, *Christopher Isherwood Inside Out* (Farrar, Straus and Giroux, 2024); Christopher Isherwood, *Christopher and His Kind* (1976; repr.

Farrar, Straus and Giroux, 2015); Christopher Isherwood, *Diaries, Volume One: 1939–1960*, ed. Katherine Bucknell (Michael di Capua Books, 1998).

39 **"Henry was the"**: Isherwood, *Christopher and His Kind*, 36.

39 **"Christopher was expected"**: Isherwood, *Christopher and His Kind*, 37.

40 **"He had once"**: Isherwood, *Christopher and His Kind*, 37.

40 **"During the years"**: Stephen Spender, *World Within World: The Autobiography of Stephen Spender* (St. Martin's Press, 1951), 121.

40 **"Sometimes [Isherwood] was"**: Spender, 126.

41 **"always approved of"**: Quoted in Bucknell, 212.

41 **"keep his mouth"**: Isherwood, *Christopher and His Kind*, 38.

41 **"Thus Christopher was"**: Isherwood, *Christopher and His Kind*, 38.

41 **"the novel that"**: Bucknell, 386.

41 **"It is too late"**: Isherwood, July 12, 1940, *Diaries*, 103.

42 **"Poor Henry—"**: Isherwood, July 12, 1940, *Diaries*, 103.

THE ART OF MOOCHING

43 **George Bernard Shaw:** Michael Holroyd, *Bernard Shaw: The One-Volume Definitive Edition* (W. W. Norton, 2006), Kindle; George Bernard Shaw, preface to *The Irrational Knot* (1905; repr. Project Gutenberg, 2004), https://www.gutenberg.org/ebooks/11354.

43 **"Because it consoles"**: Franz Kafka, October 26, 1911, in *Diaries, 1910–1923*, ed. Max Brod (1948; repr. Schocken Books, 1976), 90–91.

44 **"only to the extent"**: Kafka, October 26, 1911, *Diaries*, 91.

44 **"mesmeric conductor"**: Quoted in Holroyd, 30.

44 **"Do you know"**: George Bernard Shaw, *Misalliance* (1910; repr. Project Gutenberg, 2008), https://www.gutenberg.org/files/943/943-h/943-h.htm.

45 **"I made good"**: Quoted in Lewis Hyde, *The Gift: Creativity and the Artist in the Modern World* (1979; repr. Vintage, 2007), 66.

45 **"drudging in her"**: Shaw, *Irrational Knot*.

45 **"monstrous"**: Shaw, *Irrational Knot*.

45 **"his club, his university"**: Holroyd, 76.

46 **"inestimable"**: Holroyd, 76.

46 **James Joyce:** Kevin Birmingham, *The Most Dangerous Book: The Battle for James Joyce's "Ulysses"* (Penguin Books, 2014); Richard Ellmann, *James Joyce*, rev. ed. (Oxford University Press, 1982); Richard Ellmann, introduction to Stanislaus Joyce, *My Brother's Keeper: James Joyce's Early Years*, ed. Richard Ellmann (Viking Press, 1958). The bulk of this section comes from Ellmann's biography, with valuable additional context from Birmingham and from Ellmann's introduction to Stanislaus Joyce's memoir.

47 **"Underneath the excesses"**: Ellmann, introduction to *My Brother's Keeper*, xviii.

47 **"a most villainous"**: Quoted in Ellmann, *James Joyce*, 127.

48 **"I should be"**: Quoted in Ellmann, *James Joyce*, 132.

48 **"a naval Siberia"**: Quoted in Ellmann, *James Joyce*, 186.

49 **"extraordinary moral courage"**: Quoted in Ellmann, *James Joyce*, 137.

49 **"Stanislaus was punctual"**: Ellmann, introduction to *My Brother's Keeper*, xvi.

49 **"You who slid"**: James Joyce to Nora Barnacle, December 3, 1909, in Nadja Spiegelman, "James Joyce's Love Letters to His 'Dirty Little Fuckbird,'" *Paris Review*, February 2, 2018, https://www.theparisreview.org/blog/2018/02/02/james-joyces-love-letters-dirty-little-fuckbird/.

50 **"The tax collector":** Quoted in Birmingham, 49–50.

50 **"James saw no":** Ellmann, *James Joyce*, 213.

50 **various additional saintlike patrons:** Birmingham.

51 **Vincent van Gogh:** Julian Bell, *Van Gogh: A Power Seething* (Amazon, 2015); Leo Jansen, Hans Luijten, and Nienke Bakker, eds., *Vincent Van Gogh: The Letters* (Van Gogh Letters Project, 2009), https://vangoghletters.org/; Steven Naifeh and Gregory White Smith, *Van Gogh: The Life* (Random House, 2011). My characterization of Van Gogh's family history and path to becoming an artist is based primarily on Naifeh and Smith's biography, with additional context from Bell. For the letters, I used the digital version of the edition published by the Van Gogh Letters Project in 2009.

53 **"Thank you for":** Vincent van Gogh to Theo van Gogh, October 8, 1888, *Van Gogh: The Letters*, https://vangoghletters.org/vg/letters/let699/letter.html.

54 **"plaintive, coercive arguments":** Naifeh and Smith, 216.

54 **"an unending cycle":** Naifeh and Smith, 270.

54 **Theo was in a good position:** "Biographical & Historical Context: The Financial Backgrounds," *Van Gogh: The Letters*, https://vangoghletters.org/vg/context_3.html. All the details about Theo's finances come from the breakdown of his income and expenditures provided here.

55 **"Everything gets sold":** Quoted in Naifeh and Smith, 65.

55 **"One can't present":** Vincent van Gogh to Theo van Gogh, November 26–27, 1882, *Van Gogh: The Letters*, https://vangoghletters.org/vg/letters/let288/letter.html.

56 **"*No*, and a thousand":** Vincent van Gogh to Theo van Gogh, October 10 or 11, 1888, *Van Gogh: The Letters*, https://vangoghletters.org/vg/letters/let702/letter.html.

57 **"I have high hopes":** Jo van Gogh–Bonger, February 24, 1892, in *Diaries Jo Bonger* (Van Gogh Museum, 2019), https://bongerdiaries.org/dagboek_jo_4_section_2.

ODD JOBS

61 **Grace Hartigan:** Cathy Curtis, *Restless Ambition: Grace Hartigan, Painter* (Oxford University Press, 2015), Kindle; Mary Gabriel, *Ninth Street Women: Lee Krasner, Elaine de Kooning, Grace Hartigan, Joan Mitchell, and Helen Frankenthaler: Five Painters and the Movement That Changed Modern Art* (Little, Brown, 2018); William T. La Moy and Joseph P. McCaffrey, eds., *The Journals of Grace Hartigan* (Syracuse University Press, 2009), Kindle.

61 **the "most celebrated":** Quoted in Curtis, 1.

61 **"To be truthful":** Interview with Cindy Nemser, *Art Talk: Conversations with 15 Women Artists*, rev. ed. (Westview Press, 1995), 150.

62 **"the family often":** Curtis, 10.

62 **"I married the":** Quoted in Gabriel, 243.

62 **"conscious of art":** Quoted in Gabriel, 243.

62 **"It was love":** Quoted in Curtis, 26.

63 **"During one whirlwind":** Curtis, 39.

64 **"such vitality that":** Quoted in Curtis, 76.

64 **"Getting enough money":** La Moy and McCaffrey, April 17, 1951, loc. 283 of 2260.

65 **"I think I'm incapable":** La Moy and McCaffrey, June 6, 1953, loc. 1097 of 2260.

65 **to "live & paint":** La Moy and McCaffrey, June 19, 1953, loc. 1117 of 2260.

65 **"working as a file clerk":** La Moy and McCaffrey, May 23, 1951, loc. 317 of 2260.

65 **"The last month":** La Moy and McCaffrey, October 3, 1951, loc. 377 of 2260.

65 **"A whole month"**: La Moy and McCaffrey, March 5, 1952, loc. 463 of 2260.

65 **"Any kind of 'success'"**: La Moy and McCaffrey, March 29, 1952, loc. 494 of 2260.

65 **"Tuesday I begin"**: La Moy and McCaffrey, April 18, 1952, loc. 534 of 2260.

66 **"steady, endless poverty"**: La Moy and McCaffrey, March 6, 1953, loc. 960 of 2260.

66 **"I'm working in"**: La Moy and McCaffrey, December 17, 1951, loc. 421 of 2260.

66 **"They used to"**: Quoted in Gabriel, 329.

66 **"It takes more"**: La Moy and McCaffrey, April 9, 1952, loc. 525 of 2260.

66 **"My God how"**: La Moy and McCaffrey, November 28, 1951, loc. 410 of 2260.

66 **"Everything coming with"**: La Moy and McCaffrey, January 11, 1952, loc. 434 of 2260.

66 **"Back to work"**: La Moy and McCaffrey, March 31, 1952, loc. 501 of 2260.

66 **"The weather is singing"**: La Moy and McCaffrey, August 18, 1952, loc. 633 of 2260.

66 **"Of course I doubt"**: La Moy and McCaffrey, November 5, 1953, loc. 1303 of 2260.

66 **"I believe I am"**: La Moy and McCaffrey, December 6, 1952, loc. 848 of 2260.

66 **"worked at a job"**: La Moy and McCaffrey, December 6, 1952, loc. 858 of 2260.

67 **"tabulating job"**: La Moy and McCaffrey, May 20, 1953, loc. 1082 of 2260.

67 **"In a terrible state"**: La Moy and McCaffrey, May 20, 1953, loc. 1082 of 2260.

67 **Roberto Bolaño:** Natasha Wimmer, introduction to Roberto Bolaño, *The Savage Detectives*, trans. Natasha Wimmer (Picador, 2008), ix–xxiii.

67 **Jorge Luis Borges:** Jorge Luis Borges, "Autobiographical Notes," *New Yorker*, September 11, 1970, https://www.newyorker.com/magazine/1970/09/19/jorge-luis-borges-profile-autobiographical -notes.

67 **Charlotte Brontë:** Margaret Smith, ed., *The Letters of Charlotte Brontë, Volume One: 1829– 1847* (Clarendon Press, 1995).

67 **Octavia Butler:** Octavia Butler, *Bloodchild and Other Stories*, 2nd ed. (Seven Stories Press, 2005).

67 **Joseph Cornell:** Deborah Solomon, *Utopia Parkway: The Life and Work of Joseph Cornell* (Farrar, Straus and Giroux, 1997).

68 **Petah Coyne:** Telephone interview with the author, February 22, 2017. I interviewed Coyne for my previous book, *Daily Rituals: Women at Work* (Alfred A. Knopf, 2019).

68 **James Dickey:** Henry Hart, *James Dickey: The World as a Lie* (Picador, 2000).

68 **Philip Glass:** Lola Fadulu, "How Philip Glass Went from Driving Taxis to Composing," *The Atlantic*, April 20, 2018, https://www.theatlantic.com/business/archive/2018/04/philip-glass -taxi-driver-composer/558278/.

68 **Harriet Jacobs**: Jean Fagan Yellin, *Harriet Jacobs: A Life* (Basic Civitas Books, 2004).

68 **László Krasznahorkai:** Interview with Adam Thirlwell, "The Art of Fiction No. 240: László Krasznahorkai," *Paris Review*, Summer 2018, https://www.theparisreview.org/interviews /7177/the-art-of-fiction-no-240-laszlo-krasznahorkai.

68 **Agnes Martin:** Agnes Martin, "Agnes's Relevant Biography," in Arne Glimcher, *Agnes Martin: Paintings, Writings, Remembrances* (Phaidon, 2012), 242.

68 **Lorine Niedecker:** Jenny Penberthy, ed., *Lorine Niedecker: Collected Works* (University of California Press, 2002).

69 **Henry Taylor:** Bennett Simpson, ed., *Henry Taylor: B Side* (Museum of Contemporary Art, Los Angeles, 2022).

69 **Anthony Trollope:** Anthony Trollope, *An Autobiography* (1883; repr. Dodd, Mead, 1922).

69 **Kurt Vonnegut:** Dan Wakefield, ed., *Kurt Vonnegut: Letters* (Delacorte Press, 2012), Kindle.

69 **Robert Walser:** Susan Bernofsky, *Clairvoyant of the Small: The Life of Robert Walser* (Yale University Press, 2021).

69 **Tennessee Williams:** Lyle Leverich, *Tom: The Unknown Tennessee Williams* (Sceptre, 1995).

69   **"I was often unemployed":** Quoted in Carl Seelig, *Walks with Walser*, trans. Anne Posten (New Directions, 2017).

70   **"oatmeal and bacon ends":** Quoted in Curtis, ix.

70   **"Her prices remained":** Curtis, 162.

70   **"It would be impossible":** La Moy and McCaffrey, February 23, 1954, loc. 1532 of 2260.

70   **Emily Carr:** Emily Carr, *Growing Pains: The Autobiography of Emily Carr* (1945; repr. Rare Treasures, 2024), Kindle; Emily Carr, *The House of All Sorts* (Douglas & McIntyre, 2006), Kindle; Emily Carr, *Hundreds and Thousands: The Journals of Emily Carr* (Douglas & McIntyre, 2006), Kindle; Maria Tippett, *Emily Carr: A Biography* (1979; repr. Stoddart, 1994).

71   **"a cluster of":** Carr, *Growing Pains*, 232.

71   **"made my undies":** Carr, September 7, 1933, *Hundreds and Thousands*, 85.

72   **"I never painted":** Carr, *Growing Pains*, 263.

72   **"No matter how":** Carr, *Growing Pains*, 261.

72   **"*screwed* into the house":** Carr, *House of All Sorts*, 27.

72   **"she performed the":** Tippett, 120.

72   **"I loathed being":** Quoted in Tippett, 119.

72   **"those filthy tenants":** Quoted in Tippett, 248.

73   **"Oh dear, oh dear":** Carr, November 16, 1935, *Hundreds and Thousands*, 279.

73   **"Now go out":** Carr, November 16, 1935, *Hundreds and Thousands*, 281.

73   **Kathy Acker:** Chris Kraus, *After Kathy Acker: A Literary Biography* (Semiotext(e), 2017); Jason McBride, *Eat Your Mind: The Radical Life and Work of Kathy Acker* (Simon & Schuster, 2022), Kindle; Amy Scholder and Douglas A. Martin, eds., *Kathy Acker: The Last Interview and Other Conversations* (Melville House, 2018), Kindle.

73   **"A straight job":** Quoted in Maggie Doherty, "Kathy Acker's Art of Identity Theft," *New Yorker*, November 28, 2022, https://www.newyorker.com/magazine/2022/12/05/kathy-ackers -art-of-identity-theft.

74   **"You see people":** Interview with Sylvère Lotringer, 1989–90, *Last Interview*, 73.

74   **"I couldn't have cared":** Interview with Sylvère Lotringer, 1989–90, *Last Interview*, 81.

74   **"It was task work":** Interview with Sylvère Lotringer, 1989–90, *Last Interview*, 82.

74   **"I'm trying to get away":** Kathy Acker, *The Childlike Life of the Black Tarantula by the Black Tarantula*, 1973, in *Portrait of an Eye: Three Novels* (Grove Press, 1998), 86.

75   **"a whole range":** Interview with Andrea Juno and V. Vale, 1991, *Last Interview*, 154.

75   **"I was working":** Interview with Sylvère Lotringer, 1989–90, *Last Interview*, 77.

75   **"My last job":** Quoted in McBride, 163.

75   **"As soon as I":** Quoted in McBride, 163.

DOUBLE LIVES

77   **Wallace Stevens:** J. Donald Blount, ed., *The Contemplated Spouse: The Letters of Wallace Stevens to Elsie* (University of South Carolina Press, 2006); Peter Brazeau, *Parts of a World: Wallace Stevens Remembered* (Random House, 1983); Paul Mariani, *The Whole Harmonium: The Life of Wallace Stevens* (Simon & Schuster, 2016).

78   **"the business was":** Quoted in Blount, introduction to *The Contemplated Spouse*, 3.

78   **"He was only":** Mariani, 33.

78   **"I wish that I":** Wallace Stevens to Elsie Kachel Stevens, August 29, 1915, *The Contemplated Spouse*, 340.

79   **"quickly established":** Brazeau, 8.

79 **"I miss New-York":** Quoted in Brazeau, 7.

79 **"I have not had":** Quoted in Mariani, 121.

79 **his "royalties for":** Quoted in Mariani, 164.

79 **a "terrible blow":** Quoted in "Wallace Stevens," Poetry Foundation, https://www.poetry foundation.org/poets/wallace-stevens.

79 **"I rise at day-break":** Quoted in Mariani, 167.

80 **"He arrived at":** Marguerite Flynn in Brazeau, 34.

80 **"He most always":** Richard Sunbury in Brazeau, 38.

80 **"They're pretty indecipherable":** Interview with Lewis Nichols, "Talk with Mr. Stevens," *New York Times*, October 3, 1954, https://archive.nytimes.com/www.nytimes.com/books/97/12/21/home/stevens-talk.html.

80 **"He had a peculiar":** Richard Sunbury in Brazeau, 38.

81 **"I find that having":** Quoted in Milton J. Bates, *Wallace Stevens: A Mythology of Self* (University of California Press, 1985), 157.

81 **"Poetry and surety":** Interview with Nichols.

81 **"not even begun":** Quoted in Mariani, 344.

81 **"Please don't allow":** Quoted in Blount, introduction to *The Contemplated Spouse*, 19.

81 **William Carlos Williams:** Linda Welshimer Wagner, ed., *Interviews with William Carlos Williams: "Speaking Straight Ahead"* (New Directions, 1976); William Carlos Williams, *The Autobiography of William Carlos Williams* (Random House, 1951).

82 **"Would it add":** Williams, *Autobiography*, 49.

82 **"No one was ever":** Williams, *Autobiography*, 49.

82 **"it was money":** Williams, *Autobiography*, 51.

83 **"to give her":** Williams, *Autobiography*, 69.

83 **"elucidate" the interior:** Williams, *Autobiography*, 288.

83 **"my 'medicine' was":** Williams, *Autobiography*, 288–89.

83 **"The sheer sense":** Quoted in Linda Welshimer Wagner, introduction to *Interviews*, xi.

83 **"Five minutes, ten":** Williams, *Autobiography*, xiii–xiv.

83 **"Meanwhile I receive":** Quoted in "William Carlos Williams," Poetry Foundation, https://www.poetryfoundation.org/poets/william-carlos-williams.

84 **"In my case":** William Carlos Williams, "On Writing," *Interviews*, 84.

84 **"They do not grasp":** Williams, *Autobiography*, 359.

84 **"As far as the writing":** Williams, *Autobiography*, 359.

85 **Charles Ives:** Vivian Perlis, *Charles Ives Remembered: An Oral History* (Yale University Press, 1974); Jan Swafford, *Charles Ives: A Life with Music* (W. W. Norton, 1996).

85 **"funny money-man":** John Berryman, "Dream Song 219: So Long? Stevens," *The Dream Songs* (1969; repr. Farrar, Straus and Giroux, 2007), 238.

85 **"partially ashamed":** Quoted in Swafford, 55.

85 **"When other boys":** Quoted in Swafford, 55.

85 **"one of the finest":** Swafford, 134.

86 **"continue groping":** Swafford, 134.

86 **"to let the children":** Quoted in Swafford, 143.

86 **"It is still read":** Swafford, 203.

87 **"Mr. Ives would":** Christine Loring in Perlis, 116.

87 **"had learned to adjust":** Christine Loring in Perlis, 116.

88 **"Any artist who":** Bernard Herrmann in Perlis, 162.

88 **Franz Kafka:** Louis Begley, *The Tremendous World I Have Inside My Head: Franz Kafka: A*

Biographical Essay (Atlas, 2008); Max Brod, *Franz Kafka: A Biography*, 2nd ed., trans. G. Humphreys Roberts and Richard Winston (Schocken Books, 1960); Franz Kafka, *Diaries, 1910–1923*, ed. Max Brod, trans. Joseph Kresh and Martin Greenberg (1948; repr. Schocken Books, 1976); Franz Kafka, *Letters to Felice*, ed. Erich Heller and Jürgen Born, trans. James Stern and Elisabeth Duckworth (Schocken Books, 1973).

88 **"Kafka's plan"**: Begley, 27.

88 **"Law was the"**: Quoted in Begley, 27.

89 **"supervisors were"**: Begley, 29.

89 **"19 February"**: Kafka, February 19, 1911, *Diaries*, 37–38.

90 **"most of the time"**: Kafka, October 4, 1911, *Diaries*, 62–63.

90 **"I finish nothing"**: Kafka, October 17, 1911, *Diaries*, 80.

90 **"I explain it"**: Kafka, November 5, 1911, *Diaries*, 105.

90 **"a room more like"**: Begley, 19.

90 **"the very headquarters"**: Kafka, November 5, 1911, *Diaries*, 104.

91 **"For the past six"**: Franz Kafka to Felice Bauer, November 1, 1912, *Letters to Felice*, 22.

91 **"The truth was"**: Begley, 44.

91 **"Only *in this way*"**: Kafka, September 23, 1912, *Diaries*, 213.

91 **"In one of the corridors"**: Franz Kafka to Felice Bauer, November 1, 1912, *Letters to Felice*, 22.

92 **"I stood at the window"**: Quoted in Brod, 93.

92 **"and so find a means"**: Kafka, March 9, 1914, *Diaries*, 264.

93 **"I shall never"**: Franz Kafka, "Investigations of a Dog," trans. Willa and Edwin Muir, in *The Complete Stories*, ed. Nahum N. Glatzer (Schocken Books, 1971), 309–10.

CULTURE WORKERS

94 **"Do not aspire"**: Quoted in "Accept Crisis and Enjoy It, Advises Famed Author," *New Haven Register*, October 19, 1958, in *Conversations with Thornton Wilder*, ed. Jackson R. Bryer (University Press of Mississippi, 1992), 83.

94 **"An outside job"**: Cyril Connolly, *Enemies of Promise*, rev. ed. (1949; repr. University of Chicago Press, 2008), 88–89.

95 **"When it came"**: Max Brod, *Franz Kafka: A Biography*, 2nd ed., trans. G. Humphreys Roberts and Richard Winston (Schocken Books, 1960), 78–79.

95 **Frank O'Hara**: Brad Gooch, *City Poet: The Life and Times of Frank O'Hara* (Alfred A. Knopf, 1993); Joe LeSueur, *Digressions on Some Poems by Frank O'Hara* (Farrar, Straus and Giroux, 2003).

96 **"Often this poet"**: Frank O'Hara, *Lunch Poems* (City Lights, 1964), back cover.

96 **"It seemed like Frank"**: Interview with Carl Little, "An Interview with James Schuyler," *Agni*, no. 37 (1993), https://www.jstor.org/stable/23009297.

96 **"Stationed at one"**: Gooch, 207–8.

97 **"it was still"**: Gooch, 258.

97 **"As far as I"**: LeSueur, xv.

97 **"I'm not saying"**: Frank O'Hara, "Personism: A Manifesto," September 3, 1959, in *Standing Still and Walking in New York*, ed. Donald Allen (Grey Fox Press, 1983), 110.

97 **"led later commentators"**: LeSueur, 275–76.

97 **Others included**: Michelle Harvey, "Art Work: Former Famous Staff," *MoMA Inside/Out* (blog), July 1, 2010, https://www.moma.org/explore/inside_out/2010/07/01/art-work-famous

-former-staff/. These two paragraphs describing various artists who worked at MoMA—and the quotes from Lucy Lippard and Sol LeWitt—all come from this MoMA blog post.

98 **Jeff Koons:** Interview with Claire Dienes and Lilian Tone, Museum of Modern Art Oral History Program, May 26, 1999, https://www.moma.org/momaorg/shared/pdfs/docs/learn/archives /transcript_koons.pdf; *The Jeff Koons Show*, documentary, YouTube video, 49:44, posted by Kino Lorber, August 30, 2022, https://www.youtube.com/watch?v=y4bgLQm7u8Y; Alice Rawsthorn, "Mr Big Stuff: Jeff Koons at Work and Play," *Esquire*, February 7, 2019, https:// www.esquire.com/uk/design/a26189100/mr-big-stuff-jeff-koons-at-work-and-play/; Ingrid Sischy, "Jeff Koons Is Back!," *Vanity Fair*, July 2014, https://archive.vanityfair.com/article/2014 /7/jeff-koons-is-back; Calvin Tomkins, "The Turnaround Artist," *New Yorker*, April 16, 2007, https://www.newyorker.com/magazine/2007/04/23/the-turnaround-artist.

98 **It "was a little":** Interview with Dienes and Tone, 11.

98 **"I often spied":** Sischy.

99 **"like part clown":** *The Jeff Koons Show.*

99 **"They'd come up":** Quoted in Rawsthorn.

99 **"After school, I":** *The Jeff Koons Show.*

99 **"No!" he said:** Quoted in Rawsthorn.

100 **Howardena Pindell:** Interview with Alayo Akinkugbe, "Howardena Pindell: 'The Racism in the Art World Drove Me Out,'" *AnOther*, March 7, 2023, https://www.anothermag.com /art-photography/14714/howardena-pindell-the-racism-in-the-art-world-drove-me-out; interview with Louisa Buck, "Howardena Pindell: 'In Terms of Museums, I'm Optimistic; In Terms of the World, I'm Pessimistic,'" *Art Newspaper*, July 1, 2022, https://www .theartnewspaper.com/2022/07/01/howardena-pindell-interview-kettles-yard-cambridge; Jonathan Griffin, "Full Circle—Howardena Pindell Comes into Her Own," *Apollo*, January 2022, https://www.apollo-magazine.com/howardena-pindell-interview-abstract-painter -retrospective/; *Howardena Pindell: Inner Circle*, documentary, YouTube video, 14:44, posted by Art21, November 20, 2024, https://www.youtube.com/watch?v=2A1QWE18SWM; *Howardena Pindell: What Remains to Be Seen*, documentary, YouTube video, 9:04, posted by Museum of Contemporary Art Chicago, February 23, 2018, https://www.youtube.com /watch?v=7TIOXNCnA-Q; Alana Pockros, "Howardena Pindell's Decades-Long Fight to Integrate the Art World," *Nation*, March 15, 2022, https://www.thenation.com/article /activism/howardena-pindell/.

100 **"I would say":** Quoted in Pockros.

101 **"Everyone was mad":** Interview with Buck.

101 **"I wanted to be playful":** *Howardena Pindell: What Remains to Be Seen.*

102 **"The racism in":** Interview with Akinkugbe.

102 **"the whites freaked":** *Howardena Pindell: Inner Circle.*

102 **"And the Modern":** *Howardena Pindell: Inner Circle.*

102 **"It is spiritually pooping":** Kurt Vonnegut to Carolyn Blakemore, November 17, 1966, in *Kurt Vonnegut: Letters*, ed. Dan Wakefield (Delacorte Press, 2012), Kindle, 156.

103 **"I am sick of teaching":** Quoted in Mark McGurl, *The Program Era: Postwar Fiction and the Rise of Creative Writing* (Harvard University Press, 2009), 1.

103 **"The sad truth":** Interview with Sarah Anne Johnson, January 2002, in *Conversations with American Women Writers* (University Press of New England, 2004), 132.

103 **"I wanted a job":** Interview with Johnson, 132.

104 **"The plan was":** Quoted in Amanda Petrusich, "Digital Memory," *New Yorker*, September 25,

2023, https://www.newyorker.com/magazine/2023/10/02/the-emotionally-haunted-electronic
-music-of-oneohtrix-point-never.

104 **John Berryman:** Richard J. Kelly, ed., *We Dream of Honour: John Berryman's Letters to His Mother* (W. W. Norton, 1988); Paul Mariani, *Dream Song: The Life of John Berryman* (William Morrow, 1990); Eileen Simpson, *Poets in Their Youth: A Memoir* (1982; repr. Farrar, Straus and Giroux, 2014).

104 **"We have nothing":** John Berryman to Martha Berryman, April 4, 1943, *We Dream of Honour*, 178.

105 **"a plan of prudent":** John Berryman to Martha Berryman, June 13, 1943, *We Dream of Honour*, 192.

105 **"Every day I'm":** Quoted in Simpson, 52.

105 **"POET, 28, married":** Quoted in Mariani, 152.

105 **"trembling & half-mad":** Quoted in Mariani, 152.

105 **"This is not":** John Berryman to Martha Berryman, September 9, 1943, *We Dream of Honour*, 194.

106 **"The headmaster reprimanded":** Simpson, 72.

106 **"Hell-in-New Rochelle":** Quoted in Mariani, 154.

106 **"I have *no* savings":** John Berryman to Martha Berryman, November 15, 1961, *We Dream of Honour*, 343.

106 **"Each year it is":** Quoted in Mariani, 161.

106 **"So easy:—only":** John Berryman to Martha Berryman, September 4, 1963, *We Dream of Honour*, 360.

106 **"to be rid of that":** Quoted in Mariani, 443.

107 **"He might say":** Simpson, 73.

107 **"The secret is not":** John Berryman, "Dream Song 340," *The Dream Songs* (1969; repr. Farrar, Straus and Giroux, 2007), 362.

ELITE STATUS

111 **"I don't really care":** Grace Hartigan, October 8, 1953, *The Journals of Grace Hartigan*, William T. La Moy and Joseph P. McCaffrey, eds. (Syracuse University Press, 2009), Kindle, loc. 1246 of 2260.

111 **a foundational example [Petrarch]:** Morris Bishop, *Petrarch and His World* (Indiana University Press, 1963); Christopher S. Celenza, *Petrarch: Everywhere a Wanderer* (Reaktion Books, 2017), Kindle; "Petrarch's Coronation Oration," trans. Ernest H. Wilkins, *PMLA* 68, no. 5 (December 1953): 1241–50, https://www.jstor.org/stable/460017; "Francis Petrarch: Selections from His Correspondences," in *Petrarch: The First Modern Scholar and Man of Letters*, ed. and trans. James Harvey Robinson (G. P. Putnam, 1898), from Hanover Historical Texts Project, https://history.hanover.edu/texts/petrarch.html.

111 **"the greatest and":** "Petrarch's Coronation Oration," 1242.

112 **"But the good poet":** Quoted in "Petrarch's Coronation Oration," 1243–44.

112 **"blushed to accept":** Petrarch, "To Posterity," in "Selections from His Correspondences."

112 **"How hard and":** "Petrarch's Coronation Oration," 1243.

113 **"I gave myself":** Quoted in Bishop, 21.

113 **"In my law studies":** Quoted in Bishop, 26.

113 **"burst out in cries":** Quoted in Bishop, 27.

113   **"two volumes already":** Quoted in Bishop, 27.

113   **"I couldn't reconcile":** Quoted in Bishop, 38.

114   **"either mismanaged or":** Celenza, 32.

114   **"affability is so":** Quoted in Bishop, 52.

114   **"the happiest summer":** Quoted in Bishop, 87.

114   **"Serving him was":** Quoted in Bishop, 90.

115   **"Petrarch's benefices":** Bishop, 277.

116   **a $35,000 annual stipend:** Hillel Italie, "Ada Limón Named 24th U.S. Poet Laureate," Associated Press, July 12, 2022, https://apnews.com/article/entertainment-poetry-joy-harjo-library-of-congress-dc5898051eab5d19349beb6ac54d52ee.

116   **Joseph Haydn:** Karl Geiringer with Irene Geiringer, *Haydn: A Creative Life in Music*, 3rd rev. ed. (University of California Press, 1982); Vernon Gotwals, ed. and trans., *Haydn: Two Contemporary Portraits* (University of Wisconsin Press, 1968); Jan Swafford, "Franz Joseph Haydn," in *The Vintage Guide to Classical Music* (Vintage, 1992), 124–41.

116   **"one of the most":** Geiringer, 4.

116   **"Strange that so":** Quoted in Geiringer, 7.

117   **"more floggings":** Quoted in Geiringer, 15.

117   **"I could not help":** Quoted in Geiringer, 15.

117   **"Joseph's stomach":** Quoted in Geiringer, 19.

117   **"crowing like a":** Quoted in Geiringer, 23.

118   **"He played at":** Geiringer, 27.

118   **"old worm-eaten":** Quoted in Georg August Griesinger, *Biographical Notes Concerning Joseph Haydn* (Breitkopf and Härtel, 1810), in Gotwals, 12.

118   **"Many a genius":** Quoted in Geiringer, 68.

118   **"making something":** Quoted in Geiringer, 34.

118   **"Proper teachers I":** Quoted in Geiringer, 21.

118   **"listened attentively":** Quoted in Geiringer, 21.

118   **"the genuine fundamentals":** Quoted in Geiringer, 34.

118   **"had to eke out":** Quoted in Geiringer, 26.

119   **Haydn's employment contract:** Quoted in Geiringer, 43–45.

120   **"The number and variety":** Geiringer, 46.

120   **"The most welcome":** Quoted in Geiringer, 62–63.

120   **"He entered the":** Swafford, 128.

121   **"I had a gracious":** Quoted in Geiringer, 49.

121   **"It was a desolate":** Geiringer, 57.

121   **"vexatious, penetrating":** Quoted in Geiringer, 60.

121   **"It is scarcely credible":** Quoted in Geiringer, 66.

121   **"My prince was always":** Quoted in Geiringer, 71.

121   **"It cannot be denied":** Geiringer, 73.

122   **"Well here I sit":** Quoted in Geiringer, 90.

122   **"It is indeed sad":** Quoted in Geiringer, 95.

122   **James Abbott McNeill Whistler:** Roy McMullen, *Victorian Outsider: A Biography of J. A. M. Whistler* (E. P. Dutton, 1973); Stanley Weintraub, *Whistler: A Biography* (1974; repr. Truman Talley, 1988). This section is based primarily on Weintraub's biography, with additional context from McMullen.

123   **"Why don't you":** Quoted in Weintraub, 169–70.

123   **"I know I'd do":** Quoted in Weintraub, 170.

123 **"at the best"**: Quoted in Weintraub, 171.

124 **"Concluding a hasty"**: Weintraub, 172.

124 a **"*mélange*"**: Weintraub, 173.

124 **"*Mon cher Baron*"**: Quoted in Weintraub, 172.

125 **"harmony in blue"**: Quoted in Weintraub, 175.

125 **"It is a *noble*"**: Quoted in Weintraub, 173.

125 **"until their hair"**: Weintraub, 174.

126 **"Leyland, you see"**: Quoted in Weintraub, 177.

126 **"Tell Freddie that"**: Quoted in Weintraub, 177.

126 **"These people are"**: Quoted in Weintraub, 177.

127 **"stumbled home in grief"**: Weintraub, 177–78.

127 **"To be sure"**: Quoted in Weintraub, 179.

GOVERNMENT CHECKS

129 **aligned in 1935 [Federal Art Project]**: Hiag Akmakjian, *Name Dropping: The Cedar Bar in the 1950s* (Riverrun, 2012), Kindle; oral history interview with Leonard Bocour, Smithsonian Archives of American Art, June 8, 1978, https://www.aaa.si.edu/collections/interviews/oral-history-interview-leonard-bocour-12884; oral history interview with Burgoyne Diller, Smithsonian Archives of American Art, October 2, 1964, https://www.aaa.si.edu/collections/interviews/oral-history-interview-burgoyne-diller-12944; Mary Gabriel, *Ninth Street Women: Lee Krasner, Elaine de Kooning, Grace Hartigan, Joan Mitchell, and Helen Frankenthaler: Five Painters and the Movement That Changed Modern Art* (Little, Brown, 2018); Gail Levin, *Lee Krasner: A Biography* (HarperCollins, 2011), Kindle; Mark Stevens and Annalyn Swan, *De Kooning: An American Master* (2004; repr. Alfred A. Knopf, 2016); John Strausbaugh, *The Village: 400 Years of Beats and Bohemians, Radicals and Rogues: A History of Greenwich Village* (Ecco, 2013), Kindle.

130 **"When told that"**: Gabriel, 29.

130 **"They were shouting"**: Quoted in Stevens and Swan, 121. The observer here is May Rosenberg, the wife of the art critic Harold Rosenberg.

130 **US Bureau of Labor**: *Monthly Labor Review* 42, no. 3 (March 1936): 702–3, https://babel.hathitrust.org/cgi/pt?id=umn.31951d02381081b&seq=191.

130 **"ketchup, salt, pepper"**: Quoted in Levin, 81.

130 **"I can't begin"**: Interview with Bocour.

131 **"If you happened"**: Interview with Diller.

131 **"You learned to"**: Interview with Diller.

131 **"You can't imagine"**: Quoted in Gabriel, 31.

132 **"For the first time"**: Interview with Diller.

132 **"a big, flat pancake"**: Akmakjian, 23.

133 **"John and I would"**: Morton Feldman, "Liner Notes," 1962, in *Give My Regards to Eighth Street: Collected Writings of Morton Feldman*, ed. B. H. Friedman (Exact Change, 2000), 5.

133 **"The Project was"**: Quoted in "Federal Art Project of Works Progress Admin," The Art Story, https://www.theartstory.org/definition/federal-art-project-of-the-works-progress-administration/.

133 **Lee Krasner**: Gabriel; Levin; interview with Cindy Nemser, *Art Talk: Conversations with 15 Women Artists*, rev. ed. (Westview Press, 1995), 69–93.

133 **"the Mother Courage"**: Quoted in Levin, 3.

134 **"We were very poor":** Quoted in Levin, 21.

134 **"brought up to be":** Quoted in Levin, 21.

134 **"They didn't encourage":** Quoted in Levin, 33–34.

134 **"earned my own":** Quoted in Levin, 37.

134 **"I came out of":** Quoted in Gabriel, 23.

135 **"make his acquaintance":** Quoted in Levin, 166.

136 **Peggy Guggenheim:** Charlotte Gere and Marina Vaizey, "Peggy Guggenheim," in *Great Women Collectors* (Philip Wilson, 1999), 191–97; Peggy Guggenheim, *Confessions of an Art Addict* (1960; repr. Ecco, 1979), Kindle; Francine Prose, *Peggy Guggenheim: The Shock of the Modern* (Yale University Press, 2015).

136 **"used the threadbare":** Alfred H. Barr Jr., introduction to Guggenheim, 12.

136 **"For a patron":** Alfred H. Barr Jr., introduction to Guggenheim, 12.

137 **"She was rich":** Prose, 45.

137 **"In millionaire terms":** Gere and Vaizey, 194.

137 **who "was considered":** Guggenheim, 39.

137 **Mina Loy:** Carolyn Burke, *Becoming Modern: The Life of Mina Loy* (Picador, 1996).

137 **Djuna Barnes:** Phillip Herring, *Djuna: The Life and Work of Djuna Barnes* (Viking, 1995).

137 **"Barnes seemed to":** Herring, 200.

138 **"Little did I dream":** Guggenheim, 44.

138 **"This was before":** Guggenheim, 47.

138 **"might as well":** Guggenheim, 58.

138 **"a regime to buy":** Guggenheim, 63.

139 **"exciting and unusual":** Quoted in Levin, 201.

139 **"a real discovery":** Quoted in Levin, 201.

139 **"It was the first":** Prose, 145.

139 **"just about doesn't":** Quoted in Levin, 210.

139 **"Tell Lee to go":** Quoted in Levin, 210.

140 **"Lee was so":** Guggenheim, 94.

140 **"it was so cold":** Quoted in Levin, 239.

140 **"We gave her":** Quoted in Levin, 239.

142 **"in terms of a current":** Bob Friedman quoted in Gabriel, 620.

142 **"That single sale":** Gabriel, 621.

142 **"In fact, I do":** Guggenheim, 147.

TRUE FANS

143 **Alexander Pope:** Irvin Ehrenpreis, "The Powers of Alexander Pope," *New York Review of Books*, December 20, 1979, https://www.nybooks.com/articles/1979/12/20/the-powers-of-alexander-pope/; Sophie Gee, "Low Tricks and High Art," *Times Literary Supplement*, October 8, 2021, https://www.the-tls.co.uk/literature/literary-criticism/alexander-pope-pat-rogers-joseph-hone-book-review-sophie-gee; Maynard Mack, *Alexander Pope: A Life* (W. W. Norton, 1985).

143 **"I take my self":** Alexander Pope to Lord Carteret, February 16, 1723, quoted in Alvin Kernan, *Samuel Johnson & the Impact of Print* (Princeton University Press, 1989), 10.

143 **"the itch of poetry":** Quoted in Mack, 44.

143 **"a sort of rapture":** Quoted in Mack, 45.

143 **"did nothing but":** Quoted in Mack, 56.

144 **"I do not think"**: Quoted in Mack, 156.

144 **"Pope was afflicted"**: Quoted in Mack, 155–56.

144 **"As an adolescent"**: Ehrenpreis.

144 **"the first business man"**: Hugo M. Reichard, "Pope's Social Satire: Belles-Lettres and Business," *PMLA* 67, no. 4 (1952): 420–34, https://www.jstor.org/stable/459819.

145 **"more than any other"**: Mack, 124.

145 **"what is probably"**: Mack, 122–23.

145 **"What Authors lose"**: Quoted in Mack, 122.

145 **"In the early eighteenth"**: Gee.

146 **"on the finest Paper"**: Quoted in Mack, 266.

146 **"For the subscribers'"**: Mack, 267.

146 **"in the good opinion"**: Quoted in Mack, 268.

147 **"live and thrive"**: Alexander Pope, "The Second Epistle of the Second Book of Horace," *An Essay on Man; Moral Essays and Satires*, ed. Henry Morley (Cassell, 1891; repr. Project Gutenberg, 2007), https://www.gutenberg.org/ebooks/2428.

147 **newsletter from April 2023**: Mason Currey, "Why It's So Hard for Writers to Ask for Money for Their Work," *Subtle Maneuvers*, April 17, 2023, https://masoncurrey.substack.com/p/why-its-hard-for-writers-to-ask-for-money.

147 **"To be honest"**: Public comment on Substack Notes, April 17, 2023. This entire exchange took place on Substack's public social media network, in reply to a post by the author.

150 **Augusta Savage**: Romare Bearden and Harry Henderson, "Augusta Savage," in *A History of African-American Artists: From 1792 to the Present* (Pantheon, 1993), 168–80; Concepción de León, "The Black Woman Artist Who Crafted a Life She Was Told She Couldn't Have," *New York Times*, March 30, 2021, https://www.nytimes.com/2021/03/30/us/augusta-savage-black-woman-artist-harlem-renaissance.html; Augusta Savage, "An Autobiography," *The Crisis*, August 1929, 269, https://archive.org/details/sim_crisis_1929-08_36_8/.

150 **"I was born"**: Savage, "An Autobiography."

150 **"I am the seventh"**: Savage, "An Autobiography."

150 **"almost whipped all"**: Quoted in Bearden and Henderson, 168.

151 **"Democracy is a"**: Quoted in Bearden and Henderson, 170.

152 **"influence was critical"**: Bearden and Henderson, 168.

152 **"paid a heavy price"**: Bearden and Henderson, 170.

153 **"her resources"**: Bearden and Henderson, 168.

153 **"I have created"**: Quoted in Bearden and Henderson, 176.

153 **Ezra Pound [and T. S. Eliot]**: Lyndall Gordon, *T. S. Eliot: An Imperfect Life* (W. W. Norton, 1999); Donald E. Herdeck, "A New Letter by Ezra Pound About T. S. Eliot," *Massachusetts Review* 12, no. 2 (1971): 287–92, http://www.jstor.org/stable/25088114; Timothy Materer, ed., *The Selected Letters of Ezra Pound to John Quinn* (Duke University Press, 1991); James E. Miller Jr., *T. S. Eliot: The Making of an American Poet, 1888–1922* (Pennsylvania State University Press, 2005); Charles Norman, *Ezra Pound* (Macmillan, 1960).

153 **"the most generous"**: Ernest Hemingway, "Ezra Pound and His Bel Esprit," *A Moveable Feast: The Restored Edition* (Scribner, 2010), Kindle, 120.

153 **"a miracle worker"**: Quoted in Norman, 172.

153 **"He would go to"**: Quoted in Norman, 169.

154 **"To Pound, *The Waste Land*"**: Norman, 251.

154 **"There is no"**: *The Letters of Ezra Pound, 1907–1941*, ed. D. D. Paige (New Directions, 1971), 172fn.

155   **"keep one alive":** Virginia Woolf, *A Room of One's Own* (1929; repr. Penguin, 2004), Kindle, 21.

155   **"I have been":** Virginia Woolf to Lady Ottoline Morrell, August 1, 1922, in *The Letters of Virginia Woolf, Volume Two: 1912–1922*, ed. Nigel Nicolson and Joanne Trautmann (Harcourt Brace, 1976), 540.

155   **"what Tom's own":** Virginia Woolf to Lady Ottoline Morrell, August 6, 1922, in *Letters, Volume Two*, 542.

155   **"If this Circular":** Quoted in Miller, 404.

155   **"first beneficiary":** Quoted in Miller, 405.

156   **"an incessant strain":** Quoted in Miller, 405.

156   **"My whole drive":** Ezra Pound to John Quinn, March 9, 1915, *Letters*, 23.

ART AND THEFT

159   **Chantal Akerman:** *I Don't Belong Anywhere: The Cinema of Chantal Akerman*, directed by Marianne Lambert (2015; Amazon Prime Video, 2023), https://www.amazon.com/gp/video/detail/B01F9SI1NA/; interview with Gary Indiana, "Getting Ready for the Golden Eighties: A Conversation with Chantal Akerman," *Artforum*, Summer 1983, https://www.artforum.com/features/getting-ready-for-the-golden-eighties-a-conversation-with-chantal-akerman-208022/.

159   **"a lower-middle-class":** Henry Bean, "Our Lives With (and Without) Chantal Akerman," *Forward*, October 10, 2015, https://forward.com/culture/322320/our-lives-with-and-without-chantal-akerman/.

159   **2022 poll of the greatest:** "The Greatest Films of All Time," *Sight and Sound*, December 2022, https://www.bfi.org.uk/sight-and-sound/greatest-films-all-time.

160   **"I wanted to make":** Interview with Indiana.

160   **"I hid them under":** *I Don't Belong Anywhere*.

160   **"My pockets were":** *I Don't Belong Anywhere*.

161   **"That was the first":** Interview with Indiana.

161   **[Jean-Luc] Godard:** Richard Brody, *Everything Is Cinema: The Working Life of Jean-Luc Godard* (Metropolitan, 2008), Kindle; Colin MacCabe, *Godard: A Portrait of the Artist at Seventy* (Farrar, Straus and Giroux, 2004).

161   **"I lived my childhood":** Quoted in Brody, 526.

162   **"When we saw":** Quoted in Brody, 18.

162   **"stole and sold":** Brody, 30.

162   **"In Paris he had":** Quoted in Brody, 44.

162   **"By writing about":** Brody, 22.

163   **"*Cahiers* was a tiny":** MacCabe, 82.

163   **"because of the extreme":** MacCabe, 83.

163   **"Instead of working":** MacCabe, 83–84.

164   **"He spent the nights":** Quoted in Brody, 32.

164   **"a sufficiently large":** MacCabe, 84.

164   **"For two years":** Quoted in Brody, 33.

165   **"After one screening":** Brody, 47.

165   **Jean Genet:** Mohamed Choukri, *Jean Genet in Tangier* (Ecco, 1974); Jean Genet, *The Thief's Journal*, trans. Bernard Frechtman (1964; repr. Grove Press, 2018); Edmund White, *Genet: A Biography* (Alfred A. Knopf, 1993).

166 **"I perfected a trick":** Quoted in Wilson, 167.

166 **"The boredom of":** Genet, 101.

166 **"With fanatical care":** Genet, 5.

167 **"I was alone":** Quoted in White, 159.

168 **"always been writing":** Quoted in Choukri, 38.

168 **"I wrote in prison":** Quoted in White, 169.

168 **Edmund White points out:** White, 252–53.

168 **"When I have broken":** Genet, 147.

SORT OF RICH, SORT OF QUICK

169 **"Now listen to me":** Robert Musil, "Notebook 24: 1904 to 1905," in *Diaries, 1899–1941*, ed. Adolf Frisé and Mark Mirsky, trans. Philip Payne (Basic Books, 1998).

169 **Robert Musil:** Rober Kimball, "The Qualities of Robert Musil," *New Criterion*, February 1996, https://newcriterion.com/article/the-qualities-of-robert-musil/; Musil, *Diaries*.

169 **"At the age of 21":** Musil, "Notebook 24: 1904 to 1905," *Diaries*, 72.

170 **"I spent three months":** Musil, "Notebook 24: 1904 to 1905," *Diaries*, 72.

170 **"quite a nice sum":** Musil, "Notebook 24: 1904 to 1905," *Diaries*, 73.

170 **"But what a year":** Musil, "Notebook 24: 1904 to 1905," *Diaries*, 73.

172 **Romare Bearden:** Oral history interview with Romare Bearden, Smithsonian Archives of American Art, June 29, 1968, https://www.aaa.si.edu/collections/interviews/oral-history -interview-romare-bearden-11481; Mary Schmidt Campbell, *An American Odyssey: The Life and Work of Romare Bearden* (Oxford University Press, 2018); Robert G. O'Meally, ed., *The Romare Bearden Reader* (Duke University Press, 2019); Myron Schwartzman, *Romare Bearden: His Life and Art* (Harry N. Abrams, 1990); Calvin Tomkins, "Putting Something Over Some-thing Else," *New Yorker*, November 20, 1977, 53–77, https://www.newyorker.com/magazine /1977/11/28/putting-something-over-something-else.

172 **"like a thing of":** Oral history interview with Bearden.

172 **"a skylit studio":** Schwartzman, 164.

172 **"You can sit":** Quoted in Schwartzman, 165–66.

173 **"You know, when":** Quoted in Tomkins, 64.

173 **"Spend eight days":** Musil, August 29, 1910, "Notebook 5: 8 August 1910 to October 1911 or Later," *Diaries*, 121.

174 **"What you're doing":** Quoted in Schwartzman, 175.

174 **"Now I'm going":** Quoted in Schwartzman, 176.

174 **"deep discouragement":** Musil, "Notebook 24: 1904 to 1905," *Diaries*, 73.

174 **"was or became difficult":** Quoted in Kimball.

175 **"I began experimenting":** Romare Bearden, "Rectangular Structure in My Montage Paint-ings," in *Romare Bearden Reader*, 123.

176 **"I think the artist":** Quoted in Tomkins, 61.

176 **Martin Kippenberger:** Susanne Kippenberger, *Kippenberger: The Artist and His Families*, trans. Damion Searls (J&L Books, 2011).

176 **"a dandyish, articulate":** Roberta Smith, "Martin Kippenberger, 43, Artist of Irreverence and Mixed Styles," *New York Times*, March 11, 1997, https://www.nytimes.com/1997/03/11/arts /martin-kippenberger-43-artist-of-irreverence-and-mixed-styles.html.

176 **"Think today, done":** Quoted in Kippenberger, 11.

176 **"It was easy":** Oral history interview with Bearden.

176 **"If you're working"**: Interview with Myron Schwartzman, "Conversation I: Of Mecklenburg, Memory, and the Blues," in *Romare Bearden: His Life and Art*, 41.

177 **"*Nicht sparen*—"**: Kippenberger, 5.

177 **"his monthly allowance"**: Kippenberger, 151.

177 **"Warnings were always"**: Kippenberger, 108.

177 **"in the end Martin"**: Kippenberger, 151.

178 **"for lifetime free"**: Kippenberger, 133.

178 **"He played mau-mau"**: Kippenberger, 160.

178 **"It's a kind of engine"**: Kippenberger, 159–60.

179 **"always paid from"**: Kippenberger, 156.

179 **"I'm on the run"**: Quoted in Kippenberger, 156.

THE BRIDGE

180 **"had already become"**: Romare Bearden, "Rectangular Structure in My Montage Paintings," in Robert G. O'Meally, ed., *The Romare Bearden Reader* (Duke University Press, 2019), 121.

181 **"that I began to"**: Romare Bearden, "Rectangular Structure in My Montage Paintings," in *Romare Bearden Reader*, 122.

181 **"There is unfortunately"**: Romare Bearden, September 7, 1947, "The Journal of Romare Bearden, 1947 to 1949," in *Romare Bearden Reader*, 104.

181 **Robert Graves:** Interview with Malcolm Muggeridge, "Intimations . . . A Question of Influences: Malcolm Muggeridge Talks to Robert Graves," YouTube video, 29:47, posted by Bryan Helton, April 1, 2019, https://www.youtube.com/watch?v=qzLuG3tM84I; Wolfgang Saxon, "Robert Graves, Poet and Scholar, Dies at 90," *New York Times*, December 8, 1985, https://www.nytimes.com/1985/12/08/books/robert-graves-poet-and-scholar-dies-at-90.html.

182 **"I'd been let down"**: Interview with Muggeridge.

182 **"I wrote it"**: Interview with Muggeridge.

182 **"It was purely a"**: Interview with Muggeridge.

182 **"Prose books"**: Quoted in Saxon.

182 **Graham Greene:** Graham Greene, *A Sort of Life* (Touchstone, 1971); Graham Greene, *Ways of Escape* (Simon & Schuster, 1980).

183 **"There was no"**: Greene, *Ways of Escape*, 91.

183 **"an established writer"**: Greene, *A Sort of Life*, 113.

183 **"I can think of no"**: Greene, *A Sort of Life*, 180.

184 **"Both books are"**: Greene, *Ways of Escape*, 19.

184 **"If *The Man Within*"**: Greene, *A Sort of Life*, 212.

185 **"I fell back"**: Greene, *Ways of Escape*, 92.

186 **"It is not really"**: Greene, *Ways of Escape*, 92.

186 **"left my nerves"**: Greene, *Ways of Escape*, 92–93.

186 **Louisa May Alcott:** Susan Cheever, *Louisa May Alcott* (Simon & Schuster, 2010); Ann Douglas, "Mysteries of Louisa May Alcott," *New York Review of Books*, September 28, 1978, https://www.nybooks.com/articles/1978/09/28/mysteries-of-louisa-may-alcott/; Alison Lurie, "Liberated Girls," *New York Review of Books*, November 3, 2005, https://www.nybooks.com/articles/2005/11/03/liberated-girls/; John Matteson, *Eden's Outcasts: The Story of Louisa May Alcott and Her Father* (W. W. Norton, 2007); Daniel Shealy, ed., *Alcott in Her Own Time: A Biographical Chronicle of Her Life, Drawn from Recollections, Interviews, and Memoirs by Family, Friends, and Associates* (University of Iowa Press, 2005).

187 **"I *will* do something":** Alcott, "Recollections of My Childhood," 1888, in Shealy, 37.

187 **"a caged sea-gull":** Alcott, "Recollections of My Childhood," 1888, in Shealy, 37.

187 **"to know something":** Quoted in Cheever, 88.

188 **"A short romantic":** Cheever, 93.

188 **"discovered the secret":** Louisa May Alcott to Miss Churchill, December 25, 1878, in Emily Temple, "Louisa May Alcott's Letter of Advice to a Young Writer," *Literary Hub*, March 6, 2019, https://lithub.com/louisa-may-alcotts-letter-of-advice-to-a-young-writer/.

188 **"Never liked girls":** Quoted in Cheever, 4.

189 **"moral pap for":** Quoted in Shealy, viii.

189 **"The financial needs":** Lurie.

189 **"intensely private person":** Douglas.

190 **"Though I do not":** Alcott to Churchill, *Literary Hub*.

DOUBLE OR NOTHING

191 **John Cage:** John Cage, *Silence* (1939; repr. MIT Press, 1961); oral history interview with John Cage, Smithsonian Archives of American Art, May 2, 1974, https://www.aaa.si.edu/collections/interviews/oral-history-interview-john-cage-12442; interview with William Duckworth in *Talking Music: Conversations with John Cage, Philip Glass, Laurie Anderson, and Five Generations of American Experimental Composers* (Schirmer, 1995), 3–28; Richard Kostelanetz, *Conversing with Cage* (Limelight Editions, 1988); Laura Kuhn, ed., *The Selected Letters of John Cage* (Wesleyan University Press, 2022); David Revill, *The Roaring Silence: John Cage: A Life* (Arcade, 2011), Kindle.

191 **"I never made":** John Cage to Donald E. Boyd, January 19, 1973, *Selected Letters*, 426.

191 **"After I had been":** Quoted in Kostelanetz, 5.

192 **"He said, 'You'":** Quoted in Kostelanetz, 4.

192 **"I found an auto":** Quoted in Kostelanetz, 5.

192 **"Like most composers":** Quoted in Robert Adams, *Why People Photograph: Selected Essays and Reviews* (Aperture, 1994), 46.

193 **"In this way I":** Quoted in Kostelanetz, 4.

193 **"I decided that":** Quoted in Revill, 87.

193 **"I had the example":** Interview with Duckworth, 8.

194 **"You can't get":** Interview with Duckworth, 11.

194 **"I have come to":** John Cage, "Music Lovers' Field Companion," 1954, in *Silence*, 274.

194 **"Will lecture here":** John Cage to David Tudor and M. C. Richards, November or December 1958, *Selected Letters*, 198.

195 **"was besieged by":** Revill, 243.

195 **"the first consequential":** Quoted in Kostelanetz, 16.

195 **Larry Rivers:** Larry Rivers and Arnold Weinstein, *What Did I Do? The Unauthorized Autobiography* (Aaron Asher, 1992).

195 **"That began from '43":** Oral history interview with Cage.

196 **"I discovered that":** Quoted in Revill, 104.

196 **"Chance is a leap":** Quoted in Revill, 191.

196 **"I only took other":** Quoted in Kostelanetz, 14.

196 **"to limit my work":** Quoted in Revill, 177.

197 **"I long for the":** John Cage to Alan Sapp, April 5, 1966, *Selected Letters*, 341.

197 **Bernadette Mayer:** Interview with Adam Fitzgerald, "Lives of the Poets: Bernadette Mayer,"

Poetry Foundation, April 4, 2011, https://www.poetryfoundation.org/articles/69658/lives-of
-the-poets-bernadette-mayer; Rachel James, host, *The Organist* podcast, "Give Everybody Everything: The Financial Life of Bernadette Mayer," April 18, 2019, https://theorganist.org
/give-everybody-everything-the-financial-life-of-bernadette-mayer; Daniel Wenger, "How
to Look in the Mirror Without Saying 'I,'" *New Yorker*, September 1, 2016, https://www
.newyorker.com/culture/persons-of-interest/how-to-look-in-the-mirror-without-saying-i.

197 **"The only woman":** Quoted in Rivka Galchen, "Bernadette Mayer, the Poet of Escape," *New
Yorker*, December 9, 2022, https://www.newyorker.com/news/postscript/bernadette-mayer
-the-poet-of-escape.

197 **"Why is Bernadette":** *The Organist.*

197 **"As a poet":** *The Organist.*

197 **"I'm an idiot":** Quoted in Wenger.

198 **"I have never":** *The Organist.*

198 **"I was in this":** Interview with Fitzgerald.

198 **"Everybody died by":** Interview with Janique Vigier, "Bernadette Mayer," *Artforum*, May
25, 2020, https://www.artforum.com/columns/bernadette-mayer-remembers-memory-1971
-247702/.

198 **"I don't know":** Interview with Fitzgerald.

198 **"an epic poem":** Quoted in Alex Williams, "Bernadette Mayer, Poet Who Celebrated the
Ordinary, Dies at 77," *New York Times*, December 4, 2022, https://www.nytimes.com/2022
/12/04/books/bernadette-mayer-dead.html.

198 **"i write unbalanced":** Bernadette Mayer, "40–60," in *Poetry State Forest* (New Directions,
2008), 38.

199 **"Bernadette didn't have":** *The Organist.*

199 **"So my kids":** *The Organist.*

199 **"I mean, we":** *The Organist.*

199 **"My father would":** *The Organist.*

199 **"a poets and artists":** Bernadette Mayer to Rosemary Mayer, November 11, 1978, in *The
Letters of Rosemary and Bernadette Mayer, 1976–1980*, ed. Gillian Sneed and Marie Warsh
(Swiss Institute, 2022), 229.

199 **"Give everybody everything":** Bernadette Mayer, "Walking Like a Robin," 2016, Verse,
https://verse.press/poem/walking-like-a-robin-7636326586100938419. This phrase appears
in the poem's final two lines: "remember: property is robbery, give everybody / everything,
other birds walk this way too."

200 **Pina Bausch:** Pina Bausch, "What Moves Me," 2007, Pina Bausch Foundation, https://www
.pinabausch.org/post/what-moves-me.

200 **Sybille Bedford:** Brooke Allen, "A World-Class Writer and a World-Class Freeloader," *New
York Times*, February 4, 2021, https://www.nytimes.com/2021/02/04/books/review/sybille
-bedford-a-life-selina-hastings.html; Sybille Bedford, *Quicksands: A Memoir* (Counterpoint,
2005).

200 **Aphra Behn:** Janet Todd, *Aphra Behn: A Secret Life* (Fentum Press, 2017).

200 **Samuel Taylor Coleridge:** Richard Holmes, *Coleridge: Early Visions* (Viking, 1990).

200 **John O'Hara:** Ben Yagoda, *About Town: The "New Yorker" and the World It Made* (Da Capo
Press, 2000).

200 **Dorothy Parker:** Gail Crowther, *Dorothy Parker in Hollywood* (Gallery Books, 2024).

201 **Satyajit Ray:** Andrew Robinson, *Satyajit Ray: The Inner Eye* (University of California Press,
1989).

201   **Kenneth Rexroth:** Dwight Garner, *Garner's Quotations: A Modern Miscellany* (Farrar, Straus and Giroux, 2020).

201   **Titian:** Sheila Hale, *Titian: His Life* (HarperPress, 2012).

202   **"I won't say":** Charles Baudelaire to Caroline Aupick, December 20, 1855, in *The Selected Letters of Charles Baudelaire*, ed. and trans. Rosemary Lloyd (University of Chicago Press, 1986), 77.

ABOUT THE AUTHOR

Mason Currey is the author of the *Daily Rituals* books—*Daily Rituals: How Artists Work* and *Daily Rituals: Women at Work*—featuring brief profiles of the day-to-day work habits of more than three hundred brilliant minds. He has worked as the managing editor of *Metropolis*, the executive editor of *Print*, and a senior editor at *Core77*, and his freelance writing has appeared in *The New Yorker*, *The New York Times*, *The Atlantic*, and *Slate*. Currey lives in Los Angeles and writes *Subtle Maneuvers*, a twice-monthly newsletter on the creative process.

CELADON
BOOKS

Founded in 2017, Celadon Books, a division of
Macmillan Publishers, publishes a highly curated list
of twenty to twenty-five new titles a year. The list of
both fiction and nonfiction is eclectic and focuses
on publishing commercial and literary books and
discovering and nurturing talent.